Sport in the Global Society: Contemporary Perspectives

Edited by
Boria Majumdar, *University of Central Lancashire, UK*

The social, cultural (including media) and political study of sport is an expanding area of scholarship and related research. While this area has been well served by the *Sport in the Global Society* series, the surge in quality scholarship over the last few years has necessitated the creation of *Sport in the Global Society: Contemporary Perspectives*. The series will publish the work of leading scholars in fields as diverse as sociology, cultural studies, media studies, gender studies, cultural geography and history, political science and political economy. If the social and cultural study of sport is to receive the scholarly attention and readership it warrants, a cross-disciplinary series dedicated to taking sport beyond the narrow confines of physical education and sport science academic domains is necessary. *Sport in the Global Society: Contemporary Perspectives* will answer this need.

For a complete list of titles in this series, please visit https://www.routledge.com/series/SGSC

Recent titles in the series include the following:

Football, Community and Sustainability
Edited by Chris Porter, Anthony May and Annabel Kiernan

From Olympic Administration to Olympic Governance
Edited by Emmanuel Bayle and Jean-Loup Chappelet

Junior and Youth Grassroots Football Culture
The Forgotten Game
Edited by Jimmy O'Gorman

Gender in Physical Culture
Crossing Boundaries – Reconstituting Cultures
Edited by Natalie Barker-Ruchti, Karin Grahn and Eva-Carin Lindgren

DIY Football
The Cultural Politics of Community Based Football Clubs
Edited by David Kennedy and Peter Kennedy

A Social and Political History of Everton and Liverpool Football Clubs
The Split, 1878–1914
David Kennedy

Football Fandom in Italy and Beyond
Community through Media and Performance
Matthew Guschwan

Numbers and Narratives
Sport, History and Economics
Wray Vamplew

Junior and Youth Grassroots Football Culture

Football is ubiquitously acknowledged as 'The Global Game' and/or 'The People's Game' – everyday all-encompassing terms familiar to anyone with an interest in football which illustrate, albeit nebulously, the game's international reach and popularity. Yet much academic and popular attention has been, and continues to be, narrowly centred on topics pertaining to the elite and professional aspects of the game. At a time when there appears to be an ever-widening gap between the grassroots and elite levels of the sport, this book brings together, for the first time, a collection of research articles dedicated solely to youth and junior grassroots football. The intention is to generate future inquiry, encourage theoretical debate and stimulate empirical research on topics and issues within the relatively marginalised area of the game that is youth and junior grassroots football. The collection represents a preliminary consideration of what is already currently known about grassroots football and, no less importantly, point towards what remains unknown and under-researched but which deserves much more attention than has been given hitherto. As such, the collection includes contributions from practitioners and researchers alike. Topics included range from the provision, organisation and development of grassroots football in one national association, to broader issues such as the sources of enjoyment in participation, the lived experiences of junior players and coaches, to the causes of youth dropout from football. In addition, the significance of social stratification and various forms of social division which structure children's participation in grassroots football are discussed. These include female participation and the role of elite female role models, and issues relating to the participation of immigrant youth. The book is intended to appeal to practitioners, academics and football enthusiasts alike. This book was originally published as a special issue of *Soccer & Society*.

Jimmy O'Gorman is a Senior Lecturer in Sport Development at Edge Hill University, UK. His research interests and expertise focus on the development and implementation of youth sport policy and programmes, ranging from community/grassroots settings to the development of participation and performance. He has undertaken research and consultancy on behalf of local and national organisations in this context.

Junior and Youth Grassroots Football Culture

The Forgotten Game

Edited by
Jimmy O'Gorman

Routledge
Taylor & Francis Group

LONDON AND NEW YORK

First published 2018
by Routledge
2 Park Square, Milton Park, Abingdon, Oxon, OX14 4RN, UK

and by Routledge
711 Third Avenue, New York, NY 10017, USA

Routledge is an imprint of the Taylor & Francis Group, an informa business

British Library Cataloguing in Publication Data
A catalogue record for this book is available from the British Library

ISBN 13: 978-1-138-04757-0

Typeset in TimesNewRomanPS
by diacriTech, Chennai

Publisher's Note
The publisher accepts responsibility for any inconsistencies that may have arisen during the conversion of this book from journal articles to book chapters, namely the possible inclusion of journal terminology.

Disclaimer
Every effort has been made to contact copyright holders for their permission to reprint material in this book. The publishers would be grateful to hear from any copyright holder who is not here acknowledged and will undertake to rectify any errors or omissions in future editions of this book.

Junior and Youth Grassroots Football Culture

Football is ubiquitously acknowledged as 'The Global Game' and/or 'The People's Game' – everyday all-encompassing terms familiar to anyone with an interest in football which illustrate, albeit nebulously, the game's international reach and popularity. Yet much academic and popular attention has been, and continues to be, narrowly centred on topics pertaining to the elite and professional aspects of the game. At a time when there appears to be an ever-widening gap between the grassroots and elite levels of the sport, this book brings together, for the first time, a collection of research articles dedicated solely to youth and junior grassroots football. The intention is to generate future inquiry, encourage theoretical debate and stimulate empirical research on topics and issues within the relatively marginalised area of the game that is youth and junior grassroots football. The collection represents a preliminary consideration of what is already currently known about grassroots football and, no less importantly, point towards what remains unknown and under-researched but which deserves much more attention than has been given hitherto. As such, the collection includes contributions from practitioners and researchers alike. Topics included range from the provision, organisation and development of grassroots football in one national association, to broader issues such as the sources of enjoyment in participation, the lived experiences of junior players and coaches, to the causes of youth dropout from football. In addition, the significance of social stratification and various forms of social division which structure children's participation in grassroots football are discussed. These include female participation and the role of elite female role models, and issues relating to the participation of immigrant youth. The book is intended to appeal to practitioners, academics and football enthusiasts alike. This book was originally published as a special issue of *Soccer & Society*.

Jimmy O'Gorman is a Senior Lecturer in Sport Development at Edge Hill University, UK. His research interests and expertise focus on the development and implementation of youth sport policy and programmes, ranging from community/grassroots settings to the development of participation and performance. He has undertaken research and consultancy on behalf of local and national organisations in this context.

Sport in the Global Society: Contemporary Perspectives

Edited by
Boria Majumdar, *University of Central Lancashire, UK*

The social, cultural (including media) and political study of sport is an expanding area of scholarship and related research. While this area has been well served by the *Sport in the Global Society* series, the surge in quality scholarship over the last few years has necessitated the creation of *Sport in the Global Society: Contemporary Perspectives*. The series will publish the work of leading scholars in fields as diverse as sociology, cultural studies, media studies, gender studies, cultural geography and history, political science and political economy. If the social and cultural study of sport is to receive the scholarly attention and readership it warrants, a cross-disciplinary series dedicated to taking sport beyond the narrow confines of physical education and sport science academic domains is necessary. *Sport in the Global Society: Contemporary Perspectives* will answer this need.

For a complete list of titles in this series, please visit https://www.routledge.com/series/SGSC

Recent titles in the series include the following:

Football, Community and Sustainability
Edited by Chris Porter, Anthony May and Annabel Kiernan

From Olympic Administration to Olympic Governance
Edited by Emmanuel Bayle and Jean-Loup Chappelet

Junior and Youth Grassroots Football Culture
The Forgotten Game
Edited by Jimmy O'Gorman

Gender in Physical Culture
Crossing Boundaries – Reconstituting Cultures
Edited by Natalie Barker-Ruchti, Karin Grahn and Eva-Carin Lindgren

DIY Football
The Cultural Politics of Community Based Football Clubs
Edited by David Kennedy and Peter Kennedy

A Social and Political History of Everton and Liverpool Football Clubs
The Split, 1878–1914
David Kennedy

Football Fandom in Italy and Beyond
Community through Media and Performance
Matthew Guschwan

Numbers and Narratives
Sport, History and Economics
Wray Vamplew

First published 2018
by Routledge
2 Park Square, Milton Park, Abingdon, Oxon, OX14 4RN, UK

and by Routledge
711 Third Avenue, New York, NY 10017, USA

Routledge is an imprint of the Taylor & Francis Group, an informa business

© 2018 Taylor & Francis

British Library Cataloguing in Publication Data
A catalogue record for this book is available from the British Library

ISBN 13: 978-1-138-04757-0

Typeset in TimesNewRomanPS
by diacriTech, Chennai

Publisher's Note
The publisher accepts responsibility for any inconsistencies that may have arisen during the conversion of this book from journal articles to book chapters, namely the possible inclusion of journal terminology.

Disclaimer
Every effort has been made to contact copyright holders for their permission to reprint material in this book. The publishers would be grateful to hear from any copyright holder who is not here acknowledged and will undertake to rectify any errors or omissions in future editions of this book.

Junior and Youth Grassroots Football Culture

The Forgotten Game

Edited by
Jimmy O'Gorman

Routledge
Taylor & Francis Group

LONDON AND NEW YORK

Contents

Citation Information   vii

Notes on Contributors   ix

Introduction: developing the research agenda in junior and youth
grassroots football culture   1
Jimmy O'Gorman

1   The English Football Association Charter for Quality: the development
    of junior and youth grassroots football in England   8
    Les Howie and Wayne Allison

2   Children's voices in mini soccer: an exploration of critical incidents   18
    Jimmy O'Gorman and Kenny Greenough

3   Enjoyment in youth soccer: its portrayals among 12- to 14-year-olds   35
    Hege E. Tjomsland, Torill Larsen, Ingrid Holsen, Lars T. Ronglan,
    Oddrun Samdal and Bente Wold

4   Elite footballers as role models: promoting young women's football participation   51
    Carrie Dunn

5   A systematic review of drop-out from organized soccer among children
    and adolescents   64
    Viviene A. Temple and Jeff R. Crane

6   Transcultural football. Trajectories of belonging among immigrant youth   90
    Max Mauro

7   A generational divide within the class-based production of girls in American
    youth soccer   106
    Lisa Swanson

CONTENTS

8   Exploring the everyday realities of grass-roots football coaching:
    towards a relational perspective   118
    Paul Potrac, Lee Nelson and Jimmy O'Gorman

    Index   135

Citation Information

The chapters in this book were originally published in *Soccer & Society*, volume 17, issue 6 (November 2016). When citing this material, please use the original page numbering for each article as follows:

Introduction
Introduction: developing the research agenda in junior and youth grassroots football culture
Jimmy O'Gorman
Soccer & Society, volume 17, issue 6 (November 2016) pp. 793–799

Chapter 1
The English Football Association Charter for Quality: the development of junior and youth grassroots football in England
Les Howie and Wayne Allison
Soccer & Society, volume 17, issue 6 (November 2016) pp. 800–809

Chapter 2
Children's voices in mini soccer: an exploration of critical incidents
Jimmy O'Gorman and Kenny Greenough
Soccer & Society, volume 17, issue 6 (November 2016) pp. 810–826

Chapter 3
Enjoyment in youth soccer: its portrayals among 12- to 14-year-olds
Hege E. Tjomsland, Torill Larsen, Ingrid Holsen, Lars T. Ronglan, Oddrun Samdal and Bente Wold
Soccer & Society, volume 17, issue 6 (November 2016) pp. 827–842

Chapter 4
Elite footballers as role models: promoting young women's football participation
Carrie Dunn
Soccer & Society, volume 17, issue 6 (November 2016) pp. 843–855

Chapter 5
A systematic review of drop-out from organized soccer among children and adolescents
Viviene A. Temple and Jeff R. Crane
Soccer & Society, volume 17, issue 6 (November 2016) pp. 856–881

CITATION INFORMATION

Chapter 6

Transcultural football. Trajectories of belonging among immigrant youth
Max Mauro
Soccer & Society, volume 17, issue 6 (November 2016) pp. 882–897

Chapter 7

A generational divide within the class-based production of girls in American youth soccer
Lisa Swanson
Soccer & Society, volume 17, issue 6 (November 2016) pp. 898–909

Chapter 8

Exploring the everyday realities of grass-roots football coaching: towards a relational perspective
Paul Potrac, Lee Nelson and Jimmy O'Gorman
Soccer & Society, volume 17, issue 6 (November 2016) pp. 910–925

For any permission-related enquiries please visit:
http://www.tandfonline.com/page/help/permissions

Notes on Contributors

Wayne Allison is a Coach Inclusion and Diversity Manager at FA Education, Technical Directorate, The FA Group, UK.

Jeff R. Crane, Assistant Teaching Professor, is based at the School of Exercise Science, Physical and Health Education, University of Victoria, Canada.

Carrie Dunn is a journalist and researcher at the Faculty of Arts and Digital Industries, University of East London, UK.

Kenny Greenough works at the Department of Sport and Physical Activity, Edge Hill University, UK.

Ingrid Holsen is an Associate Professor at the Department of Health Promotion and Development, University of Bergen, Norway.

Les Howie is the FA's Head of Grassroots Delivery at Grassroots Coaching, Technical Directorate, The FA Group, UK.

Torill Larsen is a Professor at the Department of Health Promotion and Development, University of Bergen, Norway.

Max Mauro is a Lecturer in Sports Studies at Southampton Solent University, UK.

Lee Nelson is a Reader in Sports Coaching at the Department of Sport and Physical Activity, Edge Hill University, UK.

Jimmy O'Gorman is a Senior Lecturer in Sport Development at Edge Hill University, UK.

Paul Potrac is a Professor at the Department of Sport and Physical Activity, Edge Hill University, UK.

Lars T. Ronglan is a Professor based at the Department of Rectorate, Norwegian School of Sport Sciences, Norway.

Oddrun Samdal is a Professor and the Vice-Rector for education at the Department of Health Promotion and Development, University of Bergen, Norway.

Lisa Swanson is a Professor of Sociology at the Department of Sociology and Anthropology, Goucher College, USA.

Viviene A. Temple is based at the School of Exercise Science, Physical and Health Education, University of Victoria, Canada.

Hege E. Tjomsland is an Associate Professor based at the Department of Education, University of Bergen, Norway.

Bente Wold is a Professor at the Department of Health Promotion and Development, University of Bergen, Norway.

Introduction: developing the research agenda in junior and youth grassroots football culture

Jimmy O'Gorman

Department of Sport and Physical Activity, Edge Hill University, Ormskirk, UK

According to data obtained from its 207 member associations, in 2007 the Fédération Internationale de Football Association (FIFA) noted that an estimated 265 million people play association football (soccer) in organized or recreational settings worldwide. Of this number, 9.4 million youth under the age of 18 worldwide were registered in football clubs.[1] In very many countries, the overwhelming majority of people who play football are children and adolescents who participate in various youth and junior grassroots settings, with varying degrees of formality, and for a whole range of purposes and motivations. The sport of football also has a great deal of social and cultural traction globally and much attention has been, and continues to be, paid to the professional level of the game. Most recently, particular attention has been paid to the allegations of corruption faced by the world governing body, FIFA, the hosting of the 2018 and 2022 World Cup in Russia and Qatar, and the relative success of the 2015 Women's World Cup held in Canada. To these can be added many other matters which have been of long-standing concern in studies of the professional game, including: talent identification and development, commercial sponsorship, fandom and player wages, spectator behaviour, racism, national identity and nationalism and standards of coaching and team success.

Much of the academic research – located in a variety of disciplines (e.g. sociology, psychology, sports management, business and media studies) – on professional football has typically been narrowly focused around the experiences of adult players and, increasingly, elite young footballers. Indeed, much has been written on a variety of matters relating to player and coach experiences of youth development programmes,[2] player welfare, and identity[3] and migration[4] in professional youth football academies. In addition, the influence of parents[5] and the experiences and education of elite level youth coaches have also received particular attention. Other work has focused on the organizational,[6] cultural and environmental[7] dimensions of elite youth player development.[8] Most recently, Nesti and Sulley[9] examined a selection of youth football development programmes around the world to offer recommendations for future improvement based on best practice.

Notwithstanding the bias in academic work towards professional football, the players, coaches and adults who are the focus of such work will have at some point participated in, and had their formative experiences shaped by, youth and junior grassroots football. The pre-occupation with elite youth level players and the governance of professional football[10] has been accompanied by a relative academic neglect of football at youth and junior grassroots level. Even Giulianotti's purportedly thoroughly sociological analysis of all aspects of football does not address junior and youth grassroots football,[11] while Golblatt's[12] comprehensive history of football provides nothing other than a cursory acknowledgement of it. Some might argue that this academic bias is not surprising, though as the football historian James Walvin has noted, the cultural significance of grassroots football is crucial because in comparison to studies of the professional game:

> there is another football story to tell; about ordinary, run-of-the-mill football, about boys in the park, schoolchildren driven to games by parents, older men (long past their prime) struggling on bleary-eyed Sunday mornings to recapture their footballing best, and millions more simply kicking a ball against a back wall. It is generally untold because it is part and parcel of the world we live in. We see it, know it, have taken part in it, as children, parents, as players or as spectators. At this level football is just another feature of life's weekly routines and scarcely warrants a passing thought. Yet it is this massive, incalculable substratum of popular football that sustains the professional game; the millions of ordinary players who nurture the national (and global) interest in the high-powered, commercially driven world of successful professional soccer. More than that, this popular attachment to the game takes us right back to the origins of the game itself. This is how football has always been; a simplicity and ease of play embedded deep in the routines and habits of ordinary people. That is why the game of football remains the people's game, however lavish and often absurd the antics of the wealthy minority.[13]

For Walvin and perhaps many others, youth and junior grassroots football is the lifeblood of the professional game that provides the foundations upon which future playing talent and paying supporters are often derived, and which has played a part in the development and increasing commercialization and professionalization of professional football. The grassroots level of football is also the environment in which children are typically introduced to the game at school and in junior clubs, and continue to play out their leisure time in the evenings and at weekends as adults. Grassroots football is also the source in many countries of political attention and public policy, not least because it is often seen as an important vehicle through which governments seek to achieve a whole range of social outcomes (e.g. improved community cohesion, positive youth development, enhanced social inclusion, and improved health and well-being).

This special issue of *Soccer and Society* seeks to address the obvious lacuna which exists in the social scientific literature by exploring a number of essential issues which are regarded as being significant in youth and junior grassroots football (which encompasses organized youth and junior football for males and females aged under 18 through to more informal leisure time participation). These issues are examined within particular sociocultural contexts and are expressive of the practice of grassroots football in a particular time period and space, but the various contributions included in this volume help to provide the foundations upon which future investigations may be based. The volume is necessarily selective and the contributions cannot be held to be representative of the complexity and diversity of topics which need to be better understood if we are to arrive at a more adequate understanding of grassroots football. Readers may be disappointed to see that particular topics have been omitted from the collection, and that articles have not been included from authors in a broader and more diverse set of sociocultural contexts, but this does not detract from an important fact: we currently know very little empirically and theoretically about the reality of grassroots football globally, and much work remains to be done on this important feature of the so-called 'people's game'.

The volume opens with a contribution from practitioners working for the English Football Association (FA). The article provides an account of the developments in grassroots football undertaken by one national association. The authors describe how The FA has adopted an increasingly strategic approach to football development at the junior grassroots level, and point towards the past and future challenges in implementing policies and innovations in the provision of youth football that are central to cultural change.

The paper by O'Gorman and Greenough builds on, and is located within the context of, the opening paper by Howie and Allison. The authors extend the work of Pitchford et al.[14] and seek to understand mini soccer from the perspective of the child in a social world which is increasingly shaped and structured by adults. As an alternative to the predominant developmental view of children that appears to dominate social science research,[15] audiovisual methods are used to represent children's (aged under 7–under 10) views of critical incidents in mini soccer and their experiences of those incidents in a league in north-west England. O'Gorman and Greenough argue that children's experiences are shaped by the network of social relations in which they are enmeshed and illustrate the deeply entrenched cultures that exist within mini soccer, and the game more broadly which come to impact significantly children's experiences. The views and experiences children recalled of the same critical incidents were neither homogenous nor entirely heterogeneous as such, which as the authors explain presents a variety of challenges for advocates of the game wishing to introduce future innovations which enhance the experiences children have of football.

In the next essay, Tjomsland and colleagues provide an account of the sources of enjoyment in grassroots football by 12–14-year-olds in Norway. Set in the context of Norwegian grassroots football culture which, the authors suggest, is predominantly focused on participation rather than competition, the study reports data from participants recruited from the Promoting Adolescent Physical Activity (PAPA) project. The PAPA project seeks to encourage grassroots coaches to implement a supportive, engaging and enjoyable culture on the assumption that this will enhance and sustain long-term participation in football by children who, it is assumed, will subsequently engage in healthy physical activity through grassroots football.[16]

Dunn's essay also explores the cultural significance of grassroots football via her analysis of elite female footballers' perceptions of being role models and the role this is believed to play in stimulating participation by females in grassroots football. She argues that much research on female football generally has been driven by success and the increasing public profile of elite adult national clubs and teams.[17] To date, evidence that role models have a positive influence on the propensity for children and adolescents to take part in sport has been scant but Dunn's contribution sheds light on two issues. First, Dunn explores elite women footballers' recollections about how female role models influenced their own participation in grassroots football. Second, this selection of footballers discuss how they perceive their role model status in influencing mass participation, and in doing so highlight some of the known cultural barriers to female participation in grassroots football. The paper offers a different insight than other studies that focus on girls' participation and provision.

Following on from cultural components that mediate participation in grassroots, Temple and Crane draw on Bronfenbrenner's bioecological model of human development to offer a systematic review of the literature on dropout among children and adolescents. The process of undertaking the review itself is revealing regarding the lack of research and available literature on grassroots youth soccer more generally. Of the 137 studies identified by Temple and Crane, only 14 met the keyword search and inclusion criteria devised for the study. The majority of the studies simply investigated the personal characteristics of children and adolescents, and few recognized the contextual and cultural factors associated with dropout. While it is highlighted that the dropout rate of children from soccer is consistent with dropout in child and adolescent sport more generally, the authors suggest that future research on dropout needs to expand the scale and scope of enquiry to include, among other things, the interactions between the individual and the environment. This, they argue, will help develop a deeper understanding of the cultural constraints that help explain why children and adolescents dropout of football, and better inform future policy intended to stimulate participation in grassroots football.

The next two essays explore the significance of social stratification and various forms of social division which structure children's participation in grassroots football, though there is of course a need to better understand the intersection of these with other social divisions (such as sexuality and age) which also structure grassroots participation. Many of the issues explored by the authors in this volume are not new, and there exists a large body of literature which examines issues of 'race' and ethnicity within grassroots football,[18] which has pointed towards particular expressions and forms of resistance and identity.[19] However, as football is a global game in an increasingly global society in which cultural and human flows are becoming increasingly prominent and intense, the integration of groups from different cultural backgrounds in grassroots football remains an under-explored area of research. To this end, Mauro's contribution explores the nuances of social stratification that mediate the assimilation of immigrant youth expressions of identity, resistance and acceptance in the grassroots football arena in Ireland. Mauro suggests that, for the participants in his study, grassroots football provides an important arena in which their transcultural encounters find expression and are negotiated in the context of their relations with others.

Swanson then examines class-based production in girls' football in the United States. Drawing upon Bourdieu's work on the reproduction of social class, Swanson illustrates how young females' involvement in football is to a large extent shaped by intersections of class and gender in the US. Notably, grassroots soccer appears to be connected to the reproduction of pre-existing inequalities as participation is viewed as a symbolic indication of class and status, and as something which is socially desired by parents. As well as exploring the links between grassroots participation and inequality, Swanson draws upon the youth and politics of culture literature to examine the discrepancies that exist between the expectations of mothers and parents in shaping their children's participation, and the experiences and motivations of those children in participating in football. This disconnection between parents' desires for children's participation in football, it is held, represents a generational divide which is exacerbated by a misunderstanding of children's participation. A deeper understanding of the generational differences in experiences of youth football is therefore important if future policy and innovations in grassroots football are to be informed more adequately in their design and implementation.

In the final essay of this volume, Potrac and colleagues draw attention to adults who play an important role in the provision of grassroots football: volunteer coaches. Despite the scale and practice of grassroots football coaching in very many countries, little academic attention has so far been paid to grassroots coaches. Potrac et al. argue that coach education at the grassroots level is becoming increasingly important for a variety of groups seeking to realize a number of related aims and objectives, including the role coaches are believed to play in providing quality experiences which sustain participation, and enhance players' technical ability. The authors present a creative fiction as to explore their shared experiences of being coach learners in this context. In doing so, concepts from relational sociology are employed to highlight the emotional and (micro)political processes that shape grassroots coaches experiences as learners in relation to significant others within their network of social relations. To date, little, if any, attention has been afforded to the interconnections between the multiple social networks in which grassroots coaches are embedded. A relational approach is identified as one particular way that may allow researchers to not only better understand how grassroots football coaches attempt to manage their various identities, but also the wider social demands that are placed on them in providing opportunities for children and adolescents to participate in organized football. In particular, the authors call for more empirically and theoretically informed accounts of grassroots football coaches experiences.

Overall, the collection of essays in this volume represent a preliminary consideration of what is already currently known about grassroots football and, no less importantly, point towards what remains unknown and under-researched but which deserves much more attention than has been given hitherto. It is clear, for example, that grassroots football is a fertile ground for future academic analyses which seek to use a range of methods that better capture the lived experiences and realities of grassroots football for young players and the adults (e.g. coaches) to whom their care is entrusted. The persistence of social divisions in structuring opportunities for participation (whether via direct participation or indirectly through spectatorship and other forms of support), and the individual and collective impact of these, also warrants much closer investigation. How young people's welfare can be best safeguarded within the cultures which surround football, and the roles played by significant others (e.g. parents) in that endeavour, should also remain at the forefront of research in junior and youth grassroots football. Above all, however, it is essential that future enquiries give much more emphasis to the voices and experiences of young people themselves, rather than perpetuating the dominant tendency for studies to investigate their life worlds from the perspectives of adults.

Disclosure statement
No potential conflict of interest was reported by the author.

Notes
1. 'FIFA Magazine, Big Count 2007'.
2. Cushion and Jones, 'Power, Discourse, and Symbolic Violence in Professional Youth Soccer: The Case of Albion Football Club'.
3. Brown and Potrac, '"You've Not Made the Grade, Son": De-selection and Identity Disruption in Elite Level Youth Football'.

4. Weedon, '"Glocal Boys": Exploring Experiences of Acculturation among Migrant Youth Footballers in Premier League Academies'.
5. Harwood, Drew, and Knight, 'Parental Stressors in Professional Youth Football Academies: A Qualitative Investigation of Specialising Stage Parents'.
6. Relvas et al., 'Organizational Structures and Working Practices in Elite European Professional Football Clubs: Understanding the Relationship between Youth and Professional Domains'.
7. Cushion and Jones, 'A Bourdieusian Analysis of Cultural Reproduction: Socialisation and the "Hidden Curriculum" in Professional Football'.
8. Mills et al., 'Identifying Factors Perceived to Influence the Development of Elite Youth Football Academy Players'.
9. Nesti and Sulley, *Youth Development in Football: Lessons from the World's Best Academies*.
10. Gammelsæter and Senaux, *The Organisation and Governance of Top Football across Europe: An Institutional Perspective*.
11. Giulianotti, *Football*.
12. Goldblatt, *The Ball is Round: A Global History of Football*.
13. Walvin, *The Only Game*, 251–2.
14. Pitchford et al., 'Children in Football: Seen but Not Heard'.
15. Wyness, *Childhood and Society: An Introduction to the Sociology of Childhood*.
16. Van Hoye et al., 'Physical Activity and Sedentary Behaviours among Grassroots Football Players: A Comparison across Three European Countries'.
17. Magee, Caudwell, and Liston, *Women, Football and Europe*.
18. Bradbury, 'From Racial Exclusions to New Inclusions: Black and Minority Ethnic Participation in Football Clubs in the East Midlands of England'; Lusted, 'Negative Equity? Amateurist Responses to Race Equality Initiatives in English Grass-roots Football'.
19. Burdsey, *Race, Ethnicity and Football: Persisting Debates and Emergent Issues*.

References

Bradbury, S. 'From Racial Exclusions to New Inclusions: Black and Minority Ethnic Participation in Football Clubs in the East Midlands of England'. *International Review for the Sociology of Sport* 46, no. 1 (2011): 23–44.

Brown, G., and P. Potrac. '"You've Not Made the Grade, Son": De-selection and Identity Disruption in Elite Level Youth Football'. *Soccer & Society* 10, no. 2 (2009): 143–59.

Burdsey, D., ed. *Race, Ethnicity and Football: Persisting Debates and Emergent Issues*. London: Routledge, 2012.

Cushion, C.J., and R.L. Jones. 'A Bourdieusian Analysis of Cultural Reproduction: Socialisation and the "Hidden Curriculum" in Professional Football'. *Sport, Education and Society* 19, no. 3 (2014): 276–98.

Cushion, C., and R.L. Jonnes. 'Power, Discourse, and Symbolic Violence in Professional Youth Soccer: The Case of Albion Football Club'. *Sociology of Sport Journal* 23, no. 2 (2006): 142–61.

FIFA. 'FIFA Magazine: Big Count 2007', http://www.fifa.com/mm/document/fifafacts/bcoffsurv/emaga_9384_10704.pdf (last accessed December 4, 2014).

Gammelsæter, H., and B. Senaux, eds. *The Organisation and Governance of Top Football across Europe: An Institutional Perspective*. Routledge, 2011.

Harwood, C., A. Drew, and C.J. Knight. 'Parental Stressors in Professional Youth Football Academies: A Qualitative Investigation of Specialising Stage Parents'. *Qualitative Research in Sport and Exercise* 2, no. 1 (2010): 39–55.

Lusted, J. 'Negative Equity? Amateurist Response to Race Equality Initiatives in English Grass-roots Football'. In *Race, Ethnicity and Football: Persisting Debates and Emergent Issues*, ed. D. Burdsey, 207–21. New York: Routledge, 2012.

Magee, J., J. Caudwell, and K. Liston. *Women, Football and Europe: Histories, Equity and Experience*, Oxford: Blackwell, 2007.

Mills, A., J. Butt, I. Maynard, and C. Harwood. 'Identifying Factors Perceived to Influence the Development of Elite Youth Football Academy Players'. *Journal of Sports Sciences* 30, no. 15 (2012): 1593–604.

Relvas, H., M. Littlewood, M. Nesti, D. Gilbourne, and D. Richardson. 'Organizational Structures and Working Practices in Elite European Professional Football Clubs: Understanding the Relationship between Youth and Professional Domains'. *European Sport Management Quarterly* 10, no. 2 (2010): 165–87.

Van Hoye, A., S. Fenton, C. Krommidas, J.P. Heuzé, E. Quested, A. Papaioannou, and J.L. Duda. 'Physical Activity and Sedentary Behaviours among Grassroots Football Players: A Comparison across Three European Countries'. *International Journal of Sport and Exercise Psychology* 11, no. 4 (2013): 341–50.

Walvin, J. *The Only Game*. Oxford: Blackwell, 2001.

Weedon, G. '"Glocal Boys": Exploring Experiences of Acculturation amongst Migrant Youth Footballers in Premier League Academies'. *International Review for the Sociology of Sport* 47, no. 2 (2012): 200–16.

The English Football Association Charter for Quality: the development of junior and youth grassroots football in England

Les Howie[a] and Wayne Allison[b]

[a]Grassroots Coaching, Technical Directorate, The FA Group, Burton-upon-Trent, UK; [b]FA Education, Technical Directorate, The FA Group, Burton-upon-Trent, UK

In this article, we provide a practitioner's account of the work undertaken by the English football association (FA) in the field of junior and youth grassroots football over the past two decades. We cover The FA's main achievements and challenges in implementing strategies and changes in the delivery and provision of grassroots football. In doing so, we draw upon some of the research The FA has commissioned and undertaken to inform the developments that have been and continue to be made. It is rare for organizations such as The FA to communicate their work and contextualize the challenges and innovations within which this work takes place. As such, we hope this contribution will inform the reader of the past and future innovations that are central to sustaining and developing the grassroots game.

Introduction

In 1997, The Football Association (FA) Technical Director at the time, Howard Wilkinson, presented The FA Charter for Quality[1] the proposal of a club based academy system was the most eye catching recommendation in the report. For grassroots football, the charter was a very clear signal from the governing body that after years of neglect they were going to provide strong leadership, linked with substantial investment. High among many concerns were the state of facilities, quality of coaching and the safety and welfare of children playing the grassroots game. To address these concerns, The FA has undertaken an increasingly strategic approach to football development at the junior grassroots level for the past 17 years. Two important recommendations were made that we argue are having a progressive impact in terms of shaping the game at grassroots level, not only for this generation of players but it has laid the foundations for raising the standard of football development for years to come. In this practitioner paper, we track the way that these two recommendations have evolved over time to reflect and support the needs of the modern grassroots game which, we argue, is having a beneficial impact on the participatory experience of those involved in junior grassroots football. That is, the proposal to introduce small-sided games for children (under 10 years of age) in what would become to be known as mini soccer, and a charter mark programme for junior football which became marketed as The FA Charter Standard programme. In doing so, we explore the impact of these changes on grassroots football through evidence-based research that has informed them. In addition, we address the challenges and opportunities they have presented and continue to present, The FA in implementing them and future innovations in grassroots football. First, we briefly overview how The FA has changed during the same period in order to be an organization capable of developing grassroots football.

The English FA – a strategic organization

In the late 1990s, many County Football Associations (CFAs) had very small staff teams and in some cases no paid staff, with the main function of governing and administering the game in their county. In order to successfully deliver on the policy objectives laid out in the Charter for Quality, CFA's were transformed from predominantly voluntary-led organizations into limited companies with full time professional paid staff with prescribed roles and responsibilities.

The FA formed the first Football Development team under the leadership of the National Football Development Manager John McDermott, whereby, five (rising to 10 in 2000) Regional Football Development Managers were appointed with the main objective of ensuring a successful implementation of mini soccer at a local level[2] through the CFA structure. The most significant development in the creation of the development infrastructure was the introduction of a network of over 60 county football development officers (FDOs), enabling The FA and CFA's to work more effectively together to strategically plan and deliver policies and programmes[3] at a local level. Each county formed a mini soccer working group, which over time in many counties evolved to become football development committees and they appointed (in many cases), a volunteer mini soccer coordinator. In line with modernizing of other national governing bodies of sport, all plans included targets and key performance indicators so that accountability and responsibility was central to implementing change.[4] The FA committed substantial funding which is now in excess of £40 m per season in to grassroots football.

The working group and coordinator would work with the regional manager to produce a county mini soccer plan. These plans would identify potential number of teams at each age group, which leagues would manage the games programmes, how schools would incorporate mini soccer and what facilities would be needed and be developed to ensure successful implementation. In addition, each CFA was given a target for the number of schools and clubs to be accredited with the Charter Standard in order to drive up standards in provision and ensure welfare.

During this period of change, The FA appointed two additional girls' and women's Regional Directors, with that team of five reporting to the National Girls' and Women's Manager, Kelly Simmons. It is worth noting that the Girls' and Women's Directors were also working with the CFA's to produce a plan for girls' football, both plans would have funding from The FA linked to implementation. Many of that original team of 12 would over the next 16 years become architects of football development in this country, leading, shaping and increasing the prominence and investment into grassroots football in England. Today women's and girls' football is prominently placed, which is ironic considering women's football was not recognized by The FA until 1990 and the development of the women's game was not encouraged at any level. Football is the number one team sport for girls and young women and according to data supplied by Sport England in 2014,[5] women's and girls' football is the fourth largest team sport in the country behind men's football, men's cricket and men's rugby. Today, The FA estimate that 1.7 m women and girls play regular football and a number of affiliated players have increased from approximately 10,000 to over 97,000.[6] Previously girls could only play mixed football up to under 11 years today this has increased to under 16s, in line with many other countries.

The FA Charter for Quality identified that women's and girls' football should be given greater attention by The FA and shortly after the publication of the report Hope Powell was appointed as the first full-time England women's manager; a structure was then developed that enabled a player pathway for young women, with the introduction of Girls' Centres of Excellences and the development of England teams at the younger age groups. To further support the Girls' Centre of Excellences and England teams, The FA has invested in a Women's Elite Performance unit which now comprises 14 full-time staff to support the England teams, centres of excellence and player development centres.

The FA Charter Standard

The Charter for Quality proposed the development of a Quality Mark across children's football to become part of a nationally recognized quality control programme. The original plan identified three categories of charter marks: holiday coaching and coaching courses, schools football and junior football.

The holiday coaching and coaching courses programme ran with limited success for five years in the early 2000s with mainly Premier League and Football League Football in the community schemes. The demise of the Footballers Further Education & Vocational Training Society and Football[7] in the community, and a rise in the number of private providers offering these types of provision such as soccer schools presented difficulties in quality assuring the kite mark. As such, the decision was taken to withdraw the kite mark for this aspect of provision which was increasingly occurring away from the jurisdiction and affiliation of The FA.

The schools Charter Standard programme ran successfully for seven years between 2001 and 2008 having a positive impact in particular on girls' football, young leadership and up skilling teachers to deliver football in their schools. Some 5500 schools achieved Charter Standard School status. The Charter Standard Schools programme was implemented in parallel with The FA TOP Sport Football Programme. The programme trained and supported over 16,000 primary school teachers over a three-year period to deliver football in the curriculum and provide much needed equipment and mini-soccer goals to play fixtures. Six million pounds was invested in to school football through this programme. In 2008, The FA decided to cease the Charter Standard Schools programme, partly because of the ability to quality assure the kite mark but mainly due to a refocus of its delivery for grassroots football through the emerging National Game Strategy.

The FA Charter Standard Clubs programme has been at heart of driving standards and developing the game at a grassroots level for the past 14 years. Established in 2001 grassroots football clubs have been encouraged and supported by the network of football development officers to devise and implement club development plans to increase the quality of provision in grassroots Junior Club Football, by among other things; screening and qualifications of coaches, implementing codes of conduct; continual professional development plans for coaches; school liaison; adopting small-sided games and devising strategies for increasing opportunities for girls football.

The initial pilot worked across six CFA's including a range of large, small, inner city and rural counties. Thirty-six clubs received The FA Charter Standard Clubs Award at its formal launch at the Lancashire FA headquarters. It was evident that the criteria would need to be reviewed and that two levels of award would be appropriate.

Following the amendments, The FA launched the programme with the introductory Charter Standard Clubs Award and the second level of Charter Standard Development Clubs that saw the need for the clubs to have boys and girls football teams, at least one Level 2 coach and a basic football development plan which was linked back to The FA Football Development Plan launched at Nottingham University in 2001. From its introduction, The Club Award proved popular, as it provided a basic operating standard, was aspirational with its two levels and helped improve quality and standards.

In 2001, Adam Crozier (then FA Chief Executive Officer), launched an FA vision document, one of the key objectives was to be the development of 300 super clubs. Charter Standard Clubs would be central to supporting this going forward and The Charter Standard Community Club status was developed which required clubs to have at least 10 teams and a pathway from youth to adult football.

We are of course aware that the requirements of the Charter Standard have represented somewhat of a cultural shift towards for those involved in the delivery of grassroots football. Despite a predominantly positive attitude towards the Charter Standard, the increasing demands placed on volunteers has caused some resistance[8] which has presented The FA with a challenge to achieve objectives regarding the number of teams to be accredited. However, research indicates that the network of FDOs have been influential in providing a consistent message and support to clubs and leagues in implementing the Charter Standard.[9] The work of the FDOs has been influential in ensuring 80% of all youth and junior football is played in Charter Standard clubs.[10]

Whilst The FA is currently involved in a number of research programmes aimed at enhancing the coaching practice at all levels of the game, the National Game Strategy report (May 2014)[11] highlighted that 75% of all youth football had a qualified coach. The growth in qualified coaches over the past 14 years is a direct consequence of the Charter Standard Programme. We recognize that volunteer coaches often experience barriers to further CPD, which is why The FA has introduced grassroots coach mentors. However, The FA recognized that while coaching numbers from Black, Asian, Minority Ethnic (BAME) communities at levels 1 and 2 were growing and consistent with the population, coaches from BAME communities were under represented at UEFA B and beyond. To try and address this imbalance, The FA introduced the Coach Bursary programme in 2011 under the direction Brendon Batson. This continues to be a challenge for The FA.

The past 17 years has seen great strides being made in the area of welfare across the game. When the Charter for Quality was first introduced, the importance of welfare was a new area for the game. In 1999, The FA introduced its first Child Protection policy followed by the first Child Protection course being delivered. It was mandatory that all volunteers, coaches and referees had to undertake The FA's safeguarding children workshop. It is now the norm for those in eligible roles working with under 18s to do a Criminal Records Check, via the Disclosure and Barring Service (DBS, formally the Criminal Records Bureau).

Every CFA, league and club with youth teams has a welfare officer. Collectively, this network works closely to make football safe for players, referees and volunteers, including handling concerns about poor practice and referring abuse to the statutory agencies and the DBS as required. The work to continually develop and improve the environment in which under 18s play, referee, coach, volunteer or watch the game, is an ongoing process, which the Child Protection in Sport Unit, run by the National Society for the Prevention of Cruelty to Children (NSPCC), has oversight of. The implementation of welfare and child protection policies and procedures in junior football has also presented a significant challenge to professional FA staff and volunteers on the ground. However, independent research[12] and research commissioned by The FA[13] indicates that the procedures and policies The FA implemented in child protection and welfare appear to have had a positive impact on attitudes and behaviour. While we are not complacent, The FA is proud of its achievements in raising awareness and educating football of the importance of Child Protection in sport.

Mini soccer

All of the above developments have provided the context in which mini soccer has developed. It seems extraordinary that less than 20 years ago we would have expected young children to play on the same size pitch, defending the same size goals as adult international players; but that was the case prior to the Charter for Quality. The proposal to introduce small-sided games for children (under 10 years of age) in what would be known as mini soccer was at the time seen as a controversial measure. Campaigns were launched opposing the idea and many leagues threatened to leave The FA if the rule became mandatory. There was even a Save Our Soccer (SOS) demonstration of The FA headquarters at Lancaster Gate, which saw the then England Manager Terry Venables meet with some of dissenters. While some were campaigning against the new rules, others were aggrieved over the perceived lack of consultation on the changes, something The FA has been mindful of and keen to engage in ever since.

However, even under this pressure, The FA in 1997 made a rule change that from the 1999–2000 season, children under 10 would play 7 v 7 Mini Soccer. The original plan also advises that U'7 and U'8's should play 5 v 5; however, it would be another 13 years until that would become mandatory through The FA Youth Review.[14] A two-year lead-in time from rule change to implementation was to allow leagues and clubs to adapt and ensure facilities was to allow a staged implementation of mini soccer to ensure success and reduce the potential barriers.

To ensure a successful implementation, therefore The FA had to:

• Promote mini soccer as the real game for children;
• ensure co-ordination at County FA level, so that leagues and clubs could deliver successfully;
• ensure that mini soccer pitches and goals were available

The promotion of mini soccer as 'The best introduction to the World's Greatest Game' would see the regional staff host a series of road shows and most importantly visit hundreds of local leagues to showcase the benefits of mini soccer. It was important that mini soccer was not just seen as a 'fad' imposed by The FA, but as the real game, adapted to meet the needs of young children. It was important that The FA highlighted and communicated the positive aspects of Mini Soccer through the network of County FAs and FDOs, which included:

- More touches of the ball
- Greater involvement in the game
- Right size goal for goal keepers
- Simple laws
- Fewer players, so simpler decisions and better understanding
- Smaller pitch so correct physical demands

In 2001, The FA and Sport England commissioned an evaluation report in to Mini Soccer conducted by Whitely International, who stated:

The results of the survey of Mini Soccer participants and their parent/guardians created a generally positive impression of the game. The strength of response in key areas suggested that Mini Soccer had been well received and is making a positive impact in terms of introducing young people to a game that encourages them to get actively involved, develop their skills levels and have fun. In particular, it is instructive to relate respondent's views to The FA's eight objectives for the game are as follows:

(1) Feel success: Although parents/guardians rated this as the least significant benefit of the game to players, it is clear from self-confidence expressed in their rating of their personal skills that Mini Soccer has made its participants feel good about themselves.

(2) Take an active part in the game: The responses on patterns of play show that a significant proportion of players feel that they spend at least 'a lot of time' running and/or passing the ball during matches.

(3) Learn to play as a team: The importance of the team ethos was underlined by all respondents indicating that they enjoyed playing as a team at least 'quite a lot'.

(4) Understand the laws of the game: 90% of respondents indicated that they know 'all' or 'most' of the rules of Mini Soccer.

(5) Develop soccer skills: The game has clearly had a positive effect on the football skills of its participants, with 52% of respondents believing that their skills have improved 'very much' and a further 46% believing that they have improved 'quite a lot'.

(6) Be able to take part whatever their ability: There is a strong endorsement for the view that players do not necessarily need to be good at football to enjoy playing Mini Soccer, with 77% of respondents believe that ability and enjoyment are not interdependent. Furthermore, almost 2% of respondents are physically less able.

(7) Develop fitness: Playing Mini Soccer has had a positive effect on the fitness levels of its participants, with 92% believing that their fitness has improved at least 'quite a lot' as a result of playing the game.

(8) Have fun: The 'fun' elements of the game are strongly endorsed, with 80% of respondents rating is as 'loads of fun', and the remainder as 'quite a lot of fun'.

From a technical point of view, the benefit of greater involvement and more touches of the ball were supported by University of Abertay[15] in their study of small-sided football in Scotland, which stated that players would touch the ball at least 50% more often in 7v7 as opposed to 11v11. In addition to enhanced enjoyment experienced by the participants, the study also indicated that 4 and 7-a-side games are the best means of developing technical and tactical attributes in preparation for the adult game, and having a positive physiological impact as the smaller game encouraged more movement and involvement.

The FA National Game Strategy (2008–2012) presented the document 'The Vision for Grassroots Football in England: Your Game, Your Say, One Goal'. This was developed after a comprehensive consultation process; one of the commitments in the strategy was to encourage and expand greater use of alternative small sided football formats. With the appointment of a National Mini Soccer and Youth Manager, Nick Levett, The FA commenced a period of consultation with Youth Leagues, coaches and young players. The consultation particularly with young players aimed to identify a number of motivations as to why children play and what they are looking for from the game. This included; 55 focus groups (approximately 2500 participants), boys majorly but including girls, aged mainly 8–12 years (included up to 14 years in some instances), from teams of all standards, in rural areas and urban areas were conducted.

The breakdown of the responses indicated that;

	TOTAL
Trying my hardest is more important to me than winning	389
I love playing football because it's fun	337
It helps keep me fit and healthy	292
I like meeting new friends through football	287
It is really a good game and I love it!	267
I like playing with my friends	243
I like learning new skills	173
I like playing matches against other teams	141
It is important to me I try to win matches	129
I really like scoring or stopping goals	113
I play because it makes my parents happy	26
I like skilling people	21
I like to show off my skills	9
It is important to me I win the league	5
Winning is more important to me than trying my hardest	0
It is important to me I win trophies and medals	0

2010 saw The FA publish a report titled 'Raising Our Game; Young Player Development and the Success of Future England Teams'. The report made a number of further recommendations across the whole game. Mini soccer has undergone several adjustments in format, rules and regulations since its inception. In promoting the child-centred approach, The FA notably claim to have undertaken research with children to inform these changes. Indeed, one of The FA's stated challenges is to give children and young people an opportunity to contribute to the running of the game.[16] Changes in format and rules include; more frequent and flexible competitions, a reduction to 5v5 for under 7s and 9v9 for under 11s and 12s before reaching the adult format of 11v11 at under 13 and the removal of league tables until under 13s at 11v11 are currently being phased in. There is no doubt that mini soccer has become a popular activity for both children and adults. Since its inception as an affiliated organized form of football, the number of mini-soccer teams increased year on year, from 21,800 to 25,932 between 2008 and 2011 (18.95% increase[17]).

This variety, it is hoped, will provide a good learning environment and opportunity for children. This, added to the greater number of coaches and varied competitions will provide a more sustainable and enjoyable introduction to the game.

Future challenges for grassroots football in England

The Charter for Quality provided the impetus for The FA's first Facilities Strategy which highlighted the importance of developing multipitch sites with appropriate size pitches and goals. It also recommended the need to develop multi use games areas (MUGA), which would develop over time with advancement in technology to third-generation artificial pitches (3G's). As a commitment to the programme, The FA and Sport England, ring-fenced £9 million over three years (1999–2001) to support the development of Mini Soccer.

Despite achievements in this area, grassroots football has historically been over reliant on the use of local authority owned pitches. Of the approximately 30,000 grass football pitches in England, it is estimated that 83% are both publicly owned and managed facilities with 52% of the total number within the education sector and 31% local authority owned and run.[18] This arrangement has become particularly acute given the current austerity measures that local authorities are being exposed to, which is pushing up pitch rent for voluntary grassroots clubs jeopardising the gains made in participation over recent years.[19] The FA Chairman's commission identified grassroots facility development as crucial to the sustainability and success of grassroots football, and the most pressing issue facing the game. Among other things, the commission has proposed that by 2020 there will be:

- Football hubs in 30 cities, increasing the number of artificial grass pitches (AGPs) in urban areas by 130% to more than 500.
- More than 150 new football-owned and managed football hubs to support the delivery of FA, County FA and professional club youth development and coach education programmes.
- More than 50% of all mini-soccer and youth football matches – about 3750 per week – being played on the best quality AGPs.

The Premier League and The FA Facilities Fund has been set up to be managed and delivered by the Football Foundation. A total of 235 grassroots projects have now benefited from a total of £44.8 m of investment from the fund since it opened to applications in January 2014 to develop new and upgrade existing community sports facilities with floodlit, all-weather 3Gs AGPs and modern changing rooms across the country.

In conclusion, the positive impact of The FA Charter for Quality has been far reaching in its developmental benefits to the grassroots game. Mini soccer is now seen as not only the norm but has been taken to its new logical step with the introduction 9V9 format. The Charter Standard Club Programme has raised standards in grassroots driving coach qualifications and child welfare. All county FAs have detailed plans delivered by a professional paid workforce. It is because of this legacy that the Charter for Quality can claim to be the birth of modern football development in England. As we look forward this year, The FA will launch a new corporate plan and National Game Strategy. These documents will set out how The FA plans to lead, support and develop the game in the future. We welcome the goal of this special issue on the culture and practice of grassroots football. It is important for any organization to keep abreast of latest trends and best practice, and the context in which these occur. A deeper understanding of these issues is important in reviewing and guiding policy and future innovations in junior and youth grassroots football.

Disclosure statement

No potential conflict of interest was reported by the authors.

Notes

1. The FA, 'A Charter for Quality'.
2. The FA, 'Football Development Strategy 2001–2006'.
3. Ibid.
4. Houlihan and Green, 'Modernization and Sport: The Reform of Sport England and UK Sport'.
5. Sport England, *Who Plays Sport – The National Picture*.
6. The FA, 'Women's and Girl's Football Strategy 2008–2012'.
7. The Footballers' Further Education and Vocational Training Society (FFE/VTS) was an organization, set up in 1980 by the combined efforts of the Professional Footballers' Association, FA and Football League to ensure clubs offer education and training opportunities to youth footballers.
8. Lusted and O'Gorman, 'The Impact of New Labour's Modernization Agenda on the English Grass-roots Football Workforce', 2010.
9. O'Gorman, 'The Changing Nature of Sports Volunteering: Modernization, Policy and Practice'.
10. The FA, 'National Game Strategy 2011–15'.
11. Ibid.
12. Brackenridge et al., *Child Welfare in Football: An Exploration of Children's Welfare in the Modern Game*.
13. Brackenridge et al., 'The Football Association's Child Protection in Football Research Project 2002–2006'.
14. The FA, 'Youth Development Review'.
15. Small, 'Small-sided Games Study of Young Football Players in Scotland'.
16. The FA, 'National Game Strategy 2011–15'.
17. Ibid.
18. Sport England, 'Active Places 2012'.
19. The FA, 'England Chairman's Commission Report'.

References

Brackenridge, C.H., J. Bringer, Claudi Cockburn, G. Nutt, Andy Pitchford, Kate Russell, and Zofia Pawlaczek. 'The Football Association's Child Protection in Football Research Project 2002–2006: Rationale, Design and First Year Results'. *Managing Leisure* 9, no. 1 (2004): 30–46.

Brackenridge, C.H., A. Pitchford, K. Russell, and G. Nutt. *Child Welfare in Football: An Exploration of Children's Welfare in the Modern Game*. London: Routledge, 2007.

The Football Association. *The FA Chairman's England Commission Report*. London: The Football Association, 2014.

The Football Association. *The Football Association National Game Strategy 2011–2015*. London: The Football Association, 2011.

The Football Association. *Football Development Strategy 2001–2006*. London: The Football Association, 2001.

The Football Association. *Women's and Girl's Football Strategy 2008–2012*. London: The Football Association, 2008.

The Football Association. *Youth Development Review*. London: The Football Association, 2010.

The Football Association Technical Department. *Football Education for Young Players: "A Charter for Quality"*. London: The Football Association, 1997.

Lusted, J., and J. O'Gorman. 'The Impact of New Labour's Modernisation Agenda on the English Grass-roots Football Workforce'. *Managing Leisure* 15, no. 1–2 (2010): 140–54.

O'Gorman, J. 'The Changing Nature of Sports Volunteering: Modernisation, Policy and Practice'. In *Managing Sport: Social and Cultural Perspectives*, ed., D. Hassan and J. Lusted, 218–38. London: Routledge, 2013.

Small, G. *Small-sided Games Study of Young Football Players in Scotland*. Dundee: University of Abertay Dundee, 2006.

Sport England. 'Active Places 2012'. Unpublished data set. http://data.gov.uk/dataset/active-places (accessed January 2015).

Sport England. *Who Plays Sport – The National Picture*. 2014. http://www.sportengland.org/research/who-plays-sport/national-picture/who-plays-sport/ (accessed January 2015).

Children's voices in mini soccer: an exploration of critical incidents

Jimmy O'Gorman and Kenny Greenough

Department of Sport and Physical Activity, Edge Hill University, Ormskirk, UK

Since being adopted by The English Football Association as the preferred format of football to be played by children aged 10 and under, mini soccer has evolved and expanded into a popular activity for children. Yet little is known about the experiences of those participating in the game. In addition, adult-organized activities such as mini soccer are increasingly seen by parents and adults as suitable pursuits for their children to participate in. Yet the perspective of the child participating in mini soccer, as with many other activities, is largely ignored in academic literature. This is especially true in the social sciences, where research has historically been done 'on' children, rather than 'with' children. In this study, we seek to address this imbalance by including children as active participants in the research process. In doing so, we devised a methodology based on audiovisual methods to create participatory conditions between children and researchers interested in investigating their experiences of mini soccer in England. Children were asked to identify aspects of their experience which they felt were noteworthy to create video recordings of critical incidents that directly involved them participating in mini soccer. These were used as a discussion tool in focus groups to explore how and why children felt the incidents were critical, and how their experience of them shaped their participation. The methodology employed helped capture children's differentiated views of the same incidents, and highlighted the diversity of their experiences. It is recommended that similar audiovisual methodologies are employed to inform future policy and strategy development in grassroots football that includes children as participants.

Introduction

Children growing up in developed societies have increasingly taken part in organized sporting activities structured by adults. For a variety of reasons and societal pressures, parents have sought to include children in such activities for the presumed pro-social development of an array of competencies preparing them for transition to adulthood.[1] In addition, participation in organized sporting activities has largely been perceived by parents as a diversionary and protective tool in ensuring children are not attracted towards negative social behaviours, or are exposed to perceptibly potentially harmful unsupervised environments.[2] Parents have also been noted to place their children in, and are increasingly willing to pay to do so; organized sporting activities under the assumption they may maximize sporting potential. Evidently, a milieu of prevailing social processes appear to have reinforced the perceived desire to offer ever increasingly routinized, structured and organized activity at ever younger ages for children. Whilst these rationalized forms of childhood activity are largely designed and organized by adults, the perspective of the child in relation to these activities has remained marginalized in both the fields of practice and academia.[3] As such, these activities appear to prioritize the interests of adults rather than children, under the assumption that they are best developed in the interests of children. Authors within the field of the sociology of childhood[4] suggest children have effectively become disempowered in losing the propensity to engage in and take responsibility for their own play.

In England, mini soccer for children aged between the ages of 7 and 11 has emerged within these wider societal processes. This coincided with an increasingly interventionist approach to achieve sport-related objectives in England by successive governments since the late 1990s.[5] Government policies and strategies modernized the English sports system[6] as The FA shifted from an administrative body to a developmental and strategic organization.[7] In addition, The FA had declared that a strategy and plan for the development of grassroots football was urgently needed to increase long-term participation and enhance the technical ability of junior players against a perceived long-term decline in the regularity and quality of schools and junior football.[8] Notably, The FA suggested a 'child centred approach' was required, and that it was 'quite appropriate … to take a lead and prescribe', in the best interests of the children, 'the most appropriate forms of organised football participation for a four year introduction to 11 aside football for children under 10 years of age'.[9] It was proposed all children should receive coaching from qualified football coaches, and play on appropriate facilities on a regular basis. In aiming to raise standards of provision in grassroots, particularly junior, football, the Charter for Quality proposed that small-sided club football marketed under 'mini soccer' be introduced for children under 10.[10]

Most recently, The FA Youth development review sought to revise the 'player pathway' and reinforce the prioritization of 'children's wants and needs at the forefront of the participatory experience' in light of a win-at-all-costs mentality perceived to have accompanied the original incarnation of mini soccer which stifled development and enjoyment.[11] The document further embedded the dualistic emphasis on sustaining and increasing participation by enhancing enjoyment, whilst developing the technical ability of players, based on the assumption that small-sided games will provide children with an increase in touches, shots, dribbles and goals.[12]

According to Brackenridge, mini soccer is a smaller version of the adult game, designed to prepare children to progress into adult 11 a side players.[13] This developmental approach to children in football underscores the traditional framework within the sociology of childhood that views children in false dichotomous and binary terms.[14] That is, what children are expected to become (adults) rather than who and what they actually are. The developmental approach views children as 'unfinished', requiring continuous involvement of adults in order to develop into full members of society; as passive beneficiaries partaking in activities that prepare them for adulthood. Socialization of the child is required to bring children within the structures of the social system, imposed, as it were, in a top-down fashion with adults tending to needs.[15]

Despite much methodological and theoretical advancement in the field of the sociology of childhood[16] an abstracting of children predominates in social scientific practice.[17] Much social science-based sports literature focusing on children tends to assume they're the objects of research, marginalizing the child voice.[18] Whilst such research is informative, it tends to subordinate children in the process, limits our understanding to largely one-sided accounts, and treats children as incomplete members of society. Yet children are valued active research collaborators,[19] and have subjective worlds worth exploring in their own right to deepen our understanding of them,[20] in developing a deeper, congruent understanding of their sporting experiences.

The inclusion of children in the research process by The FA for the youth development review is indeed a welcome step. Yet, despite the scale and intensity of mini soccer practice and changes becoming more 'child centred', children's voices still appear to be relatively marginalized. Within the sample of people The FA consulted, children constituted 50 groups of 8–12-year olds and 16 regional 'Your Kids Your Say' road shows in amongst consultation with adults from over 300 youth leagues, 1000 youth club administrators, and over 4000 volunteers and coaches.[21]

We seek to emphasize that children's experiences are as equally worthy of consideration as those that tend to shape their participatory experiences, i.e. adults. This paper therefore seeks to emphasize children's voices in exploring their experiences of adult-organized mini soccer within the social networks within which they are enmeshed. In doing so, we seek to build on the research of Brackenridge et al.,[22] and The FA[23] by understanding mini soccer from the position of the child. With the sociology of childhood in mind, we sought to employ research methods that prioritized children's voices[24] and involved children as participants in the research process. We devised a methodology to allow young children to reflect on and discuss 'critical incidents' occurring within their participation in mini soccer.

Methods

The research procedure utilized audiovisual methods to generate critical incidents as a stimuli for discussion. Visual methods to generate qualitative data are becoming more prominent in facilitating the understanding and exploration of children's experiences and perspectives of sport contexts.[25] To date, the predominant techniques appear to have centred on the use of drawings or photographs as a stimuli for subsequent discussion.[26] We encouraged child participants to reflect upon and discuss their experiences by video recording matches that directly involved them, and using the recordings as a reflective tool within a focus group setting to generate discussion. This ensured that the data collection involved children within the naturalistic setting of mini soccer, rather than contrived settings in which much research with children is depicted.[27]

The practice of identifying critical incidents is particularly suited to creating participatory conditions between researchers and participants.[28] Adapted from the field of educational research, critical incidents are straightforward accounts of commonplace events that occur in routine practice. Incidents become critical in the sense that they are indicative of underlying trends, motives and structures.[29] Complementing an interpretivist position, critical incidents are produced by the interpretation of the significance of aspects of an event. This of course requires a value judgement to be made as to what is important and what stands out, i.e. the significance we attach to the meaning of an incident. According to Tripp,[30] there are two important stages in the 'creation' of critical incidents.

Creating critical incidents in mini soccer

First, the production of an incident: the observation and recall of a particular event or happening. In creating critical incidents for analysis, we therefore attempted to ensure the voices of the children were central generating incidents perceived to be noteworthy during matches in which they had played. Three teams representing under 8s, under 9s and under 10s, mini soccer age groups were video recorded participating in organized league fixtures on a weekly basis in the north of England between January and April 2011 (Table 1). Pseudonyms have been provided in order to hide the teams' and players' identities.

Cameras were positioned in two locations in order to provide coverage of the field of play and spectators. Camera 1 was positioned at the half way line on the side-line of the team being recorded, and was operated manually to follow the ball through passages of play. The camera was also fitted with a microphone to pick up verbal noise and chatter from spectators, players and officials. Camera 2 was fixed, and positioned at a point behind the corner flag on the side-line of the spectators of respective teams being recorded. At the end of each game, players were informally asked about any moments of significance in relation to opposition players, officials and parent spectators in addition to their own team.[31] Of course, this generated significant debate. Therefore, the children were asked to identify the top three incidents they had recalled in terms of those they felt occurred not just in the match they had immediately participated in, but also those that occurred most frequently in their participation more generally. These observations were then logged in a notebook, to be identified on the video recordings to be clipped for analysis. The inclusion of children in identifying the critical incidents directly after their games was participatory in nature, and diluted the power relationship[32] between the children and adult researchers.

Examining critical incidents in mini soccer

Tripp[33] suggests there is no one immutable way to analyse critical incidents. Where the final analysis ends depends upon the interpretation of those involved, and the significance they place upon it.[34] Video recordings were clipped into 12 separate critical incidents for each team, and organized into alike categories.[35] This was undertaken to provide a semblance of structure to the clips for the purpose of generating discussion. Each clip lasted between 32 and 90seconds. Focus groups for each team were organized for one evening at the end of the season, in which each clip was visually replayed back to the children on a giant screen in a local football club social club. At the end of each clip, a verbal discussion was generated as to why the children had initially felt the incident was significant, why they felt the incident occurred and how the incident made them feel. The replication of the social context of experiencing their mini soccer participation as a team within the group also enabled the researchers to focus upon the interaction between the children.[36] The

Table 1. Sample of clubs and junior players.

Team	Age range of children	No. of focus group participants
Eastcrook	7–8	8
Harvest JFC	8–9	8
Rancher JFC	9–10	10

use of focus groups directly involving the children allowed numerous voices to be heard simultaneously, and provided an opportunity for a wide array of individual and communal perspectives to be represented.[37] Moreover, the differential, and similar experiences of group members were highlighted in recalling the same critical incident. In addition, the informal and relaxed way in which the researchers conducted the discussion facilitated the interaction between group members and researchers, allowing for elaboration where appropriate on issues wider than the context of mini soccer. This allowed the group to challenge or support each other's views, providing a potentially more realistic account[38] of the nuances of children's experiences in mini soccer. As is common in focus groups with children,[39] there was a tendency for some children at times to lose focus on the task. Therefore, probing questions and prompts were used by the researchers to refocus the children on the task discussing the video clip they had just observed.

Parents and coaches of the children were present in the room, but were not part of, or in hearing distance, of the focus group. In addition, the hosting of the focus groups in an environment familiar to the children with non-significant adult researchers (i.e. not an authoritative figure such as a parent or coach) that had been present at all of their games, also reinforced an informal atmosphere and further reduced the hierarchical adult – child relationship.[40] Encouraging children to identify and reflect upon incidents that are important to them within their mini soccer participation illuminated deep cultures and structures. Indeed, the use of video clips (children's responses being identified as C1–C10 within their respective focus group contribution) also allowed the children to recall and generalize more broadly over similar incidents they had experienced in mini soccer. For the purposes of the paper, the incidents have been grouped in relation to the actors that children focused on when originally identifying the incident such as, other child players (both opposing and team mates), referees (both adult and under 18), spectators, parents and coaches. A selection of 10 critical incidents of the 36 collated across all three teams are presented for the discussion below.[41]

Incidents with players and coaches

Children identified the following incidents with their coach as critical based upon the *manner* in which instructions and behaviour were portrayed. These included shouting tactical information and remonstrating with the decisions of officials.

Critical incident 1

An Eastrcrook player has the ball at his feet in his own penalty area, and directly in front of his own team's goal. There are a lot of players from both teams in close proximity. Directly in front of him, is an opposition player. From the side-lines, the Eastcrook coach can be heard shouting aggressively whilst waving his arms in the air 'clear it, get it away'. The player from Eastcrook stands still and hesitates before attempting to execute a 'step over' to trick the opposition player. The opposition player steps forward and dispossess the Eastcrook player and then shoots accurately into the corner of the Eastcrook goal from approximately eight yards. Whilst the opposition are celebrating, the Eastcrook coach can be seen encroaching slightly onto the playing area, and is heard shouting 'Charlie, Charlie, you need to clear it from there, what are you doing taking him on? That's stupid. You've just cost us a goal'. The coach then shakes his head, talking to parents with his arms out his side, whilst Charlie bows his head, alone, and stands still until play resumes. Some spectators can be heard shouting 'don't worry Charlie, keep going'.

When asked to explain what happened and why,
C5 stated 'He wants us to win and Charlie messed up', *C3 continued* 'yeah we lost that game'. *C1 noted* 'he shouted coz the mistake cost us', *whereas C4 added* 'I didn't mean it, but I know not to do that'.

When asked how this made the children feel,
C1 stated, 'Makes you feel bad coz they might not play coz they might feel right I'm not playing now because they feel bad'. *C2 quickly contributed* 'Not good because it can put your team off', *whilst C3 adds almost immediately* 'They shouldn't be shouting bad things, it puts you off'. *After an initial pause, other children contribute* 'If they shout good things that's ok coz that makes you feel good', *and* 'yeah when you do something good' *(C4 and C5, respectively).The interpretation continues* 'Sometimes it can make you happy if its encouragement' *(C6) but C7 notes,* 'Sometimes it can make you sad'. *C6 then adds as though in thought* 'Yeah a bit (it happens) it's your manager trying to encourage ya' *with C4 adding* 'They encourage ya a lot'.

Critical incident 2

An Eastcrook player is challenged by an opposition player in the penalty area, approximately six yards away from the goal-line, slightly to the right. It appears as though the opposition player trips the Eastcrook player without touching the ball, just as the Eastcrook player is about to shoot towards the goal. The Eastcrook coach walks forward encroaching onto the pitch, displaying emotive body language with arms in the air, shouting loudly and aggressively at the referee from approximately 20 m away 'Ay that's a penalty, you've gotta be joking ref, he's just tripped him up'. The coach then turns to the side-line of the pitch and makes mildly derogatory comments about the referee to spectator parents.

When asked to explain what happened and why,
C3 noted 'Our manager running down the pitch with his arms up' *with C5 interjecting* 'Coz he thought it was a penalty' *and C7 adding* 'He did it because he wanted a pen' *and almost immediate with their contribution C6:* 'He raised his hands up because he wanted the pen'.

When asked how this made the children feel,
C2 initially answers 'Intimidated' *with C7 adding* 'It's not ok for him to do that'. *C2, in further agreement* 'No it's not alright to do that coz it puts you off'. *C1 then explains* 'He was on the pitch, that's not ok' *with C3 saying* 'He should be off the pitch doing it because sometimes the ball can just come and hit him, he could get in the way and it could go onto the goal and they could score'. *C1 continues* 'We played this team and the manager was throwing his cap off and everything' *with C6 stating* 'He was throwing it onto the pitch. I seen him coming onto the pitch and hugging the player' *(C4). C1 then adds* 'He shouldn't do that coz it could waste time and when injury time comes it could be about half an hour and all the parents might be shouting at the manager … That wouldn't be good', *but C3 then*

contributes 'But for them (parents) sometime it is, but for him (manager) it's not'. *C2 then states* 'Its putting you off as well – if your dad went to the manager what are you doing, it could put you off coz your worrying your dad could get into trouble', *whilst C1 further notes* 'It puts you off, feels like he is going to come and do something to your parents', 'It puts the team off' (*adds C5*), 'I see it sometimes … Not a lot, not really' (*C4 responds*).

Incidents with players and parent spectators

Similar to incidents with coaches, the children identified incidents with parent spectators and commented on the *manner* of instructional and tactical information provided. In addition, the children also noted both positive and negative feelings about comments made by parent spectators towards individuals and the whole group of players (own team and the opposition).

Critical incident 3

Eastcrook score a goal. From a central position, Barrie passes the ball to Jake in a wide position in the opposition half. Jake runs past an opposition player with the ball and passes into the centre of the opposition penalty area where George runs onto the ball and shoots past the goalkeeper. All Eastcrook players except the goalkeeper run towards George celebrating by hugging George, patting George on the back and with 'hi 5s'. There is a loud cheer from the group of spectator parents on the side-line, as the children involved in the passage of play are verbally praised with audible shouts of 'well done Barrie, good pass' 'brilliant Jake, great cross' 'good goal George, well done'.

When asked to explain what happened and why,
C5 announces 'Goal by me, I scored a goal', *C3 states* 'We celebrated' *and C1 describes* 'The crowd cheered and said well done' … 'They were shouting loudly'. *C4 and C2 note, respectively,* 'We always get a clap when somebody scores' *and* 'Only if it's like another team and none of the parents were there for the other team they would clap them as well'.

When asked how this made the children feel,
C4 notes 'That's good' *with C5* 'Made me happy' *and* 'The team will feel nice' (*C2 noted*). 'Making them happy' *C1 adds, then further clarifying,* 'Makes them have more confidence'. *C2 continues* 'Everyone should get clapped not just the player who scored' *with C1 summarizing that* 'The parents were happy'.

Critical incident 4

The opposition score a goal against Harvest JFC. The parent spectators on the side-line supporting Harvest FC applaud the opposition as the players reorganize to restart the game. Parent spectators audibly praise the opposition with comments 'well done, good goal' and 'fantastic football, good stuff'. Following this, the parent spectators then audibly encourage Harvest FC players 'come on boys heads up, you can get back into this'.

When asked to explain what happened and why,

C1: 'They scored a goal and our line clapped' *and C2 added* 'That was good because it encourages the other team'. 'It shows respect' *(C5) and* 'It was a good goal so they clapped' *(C3). C7 further noted their opinion* 'I don't like our line clapping the other team, they should be clapping us' *whilst C4 positions themselves too;* 'We're clapping and they don't clap for us no because they're all from them (rival team from nearby area) they're horrible there'.

When asked how this made the children feel,

C3 starts ... 'It makes you feel alright as long as they clap us too'. 'I don't mind it' *states C5,* 'But they are not bothered about us, it's not nice' *C7 interjects.*

Incidents with opposition players

Whilst the above incidents in relation to adults generally focused on verbal instruction and comments from the side-lines, the following incidents centred on their feelings towards opposition players within the context of participating within the game. In particular, children commented in a variety of ways on perceived foul play, sportsmanship, and pro-social and anti-social behaviours by their own and opposing players alike.

Critical incident 5

A Harvest JFC tries to dribble past an opposition player. The opposition player dispossess him and moves forward into the Harvest JFC half of the field in a wide area. The Harvest JFC player turns and attempts to catch up with the opposition player. And as he approaches the opposition player from the back, he runs into him, knocking him to the ground. The referee awards the free kick. The Harvest JFC player assists the opposition player to his feet, and can be audibly heard saying 'sorry, are you ok?'

When asked to explain what happened and why,

C1 explains, 'Done a tackle' *with C6 discussing their role* 'I helped someone up after I fouled him'. *C5 now continues* 'That's good because he showed sportsmanship'. *C3 now explains the impact with* 'It's like he is apologising for the foul' *and C2 adds* 'It's like he is concerned about him' *to describe the situational event.*

When asked how this made the children feel,

C2 stated – 'it makes you feel good / better if they help you', *C1 continued* 'yeah its good when the other team are nice to you', *whereas C7 noted* 'but not when they're from them (rival team from nearby area), they're never nice and I'm never nice to them'. *C5 however, added* 'yeah but I would do it, I don't care what they do'.

Critical incident 6

An Eastcrook player is fouled in the centre of the pitch, and falls to the floor. The player stays on the floor as play continues as the referee deems that Eastcrook still have possession of the ball. The Eastcrook coach tells the Eastcrook player in possession to kick the ball out of play to stop the game, so that he can enter the field of play to assist the Eastrcrook player on the floor, who is in tears. The Eastrcrook coach attends to the player, who is assisted to his feet, and regains his composure. The opposition coach and referee instruct the player to return the ball to the Eastcrook goalkeeper. There is a round of applause from most spectator parents.

When asked to explain what happened and why,
'It was a foul and they gave the ball back to the opposition coz they played on' *opens C3. C5 notes to clarify understanding* 'They played the advantage' *and C6* 'It was good for them to give the ball back coz its sportsmanship'. *C5 further tries to explain* 'If they have done it to you it's like giving it back to them' ... 'See lots of sportsmanship' *clarifies C1. C2 then explains* 'Could try and get a goal if you get the ball back' *with C3 adding in* 'It happens quite a lot'. *C6 and C7 respond, respectively, with* 'No I don't, we usually stop and have a free kick' *and* 'I don't really see that', *whilst C4 intervenes* 'I see it sometimes ...'

When asked how this made the children feel,
C2 continues 'It could make you sad if you do it if they score, you could lose' *but with C5 adding* 'It makes you feel good coz its friendly', *C7 then quickly responds with* 'You have to do it coz the ref tells you' *before the conversation ceases.*

Critical incident 7

A Rancher JFC player is attempting to tackle an opposition player in a position close to the corner of the pitch towards the opposition's goal line. The Rancher JFC player wins the tackle, and in the process knocks the opposition player to the side with his upper body. The opposition player falls on his side. The opposition player quickly regains a standing position, and jumps forward with his legs together whilst simultaneously dropping to the floor in a seated position. His feet collide with the feet of the Rancher JFC player who, on seeing this movement, has moved the ball away and is fouled. The Rancher JFC player falls to the floor. Spectator parents and the Rancher coach shout loudly at the referee for a foul and complain to the referee as to the fierceness of the tackle. A free kick is awarded and the referee ensures the opposition player and the Rancher JFC player shake hands.

When asked to explain what happened and why,
'There was a foul, in the corner and he got back up and fouled the other one' (*C5*). 'That's cheeky coz he thinks he got me so I will get him' (*C4 further adds*). *C1 now tries to explain* 'He's got up just to get him down' *and C2 carries on the discussion* 'He did it because he was angry'. *Here though C3 adds* 'I don't see it much' *yet C2 now explains* 'I tackled him and he slid in two footed and put me into the corner flag, it made me feel bad and sad'.

When asked how this made the children feel,
C1 begins with their emotions: 'It's our team and makes me feel bad coz it's not sportsmanship', *whilst C4 contributes* 'If someone from the other has hit them first it is not that bad, there is a reason what they will do it for'. *C3 now tries to explain the situation*: 'There is a reason coz he has done it to you' ... 'Or you could just ask for the free kick' (*C2* 'chips in'). *C7 continues* 'Yeah you have to get him back

or he thinks he is better than you', *whilst C3 builds upon this reasoning with* 'It's not good but you have to do it'. *C2 however, contradicts one or two answers with* 'It's not ok to do that though ...'

Incidents with officials

The majority of incidents identified by children relating to officials centred on the decisions made during the game. These included the reactions of team mates and adult, parent spectators commenting on referee decisions. Children also noted gamesmanship, citing examples from professional football that informed their feelings towards understanding their own behaviour, and that of opponents and adults.

Critical incident 8

A Rancher JFC player attempts to tackle an opposition player close to the opposition penalty area. The Rancher JFC player appears to trip the opposition, who falls to the ground. The Rancher JFC player takes the ball and moves forward towards the opposition goalkeeper. The referee blows his whistle and signals a foul to the opposition. The Rancher JFC player, upon hearing the whistle, kicks the ball off the field of play in an aggressive manner and throws his arms up in the air. The audio is not clear, but the Rancher JFC player is observed talking at the referee whilst shaking his head side to side.

When asked to explain what happened and why,
Almost immediately C5 offers an explanation of the events: 'The player kicked it away', *whereby C3 now clarifies* 'Player's arguing with the referee because he is angry'. *C2 states* 'We don't think that he made the right decision but the video shows that he did' *and C8 assures* 'It was the right decision'. *Yet here, C2 further notes* 'We always moan anyway because you want to get the ball', *but C4 adds* 'Because you are frustrated because we lost the ball, and we could have scored from that'. 'It's the players fault coz he can't do it properly (throw the ball in)' *and* 'Everyone would get fouled – You need the referee though otherwise everyone would get snapped' *immediately following the last remarks from C6 and C1, respectively, C4 now explains* 'If you didn't have the ref you would be able to do bad tackles' *... and concludes* 'It happens a lot'.

When asked how this made the children feel,
C4 now reasons 'It would have a bad effect because they could score', *with C7 adding* 'It's not good the way he reacted because he might get all the other players frustrated', *and* 'He might get a fine' *further noted from C3 within the group.*

Critical incident 9

An opposition player is deemed by the referee to have been fouled by a Rancher JFC player, close to the Rancher JFC penalty area, slightly right from centre. The offending player is observed questioning the referee, but accepts the decision and walks into the penalty area. On taking the free kick, an opposition player kicks the ball into the penalty area, where another opposition player strikes first time into the Rancher JFC goal. A parent spectator is observed walking aggressively form a position opposite from where the free kick was taken, towards the centre of the field where the camera is located. The parent spectator can audibly be heard to be swearing in the direction of the referee and to himself adding 'What a joke that was never a free kick'.

When asked to explain what happened and why,

C2 confidently states 'The man was swearing' *before C5 states abruptly* 'The keeper then was shit'. *C2 then explains* 'The fella was walking on the pitch, angry' … 'He was shouting what are you doing lad get on the pich and score a goal', 'what are you doing lad get on the pitch and score a goal', *with C4 contributing* 'He was throwing his arms out because it was a bad free kick'. *C3 now reflects,* 'What if it was you who took the free kick? It would make you feel bad' *and C2 again reasoning* 'It might be you that they are moaning at, and that is bad'.

C1 now mentions 'He can't give you a hug he could be a paedo', *whereas C3 states that* 'He might just be complaining about something stupid'. *At this point, C6 is critical of the incident* 'He swore, he can't do that, its bad language'… 'He shouldn't be doing that'. *But again at this point, C2 continues* 'I hear it all the time, especially the M word and the C word' *and C7 sums up their perception with* 'It's not good behaviour'. *It is at this point C1 recites their own experiences of such situations of behaviour:* 'If you're in our house you have to pay 20p', *with C2 also resorting to explain their behaviour* 'I've already been suspended 5 times for all kinds, bad tackles, shouting at the referee'. *At this point C8 tries to justify the incident with* 'It's ok to swear at the referee if he gives a very bad decision yeah'.

When asked how this made the children feel,

C5 now builds upon their understanding. 'If the ref made a very very bad decision you have got to give him training so you have to react' *and C4 interprets* 'It means they are bad supporters if they swear'. *C2:* 'You do get frustrated though, especially if they give a very bad decision and it costs you the game, yeaah', *with C6 adding* 'The whole team and the line get frustrated'. *The additional interpretations are then provided from C7:* 'You might be like losing and it might be the last couple of minutes and there is a penalty decision which he doesn't give and the line or the team might swear', *C2 now provides their interpretation,* 'You have to let the ref know if it's a bad decision don't ya'.

Critical incident 10

A Harvest JFC player dribbles forwards with the ball towards the edge of the opposition penalty area. An opposition player tries to deliberately trip up the Harvest JFC player. Despite losing his balance, the Harvest JFC player manages to stay on his feet, but is falling forwards as he shoots awkwardly towards the opposition goal. The ball trickles towards the opposition goalkeeper who picks the ball up. Parent spectators are shouting at the referee to give a free kick. The referee indicates the opposition goalkeeper to continue play.

When asked to explain what happened and why,

'They pulled him out of the way' *utters C6, and* 'They stuck his foot out to try and trip him over' *articulates C3. C2 mentions* 'They did slidey tackles', *but C1 describes* 'He stayed on his feet it was good coz he was carrying on and trying to score'. *C5 builds upon that understanding with* 'He didn't want to get a free kick he wanted to score a goal for his own or set one up'. 'It's good coz when you do that like you might get something better like you get better encouragement when you do that but when you get fouled everyone comes around and the game stops' *further contributes C7. C8 continues* 'If he had gone down he might of got a free kick and the free kick might not have been in a good area or gone anywhere so it was good for his team he is trying to win', *with C3 concluding* 'If he tripped over he couldn't pass it on'. *C7 now further adds* 'If he had of fell down the other team might have got the ball' *and* 'He would have been in trouble if he fell down coz the other team might have ran down the line and scored' (*adds C6*). *C2 continues* 'It has happened to me and I have done it to someone, they went in for a "slidey" and I jumped over his leg and nearly scored'. *C6 then interjects* 'I did it once and we scored off it coz I jumped over his leg and passed it on and we scored' *with C4 further contributing* 'Yeah Ronaldo and Drogba, coz if you tackled them they just fall over'. *C1 utters* 'It's a disgrace' *whilst C7 poses his response* 'Steven Gerrard doesn't do it'. *Thought-fully, after a couple of seconds, C3 contributes* 'Everyone does it once in a while', *but C1 concludes shortly in response* 'It is still bad doesn't matter who does it'.

When asked how this made the children feel,

C6 opens with 'Makes you nervous coz if you get past them sometimes a couple of minutes later they might snap you coz you beat them last time'. 'Yeah it's like they look silly so want to get you back' (*C8 responds*). 'I just feel the same' (*furthers C1*).

Discussion – children's perspectives of critical incidents in mini soccer

We have sought to emphasize children's experiences of mini soccer within the social networks of relations in which they are enmeshed. By seeking to understand mini-soccer from the position of the child, we sought to prioritize the voice of the child in juxtaposition to the predominant 'developmental' view in research 'on' children. As such, we have presented data in its raw unedited form that illustrates children's understanding and feelings in relation to this form of adult-organized football. Rather than passive beneficiaries of activities, we explored children's routine and common experiences of participating in grassroots football at mini soccer level by devising a methodology which allowed young children to be active participants in the research process, and reflect on and discuss 'critical incidents' in which they were involved in mini soccer. Our use of video recordings within a focus group set-ting as a visual stimulus to prompt children to discuss critical incidents that they themselves had identified was useful in understanding why children felt particular aspects of their experience were noteworthy, and how their experiences of these inci-dents made them feel. In addition, the use of authentic material appeared to engage the children in an enthusiastic and engaging manner. This not only allowed the chil-dren to recall the actual event after previously noting it as a critical incident, but also helped the children to explain and clarify their understanding and reasoning. As a result, the recollection of experiences via either group or individual perspectives were communicated[42] revealing deep cultures and structures that are not readily identifiable. Yet, whilst the children's perspectives were differentiated, their experi-ences were neither homogenized nor unique. The methodology employed exposed different interpretations and feelings regarding similar critical incidents that occur regularly in mini soccer. The children varied between their explanations and depth of answers, possibly due to variation of ages across the three clubs interviewed. However, children both agreed and disagreed with one another, whilst offering their interpretation and their own views.

Consistent with Walters et al.,[43] the children across all age ranges and teams identified fun, competition and sportsmanship, which interlaced all critical incidents. Whilst the intention of the article is to prioritize the child voice to present a more reality congruent illustration of children's experiences of mini soccer, the findings do present some theoretical pointers highlighting the often hidden and deeper culture that shape children's participatory experiences. The discussion of critical incidents in relation to opposing players and the officials appeared to centre on sportsmanship, particularly between anti-social and pro-social behaviours[44] witnessed and the different meanings and emphases attributed to them. Whilst some explained feeling anxiety regarding possible retributive behaviours of opposing players, others expressed justification and a desire for retributive behaviour not just in terms of winning, but in the context of rivalry between teams.

It is noteworthy that children predominantly identified critical incidents in relation to the adults within the network of social relations that form part of their participatory experience in mini soccer. Perhaps it was largely inevitable that the children would identify the excessive behaviours of parents and coaches[45] towards winning and competition as being an incidents worthy of note. Yet what is revealing are the differences between members of the same team as to the justification of such behaviours and how this shaped each individual's experience. Competition appeared to be desired, but in the context of rivalry between teams as an inherent part of the enjoyment. Whereas competition underpinned by an over emphasis on winning exhibited in the behaviours of those involved in the children's networks were noted as more problematic or negative. Some viewed coaches' and parents' vociferous and emotive manner in communicating with children in the context of providing tactical or technical information within the confines of a competitive match as negative, whilst others were more accepting of such behaviour. Although largely empirically anecdotal, it has been noted elsewhere that children of this age group are at risk of attrition from organized sport when perceptions of their experiences are negatively shaped by adults.[46] Those that continue to participate and tend to share the latter view are noted as conforming to a discourse of competition with an emphasis on playing to win in junior, adult-organized sporting activity.[47] Whilst informative, such dichotomous views do not expose the complexities of children's participation in organized sport. Rather than reducing children's experiences to mono-causal explanations, we have illustrated that children often have different perceptions of shared experiences such as mini soccer, in which they have been a part. In addition, the methodology illustrated the wider sociocultural context that shaped their feelings and interpretations of their participatory experience. Some children connected the more negative types of experience associated with adults, particularly spectators, with wider social fears regarding dangers to their well-being. Further evidence of the *child's voice* clearly needs to be heard, but discoveries from this particular methodological approach established that no matter what takes place in the context of mini soccer, the deeper cultural perspectives will contribute and such outside issues are actually positioned within it. In agreement with Cope and colleagues,[48] we argue that audiovisual methods of this nature, although time consuming, allow for a deeper understanding of children's experience that policy-makers and practitioners may be wise to adopt and include in the devising of policies and strategies in grassroots football. By including children, not only would policy design be more inclusive in nature, but also the efficacy of policy and strategy implementation would be better served by drawing on children's views. This is crucial since it is common that policy decisions intended to impact on young people's lifeworlds are usually informed by adults who frequently act on behalf of, and for, young people without always taking into account their needs and priorities. Future policy in junior and youth grassroots football would do well to take seriously the experiences children have of the game, not least if the intention of those who organize and administer it are concerned with providing children with positive and meaningful experiences which maximize their participation in the short and longer term.

Conclusion

We have attempted to present an authentic view of children's cognizance of mini soccer (and the environment surrounding it) in which they partake. The methodology employed allowed the possibility to galvanize and shed light on the experiences of the children, for whom this modified version of football, actually matter. The purpose of this paper was not to make claims regarding desired provision for mini soccer, but to illustrate experiences of the children that participate by providing them with a voice. This modified version of football should encompass seeing the game through *their eyes* and their perspectives, allowing greater opportunity to understand their experience.[49] The incidents with shared perspectives are an opportunity to allow adults into the children's line of thinking and understanding, whilst acknowledging the small responses and discussions that the children may have with each other. These are talking points that children no doubt discuss away from the adult 'eye', who may forget how they once seen the game of football or understood their roles, behaviours and development within it as a child. Allowing the children to contribute and not merely partake, rather than be evaluated, provided arguably a more real account.

This is not always articulated in research with children due to the interpretation of the respective author. Often, versions of events can be *lost in translation*, misinterpreted or even overlooked if children's power of speech is not acknowledged.[50] True accounts from children often go under reported or unsupported,[51] can be extremely brief, overlooked or merely glossed over in favour of an author's perspective or agenda.[52] As noted by Kirk,[53] research with children tends to be unequal in terms of the power relation between children and adults. Our methodology allowed us to utilize visual methods as a prompt to gather player perspectives, feelings and opinions via critical incidents directly involving them. Thus modestly shifting the balance of power within organized youth sport to the children.[54] As such, we encourage methodologies that prioritize a truer representation of the child voice in order to better understand the complexities of experiences within adult-organized junior sport and indeed that of the further developments within grassroots football.

Disclosure statement

No potential conflict of interest was reported by the authors.

Notes

1. Mahoney et al., 'Organized Activities as Developmental Contexts for Children and Adolescents'.
2. Weir, Etelson, and Brand, 'Parents' Perceptions of Neighborhood Safety and Children's Physical Activity'.
3. Pitchford et al., 'Children in Football: Seen but not Heard'.
4. Wyness, *Childhood and Society: An Introduction to the Sociology of Childhood.*
5. Houlihan and Lindsey, *Sport Policy in Britain.*
6. Green and Houlihan, 'Governmentality, Modernization, and the "Disciplining" of National Sporting Organizations: Athletics in Australia and the United Kingdom;' Houlihan and Green, 'Modernization and Sport: The Reform of Sport England and UK Sport'.
7. Lusted and O'Gorman, 'The Impact of New Labour's Modernisation Agenda on the English Grass-roots Football Workforce'.
8. The FA, *A Blueprint for the Future of Football*, 63.
9. The FA, *A Charter for Quality*, 9.
10. Ibid.
11. The FA, *Youth Development Review.*
12. Ibid.
13. Brackenridge et al., *Child Welfare in Football: An Exploration of Children's Welfare in the Modern Game.*
14. Wyness, *Childhood and Society: An Introduction to the Sociology of Childhood.*
15. Mayall, 'Towards a Sociology for Childhood: Thinking from Children's Lives'.
16. Qvortrup, Corsaro, and Honig, *The Palgrave Handbook of Childhood Studies.*
17. Wyness, *Childhood and Society: An Introduction to the Sociology of Childhood.*
18. Pitchford et al., 'Children in Football: Seen but not Heard'.
19. Grover, 'Why Won't They Listen To Us? On Giving Power and Voice to Children Participating in Social Research'.
20. Wyness, *Childhood and Society: An Introduction to the Sociology of Childhood.*
21. The FA, *Youth Development Review.*
22. Brackenridge et al., *Child Welfare in Football: An Exploration of Children's Welfare in the Modern Game.*
23. The FA, *Youth Development Review.*
24. Greig, Taylor, and MacKay, *Doing Research with Children: A Practical Guide.*
25. Cope, Harvey, and Kirk, 'Reflections on Using Visual Research Methods in Sports Coaching'.
26. Ibid.
27. Greig, Taylor, and MacKay, *Doing Research with Children: A Practical Guide.*
28. Angelides, 'The Development of an Efficient Technique for Collecting and Analyzing Qualitative Data: The Analysis of Critical Incidents'.
29. Tripp, *Critical Incidents in Teaching: Developing Professional Judgement*, 24–5.
30. Ibid.
31. Recordings and team discussions were undertaken by a research team consisting of students on placement from Edge Hill University and led by representatives from 'Don't X the Line' campaign http://www.dontxtheline.com/ a charity which aims to enhance the participatory experience of junior grassroots footballers and referees through a number of initiatives.
32. Greig, Taylor, and MacKay, *Doing Research with Children: A Practical Guide.*
33. Tripp, *Critical Incidents in Teaching: Developing Professional Judgement,* 43.
34. Ibid.
35. This was undertaken by the research team which included representatives from 'Don't X the line' http://www.dontxtheline.com/ and university staff with significant ongoing and lengthy experience of coaching in grassroots junior football.
36. Denscombe, *The Good Research Guide: For Small-scale Social Research Projects.*
37. Morgan et al., 'Hearing Children's Voices: Methodological Issues in Conducting Focus Groups with Children Aged 7–11 years'.
38. Bryman, *Social Research Methods*, 475.

39. Morgan et al., 'Hearing Children's Voices: Methodological Issues in Conducting Focus Groups with Children Aged 7–11 years'.
40. Ibid.
41. Those incidents that are not included in the paper were not selected due either engendering less significant discussion, or because they were similar to specific incidents presented above but again engendered less discussion than the incident included.
42. Bluebond-Langner and Korbin, *Challenges and Opportunities in the Anthropology of Childhoods: An Introduction to 'Children, Childhoods, and Childhood Studies'*.
43. Walters et al., '"It Just Makes You Feel Invincible": A Foucauldian Analysis of Children's Experiences of Organised Team Sports'.
44. Kavussanu et al., 'Observed Prosocial and Antisocial Behaviors in Male and Female Soccer Players'.
45. Shields et al., 'The Sport Behaviour of Youth, Parents and Coaches'.
46. Walters et al., "It Just Makes You Feel Invincible": A Foucauldian Analysis of Children's Experiences of Organised Team Sports'.
47. Ibid.
48. Cope, Harvey, and Kirk, 'Reflections on Using Visual Research Methods in Sports Coaching'.
49. Thomas and O'Kane, 'Discovering What Children Think: Connections between Research and Practice'.
50. Greig, Taylor, and MacKay, *Doing Research with Children: A Practical Guide*.
51. Johnson, Pfister, and Vindrola-Padros, 'Drawings, Photos, and Performances: Using Visual Methods with Children'.
52. Allison, 'Giving Voice to Children's Voices: Practices and Problems, Pitfalls and Potentials'.
53. Kirk, 'Methodological and Ethical Issues in Conducting Qualitative Research with Children and Young People: A Literature Review'.
54. Cope, Harvey, and Kirk, 'Reflections on Using Visual Research Methods in Sports Coaching'.

References

Allison, J. 'Giving Voice to Children's Voices: Practices and Problems, Pitfalls and Potentials'. *American Anthropologist* 109, no. 2 (2007): 261–72.

Angelides, P. 'The Development of an Efficient Technique for Collecting and Analyzing Qualitative Data: The Analysis of Critical Incidents'. *International Journal of Qualitative Studies in Education* 14, no. 3 (2001): 429–42.

Bluebond-Langner, M., and J.E. Korbin. 'Challenges and Opportunities in the Anthropology of Childhoods: An Introduction to "Children, Childhoods, and Childhood Studies"'. *American Anthropologist* 109, no. 2 (2007): 241–6.

Brackenridge, C.H., A. Pitchford, K. Russell, and G. Nutt. *Child Welfare in Football: An Exploration of Children's Welfare in the Modern Game*. London: Routledge, 2007.

Cope, E., S. Harvey, and D. Kirk. 'Reflections on Using Visual Research Methods in Sports Coaching'. *Qualitative Research in Sport, Exercise and Health* 7, no. 1 (2015): 88–108.

Denscombe, M. *The Good Research Guide: For Small-Scale Social Research Projects*. Maidenhead: McGraw-Hill Education, 2014.

The Football Association. *A Blueprint for the Future of Football*. London: The Football Association, 1991.

The Football Association. *The Football Association National Game Strategy 2011–2015*. London: The Football Association, 2011.

The Football Association. *Their Game: Youth Football Development Booklet U7/U8 (Individual Guidance Booklets)*. London: The Football Association, 2012.

The Football Association. *Youth Development Review*. London: The Football Association, 2010.

The Football Association Technical Department. *Football Education for Young Players: "A Charter for Quality"*. London: The Football Association, 1997.

Green, M., and B. Houlihan. 'Governmentality, Modernization, and the "Disciplining" of National Sporting Organizations: Athletics in Australia and the United Kingdom'. *Sociology of Sport Journal* 23, no. 1 (2006): 47–71.

Greig, A.D., J. Taylor, and T. MacKay. *Doing Research with Children: A Practical Guide*. London: Sage, 2012.

Grover, S. '"Why Won't They Listen To Us?" On Giving Power and Voice to Children Participating in Social Research'. *Childhood* 11, no. 1 (2004): 81–93.

Houlihan, B., and M. Green. 'Modernization and Sport: The Reform of Sport England and UK Sport'. *Public Administration* 87, no. 3 (2009): 678–98.

Houlihan, B., and I. Lindsey. *Sport Policy in Britain*. Abingdon: Routledge, 2012.

Johnson, G.A., A.E. Pfister, and C. Vindrola-Padros. 'Drawings, Photos, and Performances: Using Visual Methods with Children'. *Visual Anthropology Review* 28, no. 2 (2012): 164–78.

Kavussanu, M., R. Stamp., G. Slade, and C. Ring. 'Observed Prosocial and Antisocial Behaviors in Male and Female Soccer Players'. *Journal of Applied Sport Psychology* 21, no. 1 (2009): S62–76.

Kirk, S. 'Methodological and Ethical Issues in Conducting Qualitative Research with Children and Young People: A Literature Review'. *International Journal of Nursing Studies* 44, no. 7 (2007): 1250–60.

Lusted, J., and J. O'Gorman. 'The Impact of New Labour's Modernisation Agenda on the English Grass-Roots Football Workforce'. *Managing Leisure* 15, no. 1–2 (2010): 140–54.

Mahoney, J.L., R.W. Larson, J.S. Eccles, and H. Lord. 'Organized Activities as Developmental Contexts for Children and Adolescents'. In *Organized Activities as Contexts of Development: Extracurricular Activities, After-school, and Community Programs*, ed. J. Mahoney, R. Larson, and J.S. Eccles, 3–22. Hillsdale, NJ: Erlbaum, 2005.

Mayall, B. *Towards a Sociology for Childhood: Thinking from Children's Lives*. Buckingham: Open University Press, 2002.

Morgan, M., S. Gibbs, K. Maxwell., and N. Britten. 'Hearing Children's Voices: Methodological Issues in Conducting Focus Groups with Children Aged 7–11 Years'. *Qualitative Research* 2, no. 1 (2002): 5–20.

Pitchford, A., C.H. Brackenridge, J. Bringer, C. Cockburn, G. Nutt, Z. Pawlaczek, and K. Russell. 'Children in Football: Seen but Not Heard'. *Soccer and Society* 5, no. 1 (2004): 43–60.

Qvortrup, J., W.A. Corsaro, and M.S. Honig. *The Palgrave Handbook of Childhood Studies*. New York: Palgrave Macmillan, 2009.

Shields, D., B.L. Bredemeier, N.M. LaVoi, and F.C. Power. 'The Sport Behaviour of Youth, Parents and Coaches'. *Journal of Research in Character Education* 3, no. 1 (2005): 43–59.

Thomas, N., and C. O'Kane. 'Discovering What Children Think: Connections between Research and Practice'. *British Journal of Social Work* 30 (2000): 819–35.

Tripp, D. *Critical Incidents in Teaching (Classic Edition): Developing Professional Judgement*. London: Routledge, 2011.

Walters, S.R., D. Payne, P.J. Schluter, and R.W. Thomson. '"It Just Makes You Feel Invincible": A Foucauldian Analysis of Children's Experiences of Organised Team Sports'. *Sport, Education and Society* 20, no. 2 (2015): 1–17.

Weir, L.A., D. Etelson, and D.A. Brand. 'Parents' Perceptions of Neighborhood Safety and Children's Physical Activity'. *Preventive Medicine* 43, no. 3 (2006):212–7.

Wyness, M. *Childhood and Society: An Introduction to the Sociology of Childhood*. Basingstoke: Palgrave, 2012.

Enjoyment in youth soccer: its portrayals among 12- to 14-year-olds

Hege E. Tjomsland[a], Torill Larsen[b], Ingrid Holsen[b], Lars T. Ronglan[c], Oddrun Samdal[b] and Bente Wold[b]

[a]Department of Education, University of Bergen, Bergen, Norway; [b]Department of Health Promotion and Development, University of Bergen, Bergen, Norway; [c]Department of Rectorate, Norwegian School of Sport Sciences, Oslo, Norway

This article reports on a qualitative study that explored the experiences of adolescents in Norwegian soccer teams. The sample included players aged 12–14 years who participated in the promoting adolescence physical activity (PAPA) project. The data were generated by twelve focus groups with seven girls' teams and five boys' teams and indicated that a central component of the soccer players' experience was simply enjoyment. Their descriptions of this enjoyment resemble the psychological phenomenon of *flow*, the experience of feeling fully engaged and of having concentrated energy, focus and positive emotions. The results also suggest six components of their enjoyment of youth soccer: being with friends, collaborating with teammates, choosing to play the sport, having a supportive coach, and learning new skills and demonstrating mastery of them. The findings support previous conclusions in the literature about what constitutes enjoyment for young athletes, but enhances understanding of other aspects of adolescents' experiences specifically in Norwegian soccer. A particular emphasis on learning and enjoyment for all appears evident in Norwegian youth soccer, regardless of the level of talent or competitiveness of individual players.

Introduction

Previous studies have focused upon various features of sport participation that participants perceive as being positive and enjoyable.[1] Research from Scandinavia, however, tends to examine young people's experiences and enjoyment of sports using quantitative methods. Accordingly, much of this literature fails to account for how young people actually experience sport. This paper therefore examines in particular, Norwegian youths' soccer experiences by using qualitative methods. In particular, the paper explores: What constitutes 'enjoyment' for adolescents participating in Norwegian youth soccer?

In July 2007, 9.4 million youth under the age of 18 worldwide were registered in soccer clubs.[2] In Norway, more than a third of all children and youth (44% of boys and 33% of girls – 181,000 boys and 84,000 girls) play on a team, as the Norwegian Soccer Association (NFF) reported on its website on 12 July 2013.[3] Soccer, which in Norway has a community-based form of organization with coaching and management being the responsibility of parents, is by far the most popular sport for children and youth. It is not uncommon for children to begin playing on a team in first grade, and, because of strong parental involvement, soccer is also often the only organized sport offered throughout childhood. Research has suggested that what children enjoy at an early age they are more likely to continue doing in the future, whereas the lack of enjoyment is likely to lead them to drop out,[4] particularly in youth soccer.[5] Kjonniksen et al.'s study also showed that young people who are playing soccer at age 15 are more likely to still be playing the sport at age 23 than 15-year-olds involved in other sports.[6] A long-term commitment to a sport is desirable because sports offer personal growth and development, contributing not only to physical well-being, but also to cognitive, affective, social and moral well-being.[7] Understanding of the elements and consequences of enjoyment in youth soccer may therefore contribute to the development of enjoyment of sports in other settings, something that will prove conducive to maintaining involvement in sports beyond adolescence.

Background

Enjoyment of sports has been defined as 'a positive affective response to sport experience that reflects generalized feelings such as pleasure, liking and fun'.[8] Although qualitative and quantitative research has provided some understanding of the meaning and nature of the enjoyment of sports, McCarthy, Jones and Clark-Carter argue that there is still a gap in research regarding the developmental differences of the sources of this enjoyment.[9] Understanding how the different sources of enjoyment of sport develop from childhood through adolescence may influence the principles and practices of those who seek to use enjoyment to motivate children and youth to practice any given sport.[10]

Previous research regarding the sources of enjoyment in sports has highlighted age-related differences in what constitutes enjoyment.[11] MacPhail and colleagues demonstrated that enjoyment and fun in sport participation of younger children emanated from social elements and play, whereas for older children fun was more closely related to the excitement of competing and performing.[12] Ullrich-French and Smith's study also demonstrated that relationships with parents and peers help predict motivational outcomes among young people, thereby suggesting that enjoyment, perceived competence, and self-motivation are linked to the quality of these relationships.[13] The perception of peer acceptance was an especially important predictor as children become adolescents and their peers become increasingly important in their lives.[14]

Because soccer is a team sport involving collaboration with teammates and feedback from peers, the soccer team provides an important venue for youth to experience friendship and peer approval, to engage in bonding, and to establish social networks.[15] Wold and colleagues argue that team sports, as opposed to individual sports, tend to provide participants with greater opportunities for positive developmental experiences because of the high degree of interdependence between team members in performing tasks.[16] Hence, the social aspect of involvement in soccer seems to be an important predictor of enjoyment.

The phenomenon of *flow* has been defined as a psychological state in which people feel efficient, motivated and happy.[17] The experience of flow in team sports has received less attention than experiences of flow in individual sports, because it has been argued that individual sports are more likely to elicit flow.[18] Elbe and colleagues found, however, that participants in different exercise groups experienced high levels of flow regardless of whether the activity was collective or individual.[19] Flow is intrinsically motivating for participants and influences participants' continued commitment to being physically active.[20] Thus, the experience of flow in youth soccer is to be welcomed since it enhances young people's intrinsic motivation to remain involved in the sport.[21]

An essential component of flow is a sense of autonomy. Setting one's own goals and finding ways of achieving them,[22] may partly explain why flow has not been extensively studied in relation to team sports. Although young soccer players are often under the supervision of a coach and are not entirely free to pursue their own goals while training or during matches, adults can help promote a sense of autonomy by providing challenges that offer opportunities to youth to learn for themselves. Studies indicate that learning and 'getting better' are associated with enjoyable experiences.[23] Those coaches who can foster skills development by balancing the level of difficulty with the athletes' abilities, often contribute to the enjoyment of the sport.[24] Indeed, Bakker and colleagues indicated that performance feedback and support from the coach predict flow and peak performances during a soccer game.[25]

How the coach perceives success and values competence also determines whether or not youth sports enjoyment is enhanced by adult leadership. Duda and Nicholls associate task-oriented goals with increased enjoyment, while associating performance-oriented goals with less enjoyment.[26] Because their focus is on learning and development rather than success and superiority, task-oriented soccer coaches seem to be more likely to contribute to enjoyable experiences than performance-oriented coaches. Since such a high proportion of Norwegian youth and children plays soccer and since there is only a single recreational league through age 12, many of the Norwegian children and youth who play soccer are neither very interested in the game itself nor especially talented. They play on a team because soccer is likely to be the only organized sport offered to them in their community and because their classmates and neighbours also play on the team. The rules and regulations of this league underscore coaches' responsibilities to emphasize learning and development to promote enjoyment for all, rather than competition and superiority in order to promote excellence in a few.

There is, however, a significant dropout rate from Norwegian youth soccer during mid adolescence. This attrition could result from a lack of enjoyment, other things to do, negative interaction, dislike of the coach, or a lack of perceived success.[27] Since no previous research has employed qualitative methods to explore the experiences of middle adolescents in Norwegian youth soccer, this paper addresses this need. A qualitative approach should provide details and nuances of what it is like to play soccer at this age. The specific research questions were:

(1) What is it like to play soccer from the perspective of 12- to 14-year-olds?
(2) Which factors contribute to enjoyment of soccer for this age group?

Methods

The promoting adolescence physical activity (PAPA) project, funded by the European Commission, is an intervention study aimed at improving the quality of youth soccer in order to promote adolescent health through long-term participation in sport.[28] The PAPA project developed, delivered and evaluated a theoretically grounded and evidence-based coach education programme which guides grassroots coaches in providing quality motivation to make youth soccer more supportive, engaging and enjoyable.[29] This article reports on a qualitative Norwegian study located within the larger PAPA project. Conducting the study under the PAPA umbrella offered a pool of teams from which players could be drawn for interview. Furthermore, the quantitative data already collected within the PAPA project offered the opportunity at a later point in time to combine the qualitative data with quantitative data for a clearer understanding of emerging themes in the qualitative portion of the project.

Interview subjects and sampling procedures

This study was approved by the Norwegian Social Science Data Services, which required informed consent from the parents of the participants. The interviewees were recruited from twelve teams in three different regions in Norway: south-east, north and west. All the head coaches of these teams had been invited to participate in the larger PAPA project, and had been informed that this included research concerning the experiences of their players. Because the qualitative phase took place at the end of the soccer season, it was difficult to recruit sufficient coaches and teams for this portion of the project. Many teams ended their seasons at the beginning of October, and thus the selection of the 12 teams was primarily drawn from those who were holding practices in October. The final pool consisted of seven teams of 12-year-old players, four teams of 13-year-old players and one team of 14-year-old players. All the teams were single-sex teams from the recreational league. Five boys' teams and seven girls' teams participated in the study. The length of each player's involvement in soccer varied from 1 to 7 years, with the majority of players having begun to play soccer at age 6 or 7. Two teams were coached by female coaches, while 10 teams were coached by male coaches who typically dominate coaching positions in Norway. Given the high level of parental involvement, however, most teams enjoy a balance of men and women in the other support roles.

Each team coach recruited players for the focus groups through a hand-delivered invitation and information sheet required by the study and given to all the players on each team (approximately 180 players total). None of the players refused to participate in the focus groups, and 140 players returned consent forms. From this pool, 6–8 players per team were randomly selected to participate which resulted in a sample of 39 girls and 34 boys. Since the invitation was handed out by each coach, this may have prejudiced recruiting to some extent to please the coach.

Data collection

The preferred method of data collection was focus groups which create a safe environment and replicate the settings that children are accustomed to in the classroom. Safety and familiarity afforded participants the opportunity to share their own opinions freely. Moreover, the peer support provided by the group helps to correct the power imbalance that occurs between the researcher and the participants in one-on-one interviews.[30]

The twelve focus groups were conducted during winter 2011 in each team's club house, by the three first authors of this article. A university student acted as a non-participant in the discussion. The focus groups lasted between 25 and 40 min and were based on an interview guide informed by the research on sports enjoyment and physical activity. This guide was pre-tested with a trial sample of four boys and four girls from the same age groups and from teams not involved in PAPA. As a result of the pre-test, some of the questions were rephrased and edited to make the language less formal and more age-appropriate for the interviewees. Although the guide provided the basic structure, deviations were allowed during the focus groups in order to fully explore varying responses.

Each of the focus groups began with the researchers explaining what was being studied, and how each member's participation would contribute to a greater knowledge of youth soccer. The adult leaders explained the importance of group confidentiality and provided assurance that data would be treated anonymously. The participants provided their names and ages, and also years of soccer experience. This introductory phase of the interview helped to put the members at ease before answering questions. The participants were free to leave the focus group at any time if they did not feel comfortable.

After the introductory phase, the questions led to a discussion regarding players' enjoyment, feelings, and their interaction with the coach and teammates in practice and matches. These questions included: 'Can you describe a soccer practice that you really enjoyed?'; 'What made this practice particularly enjoyable?'; 'Can you describe a soccer practice that you did not enjoy?'; 'Why did you not enjoy this practice?'; 'Can you tell how you feel when things go well in practice?'; and, 'What do you think are the responsibilities of a youth soccer coach?'. Participants were encouraged to respond freely, and informed that no one was forced to respond to any questions. In most focus groups, the participants did speak freely and with feeling regarding the topic at hand. In two focus groups, however, the respondents were less outspoken and needed more prompting. This was probably because the two focus groups represented newly formed teams in which the teammates were new to each other. The researcher would conclude the meeting by asking the group members if they wanted to add something to important questions or topics and by asking the observer to follow up on responses which seemed unclear or add questions the researcher had missed. There was no discernible gender difference with regard to either the focus group participation or the responses to specific questions.

Data analysis

After the first focus groups had been held, the initial phase of the data analysis began and involved shared reflections and discussions among the three researchers regarding the responses given to inform subsequent focus groups. Once all discussions were completed, the following procedure recommended by Keegan[31] was undertaken:

(1) The data were transcribed verbatim.
(2) The interview transcripts were read and reread by the first, second and third author for complete familiarity with the raw data.
(3) The manuscripts from the 12 interviews were organized following the interview guide.
(4) The first author broke the responses from each focus group into units of analysis, called units of meaning[32] (for example, the following quotes are three such units: 'we play soccer because it is fun and because we get together with friends', 'a good coach sees all the players on a team', 'challenging soccer matches are more fun to win than easy matches').

(5) The units of meaning from each focus group were then compared to units of meaning from the other focus groups, and similar units of meaning were grouped into categories (such as *enjoyment is fun, enjoyment is like flow* and *the coach matters for enjoyment*) and in turn the categories were grouped into overall themes[33] (for example: being with friends, choosing to play the sport, having a supportive coach).

(6) All the three co-authors who had led focus groups, together participated in a critical assessment of the identified units of meaning, categories and themes.

(7) To ensure that identified categories and themes as well as the overall organization of the data made the most analytical sense, the co-authors continued to formulate critical questions throughout the different stages of the analysis and manuscript writing.

Although focus group member checking is recommended as one of Keegan's eight steps for qualitative data analysis,[34] this step could not be performed for validation in the current study since there had been turnover of coaches and players by the time the interviews had been transcribed. The data analysis was performed using QSR N-Vivo9 software.

Results

When the players were asked about their overall experience playing soccer, they frequently emphasized enjoyment as being central to that experience. Enjoyment was an expectation that led them to start and continue playing. The players described enjoyment on the field in terms of feelings: 'feeling good', 'feeling energized' and 'feeling happy'. They indicated experiencing these feelings both as individuals and as a team. For example, one team of 13-year-old boys' said:

It's like a boost. (Player 1)

You get in a way, I don't know how to put it. (Player 2)

It's like a flow of happiness. (Player 3)

And then you feel like working even harder. (Player 4)

You get an adrenalin kick even at training. (Player 3)

Often enjoyment was portrayed as being 'in the moment', or complete immersion in the activity, as highlighted by the comments of one 13-year-old girls' team:

I remember a training session we were really concentrated and focused. Of course, we had fun and talked together, but we were really in the moment, and this training smelled of sweat. I don't know how to explain it, but it was really a good training and I felt that the majority improved. So I like those trainings where we improve and have fun together the best. (Player 1)

What does it mean to be in the moment (Interviewer)?

Engaged. (Player 2)

And concentrated. (Player 1)

Not to fool around too much, but to have fun and concentrate at the same time. (Player 3)

And that you give it all, all that you have in a way. (Player 4)

Six main themes central to the soccer players' enjoyment emerged from the data. These were: (1) being with friends, (2) collaborating with teammates, (3) choosing to play the sport, (4) having a supportive coach, (5) learning new skills and (6) demonstrating mastery of skills.

Theme one: being with friends

The social dimension of being a member of a team was an important reason young soccer players gave for being involved in the sport. The players expressed that getting together with friends on the team made them happy even on days when they did not feel like attending training. They shared a common experience with their teammates, and enjoyed supporting each other whether they succeeded or failed. One group of 13-year-old girls' explained:

> If you miss a ball, you get this feeling in the stomach thinking, oh no, this was my mistake, but than the others support you. (Player 1)

> So if you do a mistake, you still get support (Interviewer)?

> Yes, it's not like, 'Oh my God you play so poorly!' … It'll never be like that on our team. (Player 1)

> Other teams may yell, but our team is not like that. (Player 2)

Theme two: collaborating with teammates

The soccer players described collaborating with teammates as essential to enjoyment. The most memorable matches and trainings involved good team work and a positive atmosphere among the team. The participants talked about collaboration as an inherent characteristic of the sport, and they stressed that soccer is not a sport for individuals who are interested in showing off or being egocentric. Proper and fun soccer involves working with others, regardless of how talented they are as individual players, as one group of 13-year-old girls' suggested:

> There will be no game if we don't collaborate. (Player 1)

> The players on a team can be really good individual players, but this is not enough. You also need to know how to play together. You have to learn how to pass the ball to your teammates and stuff. (Player 2)

> Yes, soccer is about collaboration, it is this kind of sport. (Player 3)

> A team sport. (Player 4)

> You can be awesome with touches, but if you want to be really, really good, then you need to collaborate with your mates. (Player 5)

> You can't play the game alone. (Player 6)

> Yes, you need to inspire your mates to work too. (Player 5)

Theme three: choosing to the play the sport

The participants indicated that a key element in their enjoyment of soccer was their ability to exercise choice in whether or not they signed up for the sport in the first place. They played soccer because they wanted to and because of the pleasure they derived from it, not from a sense of obligation. Freedom of choice was implicit in the comments of a group of 12-year-old boys', who, when asked why they played soccer, replied:

> So why do you play soccer (Interviewer)?
>
> It is fun, and it is social. (Player 1)
>
> It is fun and it is good exercise. (Player 2)
>
> Football is *the* perfect hobby. (Player 3)
>
> It is fun to play, and you get to be with your friends. (Player 4)

Some of the participants said that their parents had strongly advised participation in an organized sport (for the health benefits), but they did not say that they had been 'pressured' to play.

Theme four: having a supportive coach

As the comments of one group of 12-year-old girls' indicated, the participants frequently associated enjoyment in soccer with having a supportive and attentive coach:

> I think it is important that coaches support and encourage us, and tell us what to change, to improve, and say that it is ok even if we lose. (Player 3)
>
> Our coaches are good at that. When they say I did well, I want to perform even better. (Player 2)
>
> Yes, you get this feeling inside that you want to keep on performing better. (Player 4)

The participants also felt that it was essential that the coach made all players feel valuable and important to the team. They appreciated coaches who believe that players of different strengths and abilities play different but equally important roles on a team. A supportive coach, moreover, was seen as someone who communicates with the players in a positive and kind manner. The participants described situations in which this had not been the case, where coaches were too harsh and took things too seriously. These coaches diminished their players' enjoyment of soccer, including that of male players aged 14 who described their experiences as follows:

> We had a coach who got mad if we made mistakes. (Player 1)
>
> How did that affect your enjoyment (Interviewer)?
>
> I really wanted to quit then, but fortunately he quit. (Player 2)
>
> Why did you want to quit (Interviewer)?
>
> He yelled a lot. We practiced a particular drill once and some of us forgot what to do, and then he got mad and pushed one boy to the ground and used very bad language. (Player 1)
>
> He was so pissed off. (Player 4)
>
> He destroyed all our fun. (Player 3)
>
> He was so serious. (Player 1)

Too serious. (Player 2)

The players were also asked whether or not the coach allowed for participation in decision-making and if this mattered for enjoyment. On the field, the players were not often included in decision-making, and they said that the coaches only occasionally invited them to make choices about which drills to work on or which tactics to use. This lack of choice on the field or in training was not, however, perceived as detrimental to enjoyment, once the choice to participate in the sport had already been made.

Theme five: learning

The participants talked about learning soccer's technical skills as well as learning to collaborate with teammates. They differentiated between learning as individual players and learning as a team. It was learning to work as a team that was identified as being particularly enjoyable. The coach was key to this particular aspect of learning, because although some players could have learned and improved individual skills by themselves or with an older player, the coach was the one with a vision of what the team could do as a team, provided he or she gave specific and understandable instructions. Players perceived such vague expressions as 'good job' and 'way to go' as encouragement but not as valuable feedback which would help them learn and improve. Another aspect of the coach's role in teaching teamwork that the players mentioned was making them feel secure and organizing drills that provided opportunities for all players to learn within their individual areas of mastery. When asked to describe how their coach helped them learn, a group of 13-year-old boys' said:

Make the players feel secure. (Player 4)

And how can the coach make the players feel secure (Interviewer)?

By talking to them and offering challenges. You can give the player a challenge that he performs successfully, and then the player will feel secure and that he can accomplish this, and then you may go from there. (Player 4)

Help me feel self-confident and more secure. (Player 2)

Provide opportunities. (Player 1)

Theme six: demonstrating mastery of skills

After having learned a skill, the participants described how the experience of using a mastered skill improved their self-confidence, and how this generated a positive cycle which led to even more improvement, self-confidence, mastery and good feeling. Mastery thus emerged as the sixth and final factor in enjoyment, as one group of 13-year-old boys' made clear:

Experiencing mastery generates the good feeling. (Player 2).

This good feeling is important because it builds our self-confidence, and when our self-confidence improves, we feel like working even harder. (Player 1)

Yes, this good feeling is very important to our performance. (Player 2)

As they had for learning, the participants distinguished between experiencing individual and team mastery. In describing training sessions and matches that had been particularly enjoyable, experiences of team mastery were highlighted. Central to the concept of mastery was a feeling of being challenged, whether as an individual player or together with teammates. The participants expressed that experiences of mastery against an 'easy' opponent produced less enjoyment and excitement than mastery demonstrated against a difficult challenge. The first extract below illustrates how a 13-year-old experienced challenge and personal mastery despite his team's loss, while the second shows how a team of 12-year-old girls' experienced challenges and mastery as a team:

> I remember playing against a wing who was a real fighter. I get so much adrenalin in football. My position is back, and I love to give effort, so their wing got so pissed off. I got pissed off as well, but I handled it each time. I was so happy after this match. We lost, but I still love that I managed to tackle him. (Player 1)

> When we played against (team), it was a mini tournament and they were really, really good. This is the only team we have met who plays like us. (Player 1)

> They pass the ball like we do. We play the ball a lot, but many teams don't, but (team) passed the ball in the same way. (Player 2)

> But that probably made it harder for you to play against this team (Interviewer)?

> Yes, it was harder, but it was a lot of fun because we won by one goal. They were really good, but we still won by one. (Player 3)

Discussion

The focus groups indicated that enjoyment is central to the players' experience of soccer. The players perceived the following as contributing to their enjoyment of the sport: being with friends, collaborating with teammates, choosing to play the sport, having a supportive coach, and learning new skills, and demonstrating mastery of them. In their descriptions of enjoyment of soccer, the participants talked about how playing soccer helped them feel 'good', 'energized', 'happy', and fully concentrated and immersed in the activity. These portrayals of enjoyment, experienced both individually and collectively, resemble the phenomenon of flow. Bakker's study among talented 14- to 18-year-old male soccer players also indicated that soccer may facilitate flow.[35] The current study supports and extends Bakker's research and suggests that 12- to 14-year-old players may experience flow in soccer, and perhaps more importantly, that flow-like experiences seem to appear among all players independent of skill level and gender.

Bakker and colleagues showed that experiences of flow are more likely among teams where the athletes feel connected to their teammates and the coach.[36] The results of this study also link enjoyment with being with friends, collaborating with teammates, and having a supportive coach. Since adolescence is a period of transition in which young people begin to become more independent from their parents, social relationships with peers and other adults become increasingly important for enjoyment of activities.[37] Involvement in leisure activities may therefore provide a significant opportunity to link with friends and adults with similar interests, and to share experiences and goals.[38] Within the past 30 years, the number of Norwegian children and youth participating in soccer has tripled. In fact, 33% of households nationwide rank the soccer club as the most important meeting point in their local community after family and school.[39] It is not uncommon that all the boys in a given class at school will sign up together for a soccer team when recruiting begins in first or second grade and will all play together for six or seven years. Norwegian children and youth who choose not to be involved in the sport, therefore, miss out on a significant social experience for both players and parents. The greater social relevance of youth soccer in Norway may skew the results of our study, showing that in Norway involvement in youth soccer provides more opportunities for youth to be together, learn, and work towards shared goals than might a similar study in a country where the game of soccer plays a less significant role in the local community.

Furthermore, it is also possible that because collaboration is an integral part of team performance, and because the game requires complementary skills and competencies among the team members, soccer has the potential to produce enjoyment for youth, even when they may not be particularly skilled or talented. A good player needs to develop not only physical skills but also skills in collaboration and communication. How one moves without the ball and how one communicates with one's teammates is equally as important as one's ball-handling skills.[40] One makes other players better by moving into supporting positions and offering feedback as much as by one's passing ability. Given the multi-faceted and collaborative nature of the game, the soccer team may be the context for youth to experience enjoyment not only through social interaction as they would at a party, but also through learning together, developing together and accomplishing goals together.

The results also point to the players' positive feelings when demonstrating mastery of new skills and performing well. The link between feeling competent and experiencing enjoyment is consistent with a study by Scarpa and Nart, which indicated that perceived sport competence is a good predictor of enjoyment related to physical activity.[41] The results in the current study suggest that practice sessions and matches are especially enjoyable when mastery is demonstrated by both individuals and the team as a whole while they face a significant challenge. Elbe and colleagues suggest that for a challenge to produce an experience of mastery and flow, the difficulty of the task needs to match the skills of the individuals, since the experience of an 'easy' challenge may lead to boredom, whereas the experience of challenges that were too difficult may produce anxiety.[42] Since previous studies as well as the current one indicate that enjoyment in youth sports comes in part from achievement-related factors, these studies all suggest that coaches working with youth should foster development of skills in a way which balances the skill's level of difficulty with the athletes' abilities.[43] The NFF's vision for grassroots soccer is 'As many as possible – for as long as possible – as well as possible'. In 2012, the NFF published 10 guidelines for coaches working with children and youth. The following four guidelines seem to fit especially well with the results of this study: (1) as attentive as possible towards each and every player, (2) all players are equally important, (3) small teams to provide practice and play time for all and (4) (safety vs. challenge) + mastery = enjoyment and development.[44] The current study suggests that the players perceive the coaches as indeed carrying out this vision.

Freedom of choice emerged as being central to enjoyment. The participants expressed that they played soccer because it was fun and because they wanted to, not because they had to. Fraser-Thomas, Cote and Deakin[45] have suggested that young athletes who receive positive support and encouragement from parents as opposed to pressure, experience more enjoyment from sports, show greater preference for a challenge, and display greater intrinsic motivation, whereas Gagne[46] indicated that athletes with autonomous forms of motivation on average have more positive experiences in sport than athletes with more extrinsic forms of motivation. The feeling of being self-directed and having the freedom to choose for one's self to be involved thus seem to be an essential reason why soccer is so enjoyable.

Although choosing to play the sport was identified as significant for the players' enjoyment, having a say in practice and in matches did not turn out to be important to them. In Norwegian youth soccer, short games of six-on-six constitute a substantial amount of the practice time.[47] It may be therefore that players experience autonomous choice in that context, even if they don't report being much involved in decision-making during practice. Research on the teaching games for understanding theory[48] supports the suggestion that games with small 'half-teams' may be suitable for developing players by encouraging joint problem-solving in realistic scenarios.[49] This model recognizes the intimate relationship between decision-making and skill execution,[50] and advocates that explicit information and guidance have an essential supplement in learning through problem-solving in game situations.[51] Thus, young soccer players may take advantage of the didactic principles in teaching games for understanding theory, and coach-led activities and decision-making that employ this theory seem to enhance rather than diminish their enjoyment of soccer.[52] Since in Norway the soccer teams are coached and managed by parents in the community, (that is, adults who would be known to the players from other settings), these teams are a very safe, informal and less competitive environment where adult leadership is experienced as friendly accompaniment rather than authoritative instruction. This may also explain why players experienced un-coerced choice in their participation.

According to the self-determination theory, motivational climates which support and satisfy the innate human needs for relatedness, competence and autonomy enhance the enjoyment of individuals.[53] The results in this study also support the self-determination theory since the six themes arising from the focus groups reflect these three innate psychological needs.

Limitations and recommendations for future research

This study has a number of limitations that further research will need to address with a broader sample. Our sample was coloured by three factors. First, the soccer players were recruited from teams whose head coaches had participated in a six-hour workshop to make youth sport more engaging, empowering and enjoyable. Consequently, the coaches may have been particularly concerned about creating positive motivational climates. Two other papers reporting on Norwegian coaches involved in the PAPA project, however, indicate that the elements of the empowering coaching program had been implemented only to a certain degree. In their own evaluations of the training, the coaches themselves indicated that at least some of the training merely reinforced what they were already doing, and the workshop did not significantly change their coaching style.[54] They indicated that the empowering coaching principles introduced by PAPA fit well with values and strategies that they already employed. Hence, there is little reason to suggest that the experience of the players in the current study will deviate much from that of other Norwegian soccer players.[55]

The second limitation of the study is whether the focus groups provided an environment that was sufficiently safe and comfortable for youth to openly discuss sensitive issues. The group dynamics may have inhibited those who had different opinions from the majority of group members. With their peers present, this minority may not have felt free to discuss their negative feelings towards coaches, parents or teammates. Future research ought to explore youth soccer through the use of one-to-one interviews in order to better portray possible negative experiences.

This study's third limitation relates to the age range of the participants (12- to 14-year-olds). Since there were not an equal number of teams from each age involved in the study (with only one team of 14-year-olds), the scope of the study did not allow for separate data analyses for each of the three ages. Since the rules and regulations from the NFF allow for more competitive play at age 13, the factors for soccer enjoyment for 13- and 14-year-olds may differ significantly from those for 12-year-olds. Future studies, therefore, ought to explore possible differences in soccer enjoyment during mid adolescence. Our study did not suggest that gender differentiation would be helpful, at least not for exploring factors contributing to enjoyment of soccer in this age group in Norway.

Acknowledgement

The research leading to these results has received funding from the European Community's Seventh Framework Programme FP7/2007-2013 under grant agreement n 223600. The authors also want to acknowledge David Huegel for insightful and valuable language revision.

Disclosure statement

No potential conflict of interest was reported by the authors.

Notes

1. Bakker et al., 'Flow and Performance', 442; R.J. Keegan et al., 'Exploring the Motivational Climate', 361 and T.V. Ryba, 'Cartwheels on Ice', 58.
2. 'FIFA Magazine, Big Count 2007'.
3. Norwegian Football Federation (NFF) Facts and History about Norwegian Football. http://www.fotball.no/toppmeny/english/Facts-and-history-about-Norwegian-Football/.
4. McCarthy et al., 'Enjoyment Youth Sport', 143.
5. Kjonniksen et al., 'Tracking of Leisure-time', 2.
6. Ulrich-French and Smith, 'Relationships with Parents and Peers', 202.
7. Scanland, 'Sources of Enjoyment', 202.
8. McCarthy, 'Enjoyment Youth Sport', 143.
9. Ibid.
10. MacPhail et al., 'Young People's Socialization', 260.
11. Ibid.
12. Ulrich-French and Smith, 'Relationships with Parents and Peers', 202.
13. Ibid.
14. Allenderet al., 'Understanding Participation in Sport', 830; Ulrich-French and Smith, 'Social and Motivational Predictors', 87.
15. Wold et al., 'Comparing Self-reported Leisure-time', 328.
16. Gagne, 'Autonomy Support', 372.
17. Larson, 'Positive Youth Development', 174.
18. Bakker et al., 'Flow and Performance', 447; Ryba, 'Cartwheels on Ice', 58.
19. Ryba, 'Cartwheels on Ice', 70.
20. Bakker, 'Flow and Performance', 447.
21. Seifert and Hedderson, 'Intrinsic Motivation and Flow', 277.
22. Bakker et al., 'Flow and Performance', 443.
23. Ryba, 'Cartwheels on Ice', 70.

24. Bakker, 'Flow and Performance', 447.
25. Duda and Nicholls, 'Achievement Motivation', 290.
26. Fraser-Thomas et al., 'Adolescent Sport Dropout', 320.
27. Duda et al., 'Promoting Adolescent Health', 319.
28. Ibid., 114.
29. Hennessy and Heary, 'Exploring Children's Views', 236; Keegan et al., 'Exploring the Motivational Climate', 361.
30. Ibid.
31. Keegan et al., 'Exploring the Motivational Climate', 361.
32. Kvale and Brinkman, *InterViews*, 3.
33. Barnett et al., 'Adolescents' Perception', 275.
34. Keegan et al., 'Exploring the Motivational Climate', 364.
35. Ibid.
36. Bakker et al., 'Flow and Performance', 447.
37. Ibid.
38. Leversen, 'Leisure Activities and Adolescents', 1595.
39. Bjorneby, 'The Mission of Soccer', 1.
40. Light, 'Social Nature of Games', 289.
41. Scarpa and Nart, 'Perceived Sport Competence', 203.
42. Elbe et al., 'Experiencing Flow', 112.
43. Ryba, 'Cartwheels on Ice', 70.
44. Bjorneby, 'The Mission of Soccer', 3.
45. Fraser-Thomas et al., 'Youth Sport Programs', 28.
46. Gagne, 'Autonomy Support and Needs Satisfaction', 372.
47. Bergo, *Ferdighetsutvikling i fotball* [Skill development in football], 62.
48. Bunker and Thorpe, 'A Model for the Teaching of Games', 5.
49. Griffin et al., 'Teaching Games for Understanding', 221.
50. Light, 'The Social Nature of Games', 292.
51. Dyson et al., 'Sport Education, Tactical Games, and Cooperative Learning,' 228.
52. Griffin, et al., 'Teaching Games for Understanding', 221.
53. Deci and Ryan, 'The What and Why of Goal Pursuits', 227.
54. Larsen et al., 'Creating High-quality Motivational Climates'; T. Larsen et al., 'Coach Efficacy and Youth Soccer'.
55. Ibid.

References

Allender, S., G. Cowburn, and C. Foster. 'Understanding Participation in Sport and Physical Activity among Children and Adults: A Review of Qualitative Studies'. *Health Education Research* 21, no. 6 (2006): 826–35. http://her.oxfordjournals.org/content/21/6/826.abstract.

Bakker, A.B., W. Oerlemans, E. Demerouti, B.B. Slot, and D.K. Ali. 'Flow and Performance: A Study among Talented Dutch Soccer Players'. *Psychology of Sport and Exercise* 12, no. 4 (2011): 442–50. doi:10.1016/j.psychsport.2011.02.003.

Barnett, L., K. Cliff, P. Morgan, and E. van Beurden. 'Adolescents' Perception of the Relationship between Movement Skills, Physical Activity and Sport'. *European Physical Education Review* 19, no. 2 (2013): 271–85.

Bergo, A. *Ferdighetsutviklingifotball – handlingsvalgog handling* [Skill development in soccer – choices and action]. Oslo: Akilles forlag, 2002.

Bjorneby, S.I. 'Budskapet i Barnefotballen I 2012'. [The vision of children and youth soccer in 2012]. Oslo: NFF, 2012.

Bunker, D., and R. Thorpe. 'A Model for the Teaching of Games in Secondary Schools'. *Bulletin of Physical Education* 18, no. 1 (1982): 5–8.

Deci, E.L., and R.M. Ryan. 'The "What" and "Why" of Goal Pursuits: Human Needs and the Self-determination of Behavior'. *Psychological Inquiry* 11, no. 4 (2000): 227–68. doi:10.1207/S15327965PLI1104_01.

Duda, J.L., and J.G. Nicholls. 'Dimensions of Achievement Motivation in Schoolwork and Sport'. *Journal of Educational Psychology* 84, no. 3 (1992): 290–9.

Duda, J.L., E. Quested, E. Haug, O. Samdal, B. Wold, I. Balaguer, I. Castillo, et al. 'Promoting Adolescent Health through an Intervention Aimed at Improving the Quality of Their Participation in Physical Activity (PAPA): Background to the Project and Main Trial Protocol'. *International Journal of Sport and Exercise Psychology* 11, no. 4 (2013): 319–27. doi:10.1080/1612197X.2013.839413.

Dyson, B., L.L. Griffin, and P. Hastie. 'Sport Education, Tactical Games, and Cooperative Learning: Theoretical and Pedagogical Considerations'. *Quest* 56 (2004): 226–40. doi:10.1080/00336297.2004.10491823.

Elbe, A.M., K. Strahler, P. Krustrup, J. Wikman, and R. Stelter. 'Experiencing Flow in Different Types of Physical Activity Intervention Programs: Three Randomized Studies'. *Scandinavian Journal of Medicine & Science in Sports* 20, no. s1 (2010): 111–7. doi:10.1111/j.1600-0838.2010.01112.x.

FIFA. 'FIFA Magazine: Big Count 2007. http://www.fifa.com/mm/document/fifafacts/bcoff surv/emaga_9384_10704.pdf (accessed April 7, 2015).

Fraser-Thomas, J.L., J. Côté, and J. Deakin. 'Examining Adolescent Sport Dropout and Prolonged Engagement from a Developmental Perspective'. *Journal of Applied Sport Psychology* 20, no. 3 (2008): 318–33. doi:10.1080/10413200802163549.

Fraser-Thomas, J.L., J. Côté, and J. Deakin. 'Youth Sport Programs: An Avenue to Foster Positive Youth Development'. *Physical Education & Sport Pedagogy* 10, no. 1 (2005): 19–40. doi: 10.1080/1740898042000334890.

Gagne, M. 'Autonomy Support and Need Satisfaction in the Motivation and Well-being of Gymnasts'. *Journal of Applied Sport Psychology* 15, no. 4 (2003): 372–90. doi:10.1080/ 714044203.

Green, K. 'Mission Impossible? Reflecting upon the Relationship between Physical Education, Youth Sport and Lifelong Participation'. *Sport, Education and Society* 19, no. 4 (2014): 357–75. doi:10.1080/13573322.2012.683781.

Griffin, L.L., R. Brooker, and K. Patton. 'Working towards Legitimacy: Two Decades of Teaching Games for Understanding'. *Physical Education and Sport Pedagogy* 10, no. 3 (2005): 213–23. doi:10.1080/17408980500340703.

Hennessy, E., and C. Heary. 'Exploring Children's Views through Focus Groups'. Chap. 4 in *Researching Children's Experience. Approaches and Methods.* London: Sage, 2005.

Keegan, R.J., C.G. Harwood, Christopher M. Spray, and D.E. Lavallee. 'A Qualitative Investigation Exploring the Motivational Climate in Early Career Sports Participants: Coach, Parent and Peer Influences on Sport Motivation'. *Psychology of Sport and Exercise* 10, no. 3 (2009): 361–72. doi:10.1016/j.psychsport.2008.12.003.

Kjønniksen, L., T. Torsheim, and B. Wold. 'Tracking of Leisure-time Physical Activity during Adolescence and Young Adulthood: A 10-year Longitudinal Study'. *International Journal of Behavioral Nutrition and Physical Activity* 5, no. 69 (2008): 1–11. doi:10.1186/1479-5868-5-69.

Kvale, S., and S. Brinkman. *InterViews: Learning the Craft of Qualitative Research Interviewing.* Thousand Oaks, CA: Sage, 2009.

Larsen, T., I. Holsen, H.E. Tjomsland, B. Wold, Y.L.T. Rongland, and Y. Ommundsen. 'Coach Efficacy: A Mixed Method Study of Norwegian Youth Football Coaches Educated in the Empowering Coaching Program™'. University of Bergen, 2014.

Larsen, T., A. Van Hoye, H.E. Tjomsland, I. Holsen, B. Wold, J.P. Heuze, O. Samdal, and P. Sarrazin. 'Creating High Quality Motivational Climate among Youth Football Players: A Qualitative Study of French and Norwegian Youth Grassroots Football Coaches'. *Health Education* 115, no. 6, (2015): 570–86. University of Bergen.

Larson, R.W. 'Toward a Psychology of Positive Youth Development'. *American Psychologist* 55, no. 1 (2000): 170–83. doi:10.1037//0003-066X.55.1.170.

Leversen, I., A.G. Danielsen, M. Birkeland, and O. Samdal. 'Basic Psychological Need Satisfaction in Leisure Activities and Adolescents' Life Satisfaction'. *Journal of Youth and Adolescence* 41, no. 12 (2012): 1588–99. doi:10.1007/s10964-012-9776-5.

Light, R.L. 'The Social Nature of Games: Australian Pre-service Primary Teachers' First Experiences of TGfU'. *European Physical Education Review* 8, no. 2 (2002): 291–309. doi:10.1177/1356336X020083007.

Macphail, A., T. Gorely, and D. Kirk. 'Young People's Socialisation into Sport: A Case Study of an Athletics Club'. *Sport, Education and Society* 8, no. 2 (2003): 251–67. doi:10.1080/13573320309251.

McCarthy, P.J., M.V. Jones, and D. Clark-Carter. 'Understanding Enjoyment in Youth Sport: A Developmental Perspective'. *Psychology of Sport and Exercise* 9 (2008): 142–56.

Moneta, G.B., and M. Csikszentmihalyi. 'The Effect of Perceived Challenges and Skills on the Quality of Subjective Experience'. *Journal of Personality* 64, no. 2 (1996): 275–310. doi:10.1111/j.1467-6494.1996.tb00512.x.

Norwegian Football Federation (NFF). Facts and History about Norwegian Football, 2013. http://www.fotball.no/toppmeny/english/Facts-and-history-about-Norwegian-Football/ (accessed December 2014).

Ryba, T.V. 'Cartwheels on Ice: A Phenomenological Exploration of Children's Enjoyment in Competitive Figure Skating'. *Athletic Insight. The Online Journal of Sport Psychology* 9, no. 2 (2007): 58–73.

Scanlan, T.K., P.J. Carpenter, M. Lobel, and J.P. Simons. 'Sources of Enjoyment of Youth Sport Athletes'. *Pediatric Exercise Science* 5 (1993): 275–85.

Scarpa, S., and A. Nart. 'Influences of Perceived Sport Competence on Physical Activity Enjoyment in Early Adolescents'. *Social Behavior and Personality: An International Journal* 40, no. 2 (2012): 203–4.

Seifert, T., and C. Hedderson. 'Intrinsic Motivation and Flow in Skateboarding: An Ethnographic Study'. *Journal of Happiness Studies* 11, no. 3 (2010): 277–92. doi:10.1007/s10902-009-9140-y.

Ullrich-French, S., and A.L. Smith. 'Perceptions of Relationships with Parents and Peers in Youth Sport: Independent and Combined Prediction of Motivational Outcomes'. *Psychology of Sport and Exercise* 7, no. 2 (2006): 193–214. doi:10.1016/j.psychsport.2005.08.006.

Ullrich-French, S., and A.L. Smith. 'Social and Motivational Predictors of Continued Youth Sport Participation'. *Psychology of Sport and Exercise* 10, no. 1 (2009): 87–95. doi:10.1016/j.psychsport.2008.06.007.

Wold, B., J.L. Duda, I. Balaguer, O.R.F. Smith, Y. Ommundsen, H.K. Hall, O. Samdal, et al. 'Comparing Self-reported Leisure-time Physical Activity, Subjective Health, and Life Satisfaction among Youth Soccer Players and Adolescents in a Reference Sample'. *International Journal of Sport and Exercise Psychology* 11, no. 4 (2013): 328–40.

Elite footballers as role models: promoting young women's football participation

Carrie Dunn

Faculty of Arts and Digital Industries, University of East London, London, UK

Sportspeople are constantly urged to maintain the highest levels of conduct because of their position as 'role models' to children. This article reports from a study in progress which explores the experiences of elite female athletes in Britain, and focuses on qualitative interview responses of elite female footballers, all of whom were currently playing at top-flight domestic and international levels and took part in the 2012 Olympics. It explores what they perceive the position as 'role model' to mean, how it impinges on their sport performance, and how they work with gifted young footballers to promote sporting excellence as well as community cohesion through grass-roots outreach work. It discusses their thoughts on how role models are currently and can best be used to encourage young women's football participation from elite down to grass-roots levels, and highlights the amount of responsibility they feel to do this.

Introduction

The position of female athletes as positive 'role models' to young women was emphasized throughout the London 2012 Olympic Games and afterwards. Headmistress and president of the Girls' Schools Association Louise Robinson commented:

> We are now in the enviable position of having a phenomenal number of female role models for school girls, thanks to Team GB's performance. I do hope we can manage to maintain at least some of the tremendous media momentum behind these sportswomen so that young girls across the country can continue to see, and aspire to be, women of real achievement.[1]

This particularly seemed to be the case for women competing in traditionally 'male' sports, allowing for a contrast between the typical behaviour of a male athlete in that sport and the apparently 'new', 'refreshing' behaviour of his female counterpart. For example, after Team GB's female footballers beat Brazil 1–0, the Telegraph's Henry Winter concluded his match report with the words:

> [Hope] Powell's players had still not finished delighting Wembley. [Kelly] Smith, [Kim] Little, [Steph] Houghton and the rest stayed out for 20 min, signing autographs and posing for photographs with fans. Great role models. Great game.[2]

Yet, despite this positive coverage, historically only around 2% of national newspaper sports pages have been devoted to women's sport.[3] Thus, it is perhaps unsurprising to note that young women's participation in sports is cause for concern; by the

51

age of 15, half as many girls as boys meet the recommended activity levels, contributing towards the current health crisis in the UK.[4] This problem has led to the development of policies and strategies on local, regional and national levels aimed at encouraging the sports participation of young women.

One of those strategies has been to roll out community programmes attached to football clubs, in schools and in other community groups and led by players, drawing on their status to encourage young people to view sport as something fun, attractive and desirable. The football authorities have also been keen to use their elite female footballers for public appearances and prize givings, meaning that these women are (presented as) somewhat more approachable and much less remote than elite male footballers.

Understanding of the term 'role model' and the function of role models in women's football

In England, the well-publicized recent growth in female participation in football as promoted by the FA since 1993 tends to overshadow the formal and informal policies and practices that have excluded women from football,[5] and encourages the perception that women's involvement in football is a recent phenomenon – there is no central archive for women's football records[6]; a dedicated effort to uncover this element of sports history has been required to begin to fill in the gaps in the chronicle of women's football (see the work of Lopez[7]; Melling[8]; Newsham[9]; Tate[10]; Williams[11]; Williams and Woodhouse[12] and Williamson[13]). What is not in question, however, is that women's football has not been accorded a high profile in England, with little media coverage paralleling the governing body's historical neglect of the sport and lack of investment in marketing or grass-roots development.

Despite this absence, women's football has continued to cling to life tenaciously in England, with a new generation of footballers now having the chance to make money from playing sport in the new semi-professional FA Women's Super League.[14] These women have also been positioned by the FA as 'ambassadors', working in marketing or community departments at football clubs or governing bodies, presenting themselves as 'role models', with career paths that could be emulated by girls.

The significance of 'role models' for young women has been discussed across sport, and there have been several studies on how 'role models' affect young people; for the purposes of this article, the term means a person who is inspiring, and who can and should be emulated. Biskup and Pfister argue that role models are necessary, and 'offer essential help and orientation, for children and adolescents in particular'.[15] Craike et al.'s findings[16] reflected that family members, friends and teachers were often an important factor in encouraging sporting participation among young women; however, there was no mention of high-profile sportswomen having the same effect. Fleming et al.[17] acknowledged that sports stars could be inspiring to young people, but did not assess the specific impact of female sporting role models on girls.

As these studies suggest, elite sportswomen are often not named by young women as role models, and this may be at least partly because elite sportswomen's achievements are not reported in the media. A highly detailed study produced by GirlGuiding UK[18] indicates that young women in the UK would like to see more high-profile female role models outside of their immediate family and friendship circles. This research showed that girls aged under 11 found sport 'fun', yet on the whole, there was a 'very low level of awareness of sporting stars of any kind, and a near-total absence of female sports stars'. They pointed out: 'Female sports stars that the girls can name are in most cases known not for their sporting achievements but for celebrity appearances – on TV reality or quiz shows, in adverts, or promoting their own range of clothes or equipment'. The study also found that teenagers drew most of their female role models from the world of entertainment, and the authors concluded that this was a bias 'towards a relatively narrow group of celebrity women' which risked 'affecting expectations, confidence and views of what is normal behaviour'. Perhaps unsurprisingly, the study reported an 'assumption that women in sport are less well known because they are less successful than their male counterparts. One group was surprised to hear that the England women's football team had reached the finals in [the 2011] World Cup: "Why don't we hear about it? It's always the boys!"'

This current article draws from material gathered during a study in progress which explores the experiences of elite female athletes in Britain; the intent was to gain qualitative, experiential data from respondents narrating their experiences and memories on a variety of topics relating to their sporting careers, rather than responding directly to specific researcher-selected questions, allowing them flexibility and freedom to construct their own narratives[19] or as Stanley would term it, 'auto/biography',[20] narrating their experience as they remember it from their perspective. The focus here is thus on the qualitative semi-structured interview responses of elite female footballers who have been positioned as 'role models' by the media and by sporting authorities, and who also act as mentors in formal coaching and outreach programmes. All respondents were currently playing at top-flight domestic and international levels for one of the 'home nations' (these elements were essential for participants, ensuring their 'eliteness' and highlighting their sporting achievement), with those quoted in this article also taking part in the 2012 Olympics as part of the 18-woman Team GB squad; they were interviewed in the 15 months following London 2012. All have been pseudonymized, and any detail that could identify them specifically has been removed.

This article focuses on responses from the footballers when they were asked about their understanding of the term 'role model' for young people. It was discussed in the context of the media coverage and policy-makers stressing how important it was for young girls to have 'role models' who were high achievers, particularly in the field of sport where encouraging female participation for health reasons was common.

Harriet's response to being positioned as a role model was positive – and typical. She explained:

> I think it's really important. I think we all take it very seriously that we are considered role models, it is very strange and it is weird sometimes when you're kind of asked for your autograph, it's like why are you asking me for an autograph? So no, I think we all take it very seriously, obviously as we were growing up we didn't have the Kardashians to look up to, but we didn't tend to have a lot of women in sport, in terms of football-wise, to look up to really, so we tended to go on the male side more than anything, and so it's nice to kind of have for younger kids' aspirations and to see it more in the media, women's football on a bigger platform and role models for them to look up to, and try to achieve, and try to do as well or more than some of us have gained so far, so no, I think it's really good, and we're, like I said, we do take it really seriously and hope that we are good role models to them, really.

She found her public profile unusual and surprising, but she took it very seriously and wanted to use it to have a positive impact, giving children people 'to look up to'. Here, she mentioned the Kardashian family – American stars of a worldwide reality show – who were often invoked in the media commentary during the Olympics as the 'opposites' to female athlete role models due to their 'lack of achievement', their wealth and their 'lack of hard work'. She raises a significant point which recurred throughout the series of interviews: this generation of elite female athletes did not have female sporting role models growing up, but instead emulated men – and this will be discussed in more detail later in the article. Now that elite female sport does have some degree of profile, the athletes are very clear that they want to maintain that and behave in appropriate ways to inspire the younger generation. This, as I show in the next section, may be a particularly gendered response to a high profile.

How being a 'role model' affects elite female footballers' conduct and behaviour

In the research project so far upon which this article draws, respondents across all sports have been nothing less than positive about the opportunity to act as a role model to young people. (Indeed, Henry Winter's praise of the Team GB players during London 2012, as mentioned previously, shows that the media have been happy to latch on to this idea that female players are more community minded and worthy of praise.) As the rest of this article highlights, female footballers say that they see their position as not just beneficial for themselves and for elite sport, but a position of power that can encourage young people to participate in sport. Equally significantly, they say that they do not necessarily want to talent-spot the very best young female players; they want to encourage girls and boys to enjoy physical activity and promote good health.

This embrace of community outreach and use of a public profile in this way is not necessarily mirrored in the men's elite game, where the common narrative, reinforced by the media, is that male footballers will begrudgingly accept that they are role models but also make it plain that it is a position they do not relish. For example, Wayne Rooney accepted in 2010 that he and his England colleagues were role models and needed to improve their behaviour accordingly, saying:

> It is difficult as a footballer because you know people look up to you ... You are role models whether you like it or not. You need to try and be aware of that, try and do your best on the pitch, and try to do things well for kids to see.[21]

Similarly, former Stevenage manager Paul Fairclough argued:

> They didn't ask to be a role model but hey, if you're on big bucks and on our screens every week it's tough luck, you have no say in it.[22]

Elite female footballers, however, did not describe their public profile as any kind of burden during interviews. Terri was quick to point out that female footballers in England are not usually professional athletes in the usual sense of the term, i.e. getting paid to play football as a full-time job, and suggested that some players might forget they had a public profile because they did not get commensurate media coverage. However, like Harriet, she argued strongly that it was a privilege to be regarded by anyone in any way as a role model, and a responsibility that had to be taken seriously. She said:

It's been a hard thing to learn as you don't really see yourself as this professional in terms of media, money; you forget that you are being watched and looked up to all the time. You're representing yourself, your club and country, and with that honour comes responsibility and being a role model for the next generation isn't a big responsibility, it's kind of a privilege.

Similarly, Orla explained:

I consider myself kind of a little bit like an ambassador for the game, and anything I'm asked to do I'll happily do it. If that helps promote the sport, then it helps promote the sport, but I think you're giving the young girls an opportunity to look up to someone, or a team, it's definitely good to get it out there in the papers, on television as much as possible, and I'd love to be one of them people, one of the girls that they look up to and try to aspire to be, and try and be as professional as possible by doing as much for the game as I can.

These extracts show that the elite players have a sense of pride in being perceived as role models to young people. In contrast to the views expressed by Rooney and Fairclough, the elite female footballers saw their public profile and responsibilities as a privilege rather than any kind of unfair expectation or problem. As they imply here, they remember very clearly their own lack of female sporting role models as children, and want to step in to ensure that children now have a broad range of people to attempt to emulate or admire.

How elite female footballers engage with young people to encourage sporting participation

Elite female footballers' status as 'role models' does not rely on media coverage; it requires strong and frequent hands-on engagement and public visibility. The respondents for this study had multiple opportunities for this kind of work: at club level (with their immediate local communities) and at international level (across the country, representing their international team, and in some cases, Team GB following their Olympics selection). All interviewees talked about how much they enjoyed participating in community events as 'guests of honour', such as presenting awards at local clubs' prize givings, particularly for girls' teams; again, they saw it as a chance to give girls opportunities that they did not have themselves as children. Terri's explanation was typical: 'When it comes to functions or events I try to get along and help out; I never had that as a kid so it's always nice to do'.

As this article has previously pointed out, elite female footballers in the UK have historically not been full-time professionals, and several of them work for the community departments at either the men's club linked to their team, or another club close to them, allowing them to develop coaching skills and work flexibly around training and playing commitments. This means that many of them are involved in formal community outreach as well; such programmes entail initiatives such as 'summer schools' where different age groups of young people learn to play the game, but also literacy and numeracy promotions as well as other schemes promoting social cohesion and good citizenship for adults and young people.

Harriet enjoyed her job working as a community development coach for a men's professional club, which gave her the chance to improve her coaching skills but also to show girls that they could play football too if they wished. She explained:

> It's really nice, I work on the development side so it's really nice to go into schools and going into assemblies and the kids being very excited, not just the girls but also the boys being really excited as well, so it's really nice to see the mix of genders, and we really try to kind of not just obviously target girls but also go in and talk to the boys as well, because they are just as interested as the girls are in coming to watch women's football, they don't really have any opinions, to be honest, which is really lovely to see, so, um, yeah, we do kind of try and get a lot of the players in to coach the kids and stuff, and hopefully inspire them.

She points out here that the community work she does is not gender specific, and that boys as well as girls are excited to meet and play with an international footballer. (It is perhaps also significant that she mentions that the boys 'don't really have any opinions'; she is alluding to the frequent prejudice against women's football which has resulted in the historic lack of media coverage, and pointing out that children do not have these innate prejudices, but they learn them and have them reinforced.) The fact that an international footballer is coaching them and talking to them is enough to inspire both boys and girls to play.

Orla had a job outside professional football, but was still involved with her club's outreach work, making personal appearances in schools and community groups when she could, in her free time. (It is important to reiterate here that this is not unusual in elite women's football; the top England players in recent seasons have mostly been semi-professional while competing domestically in the semi-professional FA Women's Super League, or FAWSL, and the day job that subsidises their sport is not necessarily football related. However, as Orla shows, this does not mean that they take their football or their football responsibilities any less seriously.) She said:

> We regularly visit schools, do assemblies, we do girls-only coaching courses, so a lot of the girls are involved in them, and I think it's nice, if I were younger and, say, a [men's club] first-teamer came down to try and coach me, you'd automatically want to try and impress, you'd want to do anything they say, and try and improve as much as you possibly can, so if we can do that, put that back into the community, it's brilliant for us, it's something I really enjoy, and it's nice to go along and see the girls' faces when we put on a session, and it's nice to know that they want to learn as well.

Orla was much more focused than Harriet on the importance of encouraging girls specifically to play, and the ways that elite female footballers could contribute towards that. It is significant that neither of them discussed the need to talent-spot the next generation of international footballers; instead, they both stressed the need to encourage girls (and boys) to play sport and more importantly enjoy it. This enjoyment on the part of the children was what gave Orla her own enjoyment of her community work; but she also noted that her own status as an elite footballer might also encourage young people to perform better in order to impress her.

How 'role models' can be used specifically to encourage young women's football participation

Orla was clear that she felt that an elite footballer's presence could be inspiring for young people at varying levels of sporting achievement, drawing this from her own experience as a child. However, some scholars and commentators are sceptical about the significance of celebrity or sporting male role models for boys.[23] A survey of male primary school teachers by Brownhill indicates:

... that children are more likely to be influenced by people who are their own age (generational), who share the same experiences (experiential) and who live close by, such as friends and family, rather than by celebrities or sports stars such as Wayne Rooney. A friend who, for example, shows no fear when going on a fairground ride is more likely to be a role model for a youngster.[24]

However, as Fleming et al. point out, 'It is reasonable to suppose that some sports stars inspire young players'.[25] They address high-profile male sports stars inspiring boys and young men (they mention the likes of cricketer Shane Warne, footballer David Beckham and rugby league player Paul Sculthorpe), and the elite female footballers also feel that they can have a great impact on young people's lives with their outreach work, improving their sporting skills and their general health in particular.

Harriet was very enthusiastic about the potential that high-profile role models could have on encouraging young people's sporting participation. She talked about the positive reception she and her teammates got in schools but was keen to point out that promoting football did not mean promoting it at the expense of other sports. She explained:

> It's brilliant, and it's so lovely to see when a lot of the kids are getting very excited, some of them will start screaming and stuff, so it's very weird when you first kind of go in and think they'll kind of want your autograph, but it's really nice to see them all kind of really excited about football, or just sport in general, really. Obviously we want to encourage them to play football, but we're not discouraging them from taking part in any other sport, if anything we want them to be active, so that's the main thing, really, and to come and watch some of our games as well, so yeah, I think it works both ways, really ... I think it's been in the news so often about obesity and the kids not getting enough physical activity, so if we can go in and just kind of talk to them about the training we do, and hopefully inspire them to go out and have a kick about, or just to go out and have fun in the fresh air, really, with their friends, that's a key thing, and obviously, for us to talk about our nutrition as well to them, kids can learn a little bit more about the food and nutrition, which is also really key as well, so I think there's a lot of things that we can hit, really, in terms of talking with the children in the local communities, really.

This personal engagement with young people is key. As Lockwood and Kunda suggest,[26] elite athletes' behaviour is more likely to be imitated by young people when they are considered relevant, i.e. with some similarity to the observer. As the elite female footballers talk to and coach the young people, sharing their experiences and encouraging their sporting participation through play, this bond of similarity is enhanced. As the GirlGuiding UK study highlighted,[27] female sporting role models have been invisibilized; having personal contact with elite female athletes is likely to be inspiring to young women.

All the elite female footballers quoted in this article (and, in fact, in the broader study) were aged between 20 and 30, and grew up after the FA took control of the women's game in England in 1992. However, even as teenagers, they were not aware of the possibilities for women to play football due to the lack of marketing and media coverage. Unsurprisingly, then, they reported that their sporting role models were either male footballers or family members; this 'ungendering' of role models and the reliance on family members instead is similar to what Robert-Holmes and Brownhill[28] suggest about male sporting role models not being a particular influence on boys, but the women indicate that if they had indeed had female sporting role models, this would have been an encouragement to them.

Terri, a goalkeeper, recalled:

I was a big [Peter] Schmeichel and [Shay] Given fan until I was about 15 and Leanne Hall took a session – I finally had a girl to look up to, then when I was 17 I got to work with Rachel Brown so she became the goalkeeper I wanted to be.

Harriet highlighted the influence of her supportive family as she began her career in football, reflecting the responses of the female rugby players in Murray and Howat's study,[29] who talked about their participation being facilitated by a supportive family also involved in the sport. She also mentioned the power of role models via the media – not just reporting of women's sports, but also the fictional film 'Bend it Like Beckham', about a girls' football team, starring Keira Knightley and released in 2002. Significantly, the lead character Jess is inspired to play by David Beckham, who is Harriet's own role model. Harriet said:

Obviously I looked up to some famous people, but my mum and dad were kind of my role models, really, they, they absolutely love football. My older brother, I used to go and watch him play football, and I used to be kind of dressed in a massive snowsuit and I'd just stand there and watch, kind of thing, I used to run around, kick a football, kind of stuff. They're kind of what inspired me to take part in football and stuff … and then obviously, watching on TV, the likes of kind of Gary Lineker and David Beckham, and from watching 'Bend It Like Beckham', Mia Hamm from like the women's side.

Orla also reported little knowledge of women's football as a child, and talked about her experience of supporting a men's team and wanting to emulate the top male stars: 'No, to be totally honest I didn't have a clue. I never had a clue. My only focus was I was a [professional Football League club] supporter, so I only ever followed the men's team. I liked David Beckham and Steven Gerrard, they were the players that I kind of watched when I was younger, and I never knew who Faye White was, or Marieanne Spacey.'

Orla refers here to two long-serving players with vast international and domestic experience across careers that lasted nearly two decades. However, she only became more aware of women's football as she began to play for the women's team at the local men's club. She explains:

It was only until I was about 13, 14 when I was playing for the [club's] Centre of Excellence and I was going into the first team and kind of realised, oh, Fulham's a pro- fessional team, I'd love to be professional, kind of thing, it kind of just went from there, my knowledge of women's football kind of grew, but when I was younger, growing up, it was all male football that I looked at.

It is unsurprising that the footballers reported very limited awareness of women's football as young people, even though during this period there were professional teams in the USA, and Fulham Ladies were professional for a very limited time. Prior to the launch of the FAWSL in 2011, there were no live league games shown on television, with the FA Women's Cup being the only domestic game that could count on any kind of broadcast coverage. Even after that the matches were only shown on subscription-only digital channels, again restricting its coverage.

Terri's experience was similar, as she recalled:

If I'm honest I wasn't [aware of women's football leagues], I played with the boys. It wasn't until I saw my first women's game, I think I was 13, maybe, and Croydon played someone else in a FA Cup final on Sky or BBC maybe. That made me realise that maybe I could be doing that.

It is significant to note that although none of the respondents could have named any UK-based female footballers from their childhoods, all of them mentioned one American footballer in particular having an impact on their consciousness – the legendary Mia Hamm. In the USA, football has traditionally been seen as an acceptable sport for women to play, and Hamm's fame has crossed into the mainstream, even securing a namecheck on the hit comedy series 'Friends'.

Terri and Harriet reported that they became aware of Hamm and the professional US leagues when they began playing more seriously and tried to find out about potential career options. Terri said:

> Once I played for my first girls' team, other girls were always talking about Mia Hamm and how it was pro in the States; it was what we all wanted to do because there wasn't much talk of it being a career in the UK.

Meanwhile, Harriet explained:

> I went over to America when I was about ten or eleven, so I was more aware of it then, I met Kelly Smith out there when she was playing for Philadelphia Charge, so that was when I really became more aware of the leagues and stuff like that, really.

Orla, on the other hand, learnt about Mia Hamm by another of her mainstream media guest appearances – once again, in the film 'Bend It Like Beckham', again showing the importance of significant presence in high-profile media for women's football. She said:

> I think [I knew who] Mia Hamm was because of 'Bend It Like Beckham', the film, I only watched it because it was Beckham, I didn't have a clue what it was about. I think it was, I think that's the only reason I knew who Mia Hamm was, because of 'Bend It Like Beckham'. It's just amazing that that film was actually, put someone in there, and it started people taking notice of women's football, and yeah, that was, Mia Hamm was a brilliant player as well, she's done wonders for the women's game and probably will be the most popular player in women's football.

This significance of a single film in the lives of two of these interviewees is major. I argue that it demonstrates the impact that a positive role model and positive images of women's football in the media can have on inspiring young people's sporting participation. Although the news media should be reporting what is happening in women's football in order to raise awareness of the game, the experiences of the interviewees – who went on to participate in grass-roots football and progressed to the elite game – show that this lack of coverage does not necessarily put potential players off. However, positive media images – showing that women playing football is 'normal' and 'socially acceptable' – even in a fictional format can do a great deal to educate and to encourage potential players.

The respondents expressed a hope that their own increased media profile and their work as 'role models' would encourage girls to play football at all levels, from grass roots upwards. Terri highlighted the importance of media coverage, particularly reporting on the national team's continued success. She said: 'I think now girls have someone they can look up to and that's down to media and the success of the girls'.

As the GirlGuiding UK study[30] showed, young women valued the opportunity to have role models, but there was a problem with the media's focus being on a very small range of 'celebrity' women, meaning that they did not know about a vast array of women's achievements. Thus, sustained media coverage of women's sport could be one way in which girls and young women find out about a potentially bigger selection of role models, and even career opportunities; hence, Terri stresses on the need for this media coverage to continue, but acknowledged that this also depended on the quality of the football, adding:

> I can now safely say that as a girl footballer the future is massively bright for young-sters and there is a career to be made. As long as the football keeps moving forward the media will stay interested. Why can't it one day be as professional as the men?

Orla also took a more long-term view than her colleagues, talking in detail about the structure and organization of women's football, the recent changes and how she thought it would improve the game in the future, saying:

> At the time if you were 13 and you were playing in the first team it must have shown that there wasn't that good a standard at wherever you were. Now the girls are learning a lot more at a younger age, whether that's tactical or technical. It just gives them a chance to go and enjoy the football at a younger age and not feel that much pressure going into the first team, and just try and do as well as they can at their age, and if they excel, if they stand out in their age group, then they'll move on to the first team. I think the structure of the whole women's football is definitely improving. Hopefully it'll create winning England teams in the future.

Looking ahead

Eighty-one per cent of adults in the UK think that the female athletes at London 2012 are better role models than other celebrities,[31] and this statistic is based simply on their sporting achievement during those Games. Their profile can be increased even further; and it is apparent that the hands-on work in the community done by elite female footballers has the potential to have a huge impact: first, by encouraging young people to understand that they can be 'similar' to them and participate in sport, and second, by specifically showing girls potential achievements to emulate.

As the respondents highlight, there has been a historic lack of media coverage of women's football (and as previous studies show, women's sport in general), which has meant that their achievements have not been so widely reported as perhaps they deserve. The football authorities, clubs and the mainstream press all have a potential responsibility here to ensure that there is adequate coverage of women's sporting achievements and thus adequate representation of the 'good role models' they have been so keen to establish. However, it is important to note that this representation also needs to be appropriate; as Orla points out, there has been some less-than-help-ful coverage stressing female footballers' acceptable heteronormativity, showing them as 'girly' and enjoying typically 'feminine' pursuits such as shopping. Elite female footballers should be portrayed as athletes, judged on their sporting achieve-ments, treated with respect and taken seriously, as Orla so eloquently argues.

It is also clear that their positions as role models and their work with young peo-ple from grass roots upwards are both taken extremely seriously by elite female footballers. I suggest that they understand the possible importance and impact of their behaviour and achievements; they grew up wanting to be footballers and remember how they would have felt if they had the chance to meet an international player, male or female, and they welcome the opportunity to inspire today's young people. I also suggest that they take a lot of responsibility on themselves because they know from experience that the media, the sporting governing bodies and the education system cannot necessarily be trusted to put forward appropriate and admirable female sporting role models.

Additionally, having grown up themselves without female footballing role models, they understand how this lack might affect girls, and want to fill a gap they have obviously noted from their own experience. This is partially because they want to support a better and more successful structure for women's football in England, including better and more successful teams at the elite level, but also because they want to share their enjoyment of sport – not simply at a competitive level, but to help children get out in 'the fresh air', as Harriet puts it, and improve their health.

Conclusion

This article has reported some initial findings from an ongoing study, focusing on the qualitative interview responses of elite female footballers in England and their perception of their position as 'role model' to young people and how they use this position to promote sporting participation from grass roots upwards. It has shown that female footballers tend to welcome this position of responsibility, seeing it as an opportunity to encourage young people to play football – particularly girls. They explained that they enjoyed the chance to work with young people as they had not had similar experiences when they were children and learning to play the game. As such, several elite players had a full-time job working in community departments of men's clubs, and others regularly visited schools and local sports clubs for prize givings and coaching sessions in their free time, demonstrating how seriously they took their roles.

All respondents were highly positive about the changes to the women's game in recent years, expressing their hopes that a higher media profile and a more professional set-up would result in more girls playing the game at grass-roots level, improving their physical fitness, and potentially a higher standard of performance across the UK, even at the international level.

However, whether or not this is likely to happen is debatable. Though the FA are investing heavily in elite women's football via the FAWSL and its expansion to two divisions, many involved in the game have expressed a huge concern over the future of girls' and women's football at all levels below that (for example, the campaign to protect the Women's Premier League, which has been superseded by and neglected since the launch of the FAWSL, and the petitions to 'save grassroots football'). The women of the FAWSL may be working hard to improve their game and take advantage of their increased media profile to promote football to girls and young women, but if they are to have a real impact, they need to be supported by the actions of clubs and by the game's governing bodies – which includes financial investment from the grass roots upwards, and consistent media coverage across outlets, enabling people to see the players in action. At the moment, though, even the long-term future of elite women's football in England is in question, with the FA's strategy currently stretching only as far as 2018.[32] Although, as this research in progress indicates, elite female footballers may be willingly embracing their position as role models and explicitly expressing a desire to promote women's football from the grass roots, they cannot do this alone; and the broader lack of direction for the game is likely to negate their efforts in the long run.

Disclosure statement

No potential conflict of interest was reported by the author.

Notes

1. Girls Schools Association, 'Headmistress Praises Female Olympic Role Models – "We Must Maintain the Momentum"'.
2. Winter, 'London 2012 Olympics: Record Crowd Watches Team GB Women Beat Brazil to Reach Quarter-finals'.
3. WSFF, 'Women in Sport Audit'.
4. WSFF, 'Young Women and Girls' Physical Activity'.
5. See Dunn and Welford, *Football and the FA Women's Super League: Structure, Governance and Impact,* for an exploration of the current structure and governance of elite women's football in England; see also Williams, *Globalising Women's Football: Europe, Migration and Professionalization*, for a discussion of the issues facing women's football globally.
6. Williams, *A Game for Rough Girls? A History of Women's Football in Britain.*
7. Lopez, *Women on the Ball.*
8. Melling, '"Plucky Lasses", "Pea Soup" and Politics: The Role of Ladies Football during the 1921 Miners' lock-out in Wigan and Leigh'.
9. Newsham, *In a League of Their Own! The Dick, Kerr Ladies Football Club.*
10. Tate, *Girls with Balls: The Secret History of Women's Football.*
11. Williams, *A Game for Rough Girls? A History of Women's Football in Britain*; Williams, 'The Fastest Growing Sport? Women and Football in England'; and Williams, 'A Beautiful Game: International Perspectives on Women's Football'.
12. Williams and Woodhouse, 'Can Play, will Play? Women and Football in Britain'.
13. Williamson, 'Belles of the Ball'.
14. Dunn and Welford, *Football and the FA Women's Super League: Structure, Governance and Impact.*
15. Biskup and Pfister, 'I would Like to be Like Her/Him: Are Athletes Role-models for Boys and Girls?'.
16. Craike, Symons, and Zimmerman, 'Why do Adolescent Girls Drop Out of Sport and Physical Activity? A Social Ecological Approach'.
17. Fleming et al., '"Role Models" among Elite Young Male Rugby League Players in Britain'.
18. GirlGuiding UK, 2012.
19. Rubin and Rubin, *Qualitative Interviewing: The Art of Hearing Data.*
20. Stanley, *The Auto/Biographical I.*
21. D. Fifield, 'England Squad must be Better role Models, Says Wayne Rooney'.
22. *Evening Standard*, 2010.
23. Robert-Holmes and Brownhill, 2011
24. Phys.org, 'Is Rooney really a role model?'
25. Ibid.
26. Lockwood and Kunda, 'Superstars and me: Predicting the Impact of Role Models on the Self'; Lockwood and Kunda, 'Salient Best Selves can Undermine Inspiration by Outstanding Role Models'.
27. Ibid.
28. Ibid.
29. Murray and Howat, 'The "Enrichment Hypothesis" as an Explanation of Women's Participation in Rugby'.
30. Ibid.
31. WSFF, 'Women in Sport Audit'.
32. See Dunn and Welford, *Football and the FA Women's Super League*, 2014.

References

Biskup, C., and G. Pfister. 'I Would Like to be Like Her/Him: Are Athletes Role-Models for Boys and Girls?' *European Physical Education Review* 5, no. 3 (1999): 199–218.

Craike, C., C. Symons, and J. Zimmerman. 'Why do Adolescent Girls Drop Out of Sport and Physical Activity. A Social Ecological Approach'. *Annals of Leisure Research* 12, no. 2 (2009): 149–72.

Dunn, C., and J. Welford. *Football and the FA Women's Super League: Structure, Governance and Impact*. London: Palgrave Pivot, 2014.

Fairclough, P. 'Our Football Stars have no Choice but to be Role Models'. *Evening Standard*, September 16, 2010.

Fifield, D. 'England Squad must be Better Role Models, Says Wayne Rooney'. *The Guardian*, March 2, 2010.

Fleming, S., A. Hardman, C. Jones, and H. Sheridan. '"Role models" among Elite Young Male Rugby League Players in Britain'. *European Physical Education Review* 11, no. 1, (2005): 51–70..

Girls' School Association. 'Headmistress Praises Female Olympic Role Models – "We must Maintain the Momentum"'. 2012. http://www.gsa.uk.com/news/headmistress-praises-female-olympic-role-models-we/ (accessed December 3, 2013).

Lockwood, P., and Z. Kunda. 'Increasing the Salience of One's Best Selves can Undermine Inspiration by Outstanding Role Models'. *Journal of Personality and Social Psychology* 76 (1999): 214–28.

Lockwood, P., and Ziva Kunda. 'Superstars and Me: Predicting the Impact of Role models on the Self'. *Journal of Personality and Social Psychology* 73, no. 1 (1997): 91–103.

Lopez, S. *Women on the Ball*. London: Scarlet Press, 1997.

Melling, A. '"Plucky Lasses", "Pea Soup" and Politics: The Role of Ladies' Football during the 1921 Miners' Lock-out in Wigan and Leigh'. *The International Journal of the History of Sport* 16, no. 1 (1999): 38–64.

Murray, D., and G. Howat. 'The 'Enrichment Hypothesis' as an Explanation of Women's Participation in Rugby'. *Annals of Leisure Research* 12, no. 1 (2009): 65–82.

Newsham, Gail. *In a League of Their Own! The Dick, Kerr Ladies Football Club*. London: Scarlet Press, 1997.

Phys.org. 'Is Rooney Really a Role Model?' http://phys.org/news/2011-05-rooney-role.html (accessed December 3, 2013).

Rubin, H., and I. Rubin. *Qualitative Interviewing: The Art of Hearing Data*. London: Sage, 2005.

Stanley, L. *The Auto/Biographical I*, Manchester: University Press, 1992.

Tate, T. *Girls with Balls: The Secret History of Women's Football*. London: John Blake, 2013.

Williams, J., ed. *A Beautiful Game: International Perspectives on Women's Football*. New York: Berg, 2007.

Williams, Jean. 'The Fastest Growing Sport? Women and Football in England'. In *Soccer, Women, Sexual Liberation: Kicking Off a New Era*, ed. F. Hong and J.A. Mangan, 112–27. London: Frank Cass, 2004.

Williams, J. *A Game for Rough Girls? A History of Women's Football in Britain*. London: Routledge, 2003.

Williams, J. *Globalising Women's Football: Europe, Migration and Professionalization*. Bern: Peter Lang, 2013.

Williams, J., and J. Woodhouse. 'Can Play, will Play? Women and Football in Britain'. In *British Football and Social Change: Getting into Europe*, ed. J. Williams and S. Wagg, 85–111. Leicester University Press, 1991.

Williamson, D.J. *Belles of the Ball*. Devon: R&D Associates, 1991.

Winter, H. 'London 2012 Olympics: Record Crowd Watches Team GB Women Beat Brazil to Reach Quarter-finals'. *The Telegraph*, August 1, 2012.

Women's Sport and Fitness Foundation. 'Women in Sport Audit'. 2008. http://www.cwsportspartnership.org/files/wsff_sport_audit.pdf (accessed June 25, 2014).

Women's Sport and Fitness Foundation. 'Young Women and Girls' Physical Activity'. 2010. http://www.wsff.org.uk/system/1/assets/files/000/000/284/284/f3957f6e2/original/FACTSHEETyoung_womenand_girlsFINAL281010.pdf (accessed December 3, 2013).

A systematic review of drop-out from organized soccer among children and adolescents

Viviene A. Temple and Jeff R. Crane

School of Exercise Science, Physical and Health Education, University of Victoria, Victoria, Canada

Bronfenbrenner's bioecological model of human development was used as a framework to systematically review factors associated with drop-out from soccer among children and adolescents. Keyword searches for the population (child or youth or adolescent), sport (soccer or football) and construct of interest (drop-out or attrition or discontinued or quit) identified scholarly peer-reviewed publications from the entire contents of seven databases to 31 December 2013. Publications with participants at any level of organized soccer were eligible for inclusion. The initial search identified 137 studies with 14 ultimately meeting the inclusion criteria, 11 from Europe and 3 from the United States, and 97% ($n = 1125,001$) of study participants were male. The proportion of children and adolescents who dropped out from one season to the next ranged from 18 to 36%, except for one study of high-level players where the rate of drop-out was 60%. These players felt the time demands of soccer, especially 'travelling to compete', were onerous. Prominent person-level factors associated with drop-out were lower perceptions of competence and the lack of fulfilment of basic psychological needs. Contextual factors associated with drop-out were poor relationships with teammates or coaches, lack of enjoyment, lack of opportunity to play, competing time demands, and later birthdate in relation to competitive year. Interactions between the individual and their environment were rarely examined. Future research on drop-out from soccer would benefit from expanding the demographics of those being studied and by concurrently examining interactions between the individual and the environment.

Introduction

Children and adolescents are motivated to participate in sport by the potential for fun and challenge, the excitement of competing and opportunities to test their skills.[1] Being with their friends and making new friends[2] and being part of a team[3] are important motivating factors in and of themselves, but also contribute to perceptions that sport is fun[4] and to a sense of belongingness.[5] Children and adolescents also report that they participate in sport because they want to improve their skills and learn new skills[6] and because they want opportunities to exercise and get in shape.[7] The extent to which these motives are realized is highly dependent on qualities of the environment.[8] However, it is not just the properties of the environment that influence the developing person, but how the environment is experienced by the individual.[9] The interactions between the characteristics of the developing person (such as gender, age, social class and their previous sporting experiences) and their immediate and more remote contexts are important predictors of developmental outcomes such as engagement in, or disengagement from, sport.[10]

Evidence suggests that approximately 35% of children and adolescents disengage (i.e. drop-out) from sport annually[11] and that the proportion of children who drop-out from organized sport increases from middle- to late-childhood.[12] These patterns are consistent with soccer participation rates among children and adolescents in the United States, with nearly 21% of 6-year-olds playing soccer, compared with 14% of 12-year-olds, and approximately 9% of 17-year-olds.[13] These trends may in part reflect sampling of sports[14]; where children and adolescents are trying out or transferring between different sports. However, these trends may also signify dissatisfaction or negative experiences with sport. Given the importance of participating in sport for physical, psychological and social well-being among children and adolescents,[15] the positive influenced of childhood sport participation on adult engagement in physical activity,[16] and the very high rates of participation of youth in soccer worldwide[17]; it seems timely to review, and learn from, the literature examining why children and adolescents drop-out from soccer.

Although the majority of literature examining drop-out from sport among children and adolescents tends to focus on individual factors such as personal motivation and perceptions of competence,[18] evidence also suggests that broader social forces influence drop-out.[19] Recent studies have called for the use of multilevel models to examine factors associated with drop-out from sport among children and adolescents because discrete theories do not facilitate the development of integrated or holistic views of drop-out from sport.[20] Bronfenbrenner's bioecological theory[21] provides a multilevel model which posits that children do not develop in isolation, but in relation to their family and friends, school, community and society more generally.[22] The basic premise of Bronfenbrenner's bioecological theory is that development is a function of interactions between the individual and the settings in which they spend time.[23]

Bronfenbrenner's bioecological theory

The process-person-context-time (PPCT) model associated with Bronfenbrenner's bioecological theory[24] was used in this study as a framework to systematically review and classify factors associated with drop-out and intention to drop-out from soccer among children and adolescents. The PPCT model has particular utility for framing this review since it is a multilevel model and 'development' in the bioecological model is defined as continuity and change of the individual[25] and drop-out is in essence discontinuity, because the individual stops participating in organized soccer.

The PPCT model is comprised of four components and the interactions between these components. The central, or as Bronfenbrenner describes, the 'primary engine', of the model are the proximal processes. These are the systematic interactions between the individual and immediate or closest aspects of the environment. Proximal processes are characterized as being actively participated in by the individual on a fairly regular basis. These include interactions with objects or symbols as well as people, and involving reciprocity.[26] For example, in an interpersonal interaction between a child and a coach there is influence from both parties. But as Bronfenbrenner and Morris note, the 'form, power, content, and direction of the proximal processes effecting development vary systematically as a joint function of the characteristics of the developing person, the environment – both immediate and more remote – in which the processes are taking place'.[27] This leads us to the second 'P' in the model, the person. The person characteristics may be precursors of change or they may be developmental outcomes. Person variables include dispositions (e.g. motivation, ability to defer gratification and aggression), resources (e.g. skill, abilities and experience) and demand characteristics (characteristics that invite or discourage reaction from the social environment such as age, gender, hyperactivity and attractiveness). The third model component is context, or the ecological environment. This consists of four nested levels; the innermost of these levels is the microsystem. The microsystem is a pattern of activities, social roles and interpersonal relations experienced by the developing person in a given face-to-face setting.[28] The next level of context is the mesosystem, which captures interactions between microsystems. Children and adolescents spend time in more than one microsystem (e.g. school and sport club), and the interactions between the microsystems can have a powerful effect on development. For example, Johns and colleagues[29] found that among adolescent female gymnasts, competing demands for time (such as school, part-time jobs and sport) contributed to drop-out. The third level of context is the exosystem. The developing child or adolescent is not an active part of this level of context, but she/he may be affected by it. For example, if a parent loses their job, it may impact the family's ability to afford soccer. Finally, the macrosystem embodies the institutional systems of the culture in which the child/adolescent lives such as the socio-economic, educational, legal and political systems.[30] Time is the final aspect of the bioecological model. Time is represented in the model in terms of the stability or instability of settings over time, by the regular interactions with the environment, and by the historical period in which the individual lives.[31]

In keeping with recent calls to examine drop-out from sport at multiple levels,[32] the aim of this review is to synthesize what is known about drop-out from soccer among children and adolescents by answering the following questions: (1) What individual, contextual and time-related factors are associated with drop-out and intention to drop-out from soccer? (2) To what extent do factors associated with drop-out reflect proximal or more distal processes? (3) What are the gaps, limitations, implications and areas of research need on drop-out from soccer for children and adolescents?

Method

Data sources

Keywords for the population, context and construct of interest were identified using Medical Subject Headings of the National Library of Medicine controlled vocabulary thesaurus. The population keywords were: child* (asterisk denotes truncation that allows multiple versions of the word to be located), youth or adolescen*. The context keywords were soccer or football, and construct of interest keywords were: drop-out, attrition, discontinu* or quit. These terms identified scholarly peer-reviewed publications from the entire contents of the following databases: Academic Search Complete (1887 -), CINAHL (1981 -), ERIC (1966 -), MEDLINE (1965 -), PsycARTICLES (1895 -), PsycINFO (1597 – present, with comprehensive coverage from the 1880s), and SPORTDiscus (1800 -); until 31 December 2013.

Inclusion/exclusion criteria

A study was included in this review if it met the following criteria: (a) the research was empirical (qualitative or quantitative evidence), (b) the study was published in a peer-reviewed journal, (c) the focus was on children and/or adolescents aged between 5 and 19 years, (d) the context was organized soccer at any level, (e) drop-out or intention to drop out was assessed and (f) the paper was written in English. The initial search generated a total of 137 potential studies; however 125 were excluded for the following reasons: not published in a peer-reviewed journal ($n = 62$), duplicates ($n = 45$), drop-out (or intention to drop out) from soccer not assessed ($n = 11$), the population was not child/adolescent soccer players ($n = 2$), focused on other football codes ($n = 2$), not written in English ($n = 1$) and two studies included soccer players in the sample, but did not report findings for soccer players separately.[33] Two additional studies that met the inclusion criteria were found by hand searching the reference lists of the identified papers. Ultimately, 14 studies were included in this review.

Data extraction and synthesis

A data extraction form was used to obtain:(a) general information: study title, authors, journal title and publication date; (b) specific study characteristics: recruitment procedures, participant characteristics (age, sex and level of soccer played), study design, variables examined, validity and reliability of measures, and methods of analysis and (c) the definition of 'drop-out' or 'intention to drop-out' used. Key study characteristics and findings for each study were tabulated (see Table 1) and the overall proportion of studies exhibiting key characteristics (such as publication year, world region, participant age and sex, and sample size) were computed (see Table 2). Consistent with PPCT model, the person, context and time variables associated with drop-out (or intention to drop-out) were synthesized (Table 3).

Results

The proportion of children and adolescents dropping out from one season to the next was typically in the range of 18–36%, but was as high as 60% among players who travelled a 'great deal' to compete (see Table 1). Although documented in only one study,[34] the rate of drop-out during a season was lower (9%) than rates of drop-out from one season to the next. This figure of 9% was not confirmed with re-enrolment data, therefore it is quite possible the proportion of those who did not return in the subsequent season was higher. Similarly, neither study reporting intention to quit[35] followed up with an objective measure of drop-out and neither of these studies reported the proportion of children and adolescents who intended to quit. However, Van Yperen[36] did find that intention to quit increased significantly across a season. As Table 1 shows, adolescents with the highest intention to drop-out of soccer were those who felt the outcomes (fun/status) of their seven-month long season were outweighed by how much they had to do during the season (i.e. the cost to benefit ratio).

Overview of the studies

Table 2 provides a synthesis of the 14 studies included in this review. The vast majority of studies were undertaken in Europe (79%) and overwhelmingly the

Table 1. Studies investigating drop-out and intention to drop-out of soccer for children and adolescents.

Study	Aim and design	Participants	Measures	Results	Notes
Calvo et al.[a]	To predict drop-out using self-determination theory	Federation level (high ability) adolescent soccer players ($n = 492$). Age range 13–17 years ($M = 14.3$, $SD = 1.6$). Played competitive soccer for an average of 6.3 years. 178 had dropped out. Male = 100%	Self-determined motivation (six sub-scales), plus Relatedness, Competence, & Autonomy	Significant discriminant function analysis (those who dropped out vs. those who didn't) coefficients: amotivation (.83), external regulation (.45), relatedness (−.40), introjected regulation (.39) and perceived autonomy (−.33). Perceptions of competence not related (.09, NS). These factors accurately classified 90% of the sample as persistors or drop-outs	Unclear when in baseline season measures were administered
Spain	Cohort: 1-year follow-up		Drop-out ascertained after one year through federation records (i.e. re-enrolment)		Drop-out proportion of sample: 36.2%
Delorme et al.[b]	To examine birthdate distribution of players who stopped participating during or at the end of the season	All male players affiliated with the FSF* ($n = 1,831,524$) in the 2006–2007 season. Age categories: U7, U9, U11, U13, U15, U18 and adult. Children and adolescents = 1,116,464; $n = 195,641$ did not return in 2007–208 season. Male = 100%	FSF player license identification numbers used to group birthdates into four quarters. Chi-square compared the expected and the observed distribution of persistors and drop-outs	Players born in last half of the competitive year significantly overrepresented in drop-out for all child and adolescent age categories. No difference for U17 and Adult. Most marked in U13 and U15 categories	Highest drop-out in U18, which covers three years

Country	Study	Design/Aim	Sample	Measures	Findings	Drop-out proportion
France	Delorme et al.[c]	Cohort: 1-year follow-up To examine whether birthdate distribution accounted for female drop-out in the subsequent season	All female players affiliated to the FSF* ($n = 57,892$) in the 2006–2007 season. Age categories: U8, U10, U12, U14, U17 and adult. Children and adolescents = 35,128; $n = 8542$ children and adolescents did not return in the 2007–208 season. Male = 0%	Drop-out ascertained in following season from re-enrolment records. As per Delorme et al.[b]	Players born in last half of the competitive year significantly overrepresented in drop-out for U10, U14 and U17 categories	Drop-out proportion of child/adolescent sample: 17.5%. Drop-out proportion of child/adolescent sample: 24.3%
France	Ferreira and Armstrong[d]	Cohort: 1-year follow-up To examine factors associated with switching soccer organizations or dropping soccer and choosing anther activity	Parents ($n = 102$) of youth soccer players from a 'local' league who had dropped out. Youth age and sex not reported.	Parents' perceptions of: causal attributions (e.g. cost, time of games), importance of soccer for child; attitude towards and time with organization, and post drop-out behaviour (new soccer organization or new activity)	Drop-out of soccer for other activities was associated with parents' attitude towards the organization, cost and upper management (i.e. lack of upward communication). Attitude towards organization associated with coaches and time of practices. Intra-team factors (team mates) also 'blamed' for drop-out	Response rate to mailing was 30%. Drop-out rate cannot be calculated, but 25% of those who dropped out switched to another soccer organization

(Continued)

Table 1. (Continued).

Study	Aim and design	Participants	Measures	Results	Notes
USA	Cross-sectional: retrospective, descriptive and mixed-methods		Drop-out: unclear how authors ascertained that players had ceased participating		
Figueiredo et al.[e]	Compare baseline physical characteristics and goal orientation to soccer status	Club soccer players 11–12 years ($n = 87$) and 13–14 years ($n = 72$) at baseline. Male = 100%	Chronological age, sexual maturity, anthropometry, years of training, functional capacities (anaerobic fitness, agility, power), soccer skills, goal orientation and current status in soccer (i.e. drop-out, club player, elite)	For 11–12-year-olds, boys who dropped out had fewer years training than club or elite players. For 13–14-year-olds, boys who dropped out scored significantly less well on the wall pass skill test than the other groups	Drop-out proportion of sample: 22.6%
Portugal	Cohort: 2-year follow-up		Drop-out: participant report of discontinuation from soccer at follow-up.	22/36 who dropped out completed a follow-up survey that revealed lack of time, other interests and aspects of the soccer environment (lack of opportunity to play and lack of enjoyment in training) were important factors	
Keathley et al.[f]	Examine motivation for continuing or discontinuing soccer	Purposeful sample of 11 current (males = 5) and 11 former (males = 5) travelling team soccer players[*]; and 22 parents. Aged 15–17 years	Semi-structured interview. Former players asked about most important reasons why they stopped playing. Prompted re: personal,	Three most frequently cited reasons by former players were: time (72%), the coach (55%), conflicts with other sports (45%). Heavy time demands of	Letter sent to 217 classic division players (involves try-outs, three practices per week with professional staff, travel to games). 60% no longer playing 'classic'

Country / Author	Design / Aim	Sample	Measures / Definitions	Results	Drop-out
USA	Cross-sectional: qualitative, players dropped out aged 13–15 years. Follow-up at 15–17years retrospective	(M = 16.00). Male = 45% *Competing at highest level in their region for ≥3 years	social and environmental factors Drop-out: master list of adolescents that had played in the 'classic soccer division' in the last five years	travelling club soccer impact academic, social and recreational activities. Girls more concerned about the coach e.g. not supportive, yelling, etc. *Note.* Little data from parents on reasons for drop-out presented	
Nache et al.[g]	To predict drop-out during a soccer season using the Theory of Planned Behaviour (TPB)	Soccer players ($n = 354$), aged 13–15 years from the 2nd division in the region of Normandy. Male = 100%	TPB (attitude, normative beliefs, perceived behavioural control, intentions)	Three direct (intentions, attitudes and normative beliefs) and two indirect (normative and control beliefs) correctly predicted 61.3% of drop-outs; although specificity was weak (22.1%)	Drop-out during the season: 9%
France	Cohort: nine months (same season)		Drop-out: absent from two successive game forms and did not return. Not injury, illness or trips		
Ommundsen and Vaglum[h]	Examine group differences (drop-out vs. active at T2) in self-esteem and persistence based on how adolescents process failure the importance they attach to soccer	Representative sample of players from an organized soccer league ($n = 223$) aged 12–16 years ($M_{age} = 14.5$, SD = 1.3) from the 1983 Oslo League. Male = 100%	Attributional style (i.e. internal or external; stable or unstable), perceived importance of soccer, self-esteem and drop-out	No main effect for attributional style; however the interaction of attributional style and importance was significantly associated with drop-out ($R^2 = .06$, $p < .0001$). Effect	Drop-out proportion = 22%

(Continued)

Table 1. (Continued).

Study	Aim and design	Participants	Measures	Results	Notes
				stronger (13%) for those with high levels of perceived soccer importance. Those who attributed their failures to lack of ability and attached great importance to their ability were significantly more likely to drop out	
Norway	Cohort: ~16 months, interviewed beginning of season 1 (T1) and end of season 2 (T2)		Drop-out: player's negative answer to: 'Are you still a member of the club?', 'Are you still playing matches?' and 'Are you still training?' As well as a positive answer to 'Having ceased playing organized soccer'		
Ommundsen and Vaglum[i]	To examine the relationship of low perceived soccer and social competence with later drop-out	As per Ommundsen and Vaglum[h]	Soccer enjoyment, perceived soccer competence, perceived social competence in soccer	Among 14–16-year-olds, low perceived soccer competence and low perceived peer popularity negatively influenced soccer persistence; and low soccer enjoyment was a significant mediating factor. Among 12–13-year-olds, a low sense of interpersonal attraction and belongingness on negatively affected soccer persistence	As per Ommundsen and Vaglum[h]

Country	Study	Aim	Sample	Design	Variables measured	Results	Notes
Norway	Ommundsen and Vaglum[j]	Cohort: as per Ommundsen and Vaglum[h] To examine the psychological centrality hypothesis and the selectivity/discounting hypothesis	As per Ommundsen and Vaglum[h]	Cohort: as per Ommundsen and Vaglum[h]	Drop-out: as per Ommundsen and Vaglum[h] Coaches' perceptions of player's soccer competence and surveys of perceptions	Dropout not mediated or moderated by importance placed on soccer	As per Ommundsen and Vaglum[h]
Norway				Cohort: as per Ommundsen and Vaglum[h]	Dropout: as per Ommundsen and Vaglum[h]	Low perceived soccer competence mediated the relationship between low actual soccer competence and increased dropout among older players (14–16 years). Among younger players (12–13 years) lower perceived soccer competence at T1 predicted dropout	
France, Greece, Norway, Spain and England	Quested et al.[k]	Whether perceptions of autonomy support provided by the coach predict basic need satisfaction, soccer enjoyment and intention to drop out	Recreational European soccer players (n = 7769), aged 9–15 years (M_{age} = 11.6 years, SD = 1.4) Males = 85.5%	Cross-sectional	Autonomy support, basic need satisfaction (need for autonomy and relatedness and perceptions of competence), enjoyment, and *intentions to drop out* next season	Perceptions of autonomy support strongly predicted psychological need satisfaction, which in turn predicted enjoyment. The latter was a strong negative predictor of intention to drop out. This model fitted well Intention to drop-out was also indirectly affected by perceptions of autonomy support	Model was invariant across countries Cannot compute % of intention to drop out.

(Continued)

Table 1. (Continued).

Study	Aim and design	Participants	Measures	Results	Notes
Skard and Vaglum[l]	To examine whether certain personality, individual and situational soccer factors predict drop-out	Oslo League soccer players ($n = 300$) aged 13–16 years ($M_{age} = 14.5$, $SD = 1.3$). Male = 100%	Motive to approach success, fear of failure, sport anxiety, nervous symptoms, acting out behaviour, soccer self-confidence, soccer priority, friends in soccer, relation to coach, children's perceptions of parental attitude and soccer satisfaction	Three T1 factors accounted for 13.5% of the variance in drop-out: friends in soccer, soccer satisfaction, and acting out behaviour (e.g. police contact, vandalism and alcohol use)	Considerable sample overlap with Vaglum's other studies
Norway	Cohort: 16 months, T1 (May/June 1983) and T2 (Aug/Sep 1984)		Drop-out: participant report of discontinuation from soccer at follow-up	Significant T2 factors were: soccer satisfaction and priority, friends dropped out, acting out, frequency of play, soccer self-confidence, friends in soccer and sport anxiety. Accounted for 32% of the variance	Drop-out proportion: 22%; 47% of drop-outs continued with another organized activity
Ullrich-French and Smith[m]	To examine if perceived relationships with parents and peers predict soccer continuation over and above motivation-related variables	Travelling soccer players ($n = 148$) aged 10–4 years ($M_{age} = 11.7$, $SD = 1.0$) at baseline. Male = 49%	Soccer associated peer friendship and relationships with parents; peer acceptance; soccer enjoyment, stress, perceived competence and motivation. Drop-out: Coach reported continuation (or not) on the same soccer team	Discontinuers had significantly lower levels of perceived competence and less positive friendship quality than continuers. Also, when perceived mother relationship was low, likelihood of continuation was low except when both peer acceptance and friendship quality were high	Overall drop-out proportion: 22%; male drop-out = 25%, female drop-out = 20%

USA Van Yperen[n]	Cohort: one year	Effect of perception of inequity to vulnerability to dropping out	65 highly skilled pupils at a soccer school, M_{age} = 16.6 years. Male = 100%	T1 two weeks into season, T2 seven months later in last week of season perception of equity (ratio of outcome* vs. inputs**) and Dropout Symptoms (energy deletion and *intention to quit*)	Under benefitted participants (i.e. high inputs low outcomes) had the highest intention to quit ($p < .05$). Equity/inequity at T1 did not predict intention to quit; but at T2 equity/inequity predicted intention to quit, with under benefitted participants greatest intention to quit	Don't know if they actually dropped out
The Netherlands	Cohort: seven months (within season)			* e.g. fun/status ** e.g. how much they have to do		

* French Soccer Federation.
[a] Calvo et al., 'Using Self-determination Theory to Explain Sport Persistence'.
[b] Delorme et al., 'Relative Age and Dropout in French Male Soccer'.
[c] Delorme et al., 'Relative Age Effect in Female Sport'.
[d] Ferreira and Armstrong, 'Parents' Casual Attributions of Youth Soccer Dropout'.
[e] Figueiredo et al., 'Characteristics of Youth Soccer Players'.
[f] Keathley et al., 'Gender Similarities and Differences'.
[g] Nache et al., 'Predicting Dropout in Male Youth'.
[h] Ommundsen and Vaglum, 'The Influence of Attributional Style'.
[i] Ommundsen and Vaglum, 'The Influence of Low Perceived Soccer'.
[j] Ommundsen and Vaglum, 'Competence, Perceived Importance'.
[k] Quested et al., 'Intentions to Drop-out'.
[l] Skard and Vaglum, 'Psychosocial and Sport Factors'.
[m] Ullrich-French and Smith, 'Social and Motivational Predictors'.
[n] Van Yperen, 'Inequity and Vulnerability to Dropout'.

Table 2. Descriptive overview of studies related to drop-out.

	No. of studies (%)	No. of participants (%)
Year of publication		
<1994	3 (21.4%)	
1994–2003	3 (21.4%)	
2004–2013	8 (57.2%)	
Number of participants		1,161,248 (100%)
<500	11 (78.6%)	1887 (0.2%)
500–999	0 (0.0%)	
≥ 1000	3 (21.4%)	1159,361 (99.8%)
Publication world region		
Europe	11 (78.6%)	1,160,806 (99.9%)
North America	3 (21.4%)	442 (0.04%)
Construct of interest		
Drop-out	12 (85.7%)	1,153,414 (99.3%)
Intention to drop out	2 (14.3%)	7834 (0.7%)
Participant		
Child (<12 years)	3 (21.4%)	658,327 (56.7%)
Child (excluding studies[a,b])	1	87
Adolescent	9 (64.3%)	327,097 (28.2%)
Adolescent (excluding studies[a,b])	7	1528
Child/adolescent	3 (21.4%)	175,655 (15.1%)
Child/adolescent (excluding studies[a,b])	2	7917
Parent(s)	2 (14.3%)	124 (<.01%)
Sex of child/adolescent participants		
Male	12 (85.7%)	1,125,001(96.9%)
Female	4 (28.6%)	36,247 (3.1%)

[a]Cote et al., 'The Benefits of Sampling Sports'; and Strachan et al., 'Specializers Versus Samplers'.
[b]Bailey, 'Physical Education and Sport'; Fox et al., 'Physical Activity and Sports'; and Krustrup et al., 'Executive Summary: The Health and Fitness'.

participants were male (97%). Notably, the four studies that included female participants were published within the last five years. Table 2 also reveals that there were two especially large studies.[37] These two studies examined the influence of later birthdate in relation to the completive year (known as the relative age effect) on drop-out using soccer federation records. These two studies included data from more than one-million children and adolescents, and represented 99% of the participants in the studies included in this review. When those studies were excluded, it was evident that the remaining studies were generally small-scale and principally focused on adolescents ($n = 7$) or adolescents and children in a combined group ($n = 2$). Children were not the sole participants in any study, however a group of 11–12-year-old boys ($n = 87$) were distinguishable in one sample[38] and the two large 'relative age effect' studies[39] did stratify their samples according to the French Soccer Federation age classification system. Those samples included U7, U9 and U11 age groupings for boys and U8, U10 and U12 age groupings for girls. Parents were the informants (participants) for two of the studies, however for one of those studies,[40] very little of the parents' perspectives on reasons for drop-out were included.

Eleven of the studies were prospective cohort studies and three were cross-sectional. By design, the prospective studies assessed independent variables such as personal attributes or contextual parameters and then examined whether the player continued or discontinued with soccer (or intended to drop-out) at a further point in

Table 3. Personal, contextual and time-related factors associated with drop-out.

Person	Context	Time
Disposition	*Microsystem*	
Higher levels of amotivation and extrinsic motivation (external and introjected regulation)[b]	Lack of enjoyment[r]	Competing demands on time[ae]
Lower psychological need satisfaction,[c] specifically less satisfaction in relatedness,[d] autonomy[e] and autonomy support[f]	Poor teammate relationship[s]	Lack of opportunity to play[af]
Lower perceptions of competence[g] or self-confidence[h]	Lack of friends in soccer[t]	Early to later-in-season changes in perceptions[ag]
Lower scores on theory of planned behaviour constructs: attitude towards continuing, intention to practice, normative and control beliefs[i]	Friends dropped out of soccer[u]	
Low soccer priority[j]	Poor relationship with coach[v]	
Interaction between ability and importance[k]	Input/output (effort/reward) ratio[w]	
Anxiety towards sport[l]	Soccer dissatisfaction[x]	
Acting out behaviour[m]	Lack of opportunity to play[y]	
Resources	Too much emphasis on winning/competition[z]	
Lower soccer skills/competence[n]	*Mesosystem*	
Fewer years of soccer training[o]	Lack of time/competing interests[aa]	
Demand	Parents' concerns about cost[ab]	
Age[p] (group comparisons[a])	Parents' negative attitude towards organization and upper management[ac]	
Sex[q]	*Exosystem*	
	Later birthdate in relation to competitive year (i.e. relative age effect)[ad]	

[a]Age in years was not used as a direct predictor, but drop-out proportion or reasons for drop-out differed between age groups.
[b]Calvo et al., 'Using Self-determination Theory to Explain Sport Persistence'.
[c]Quested et al., 'Intentions to Drop-out'.
[d]Calvo et al., 'Using Self-determination Theory to Explain Sport Persistence'; and Ommundsen and Vaglum, 'The Influence of Low Perceived Soccer'.
[e]Calvo et al., 'Using Self-determination Theory to Explain Sport Persistence'.
[f]Quested et al., 'Intentions to Drop-out'.
[g]Ommundsen and Vaglum, 'The Influence of Low Perceived Soccer'; Ommundsen and Vaglum, 'Competence, Perceived Importance'; and Ullrich-French and Smith, 'Social and Motivational Predictors'.
[h]Skard and Vaglum, 'Psychosocial and Sport Factors'.
[i]Nache et al., 'Predicting Dropout in Male Youth'.
[j]Skard and Vaglum, 'Psychosocial and Sport Factors'.
[k]Ommundsen and Vaglum, 'The Influence of Attributional Style'.
[l]Skard and Vaglum, 'Psychosocial and Sport Factors'.
[m]Ibid.
[n]Figueiredo et al., 'Characteristics of Youth Soccer Players'; and Ommundsen and Vaglum, 'Competence, Perceived Importance'.
[o]Figueiredo et al., 'Characteristics of Youth Soccer Players'.
[p]Delorme et al., 'Relative Age and Dropout in French Male Soccer'; Idem, 'Relative Age Effect in Female Sport'; Figueiredo et al., 'Characteristics of Youth Soccer Players'; Ommundsen and Vaglum, 'The Influence of Low Perceived Soccer'; and Ommundsen and Vaglum, 'Competence, Perceived

Importance'.
[q]Keathley et al., 'Gender Similarities and Differences'.
[r]Figueiredo et al., 'Characteristics of Youth Soccer Players'; Ommundsen and Vaglum, 'The Influence of Low Perceived Soccer'; and Quested et al., 'Intentions to Drop-out'.
[s]Ferreira and Armstrong, 'Parents' Casual Attributions of Youth Soccer Dropout'; Ommundsen and Vaglum, 'The Influence of Low Perceived Soccer'; and Ullrich-French and Smith, 'Social and Motivational Predictors'.
[t]Skard and Vaglum, 'Psychosocial and Sport Factors'; and Ullrich-French and Smith, 'Social and Motivational Predictors'.
[u]Skard and Vaglum, 'Psychosocial and Sport Factors'.
[v]Keathley et al., 'Gender Similarities and Differences'; and Skard and Vaglum, 'Psychosocial and Sport Factors'.
[w]Figueiredo et al., 'Characteristics of Youth Soccer Players'; and Van Yperen, 'Inequity and Vulnerability to Dropout'.
[x]Skard and Vaglum, 'Psychosocial and Sport Factors'.
[y]Figueiredo et al., 'Characteristics of Youth Soccer Players'; Skard and Vaglum, 'Psychosocial and Sport Factors'.
[z]Skard and Vaglum, 'Psychosocial and Sport Factors'.
[aa]Figueiredo et al., 'Characteristics of Youth Soccer Players'; and Keathley et al., 'Gender Similarities and Differences'.
[ab]Ferreira and Armstrong, 'Parents' Casual Attributions of Youth Soccer Dropout'.
[ac]Ibid.
[ad]Delorme et al., 'Relative Age and Dropout in French Male Soccer'; Idem, 'Relative Age Effect in Female Sport'.
[ae]Figueiredo et al., 'Characteristics of Youth Soccer Players'; and Keathley et al., 'Gender Similarities and Differences'.
[af]Figueiredo et al., 'Characteristics of Youth Soccer Players'; Skard and Vaglum, 'Psychosocial and Sport Factors'.
[ag]Van Yperen, 'Inequity and Vulnerability to Dropout'.

time. Most often the follow-up period was the next season, although one study examined drop-out within a season[41] and one other study examined with development of intention to quit by the end of the season.[42] The majority of the studies used quantitative approaches (65.9%), typically examining correlates or predictors of drop-out. Two studies solicited participants' retrospective reflections of reasons for drop-out. Keathley and colleagues,[43] explored former travelling soccer players' reasons for quitting, and Ferreira and Armstrong[44] examined parents' perspectives about why their child either dropped out of soccer or switched to another club.

Person, context and time-related factors associated with drop-out

Disposition characteristics and microsystem factors were by far the most common factors associated with drop-out (see Table 3). At the individual level, lower perceptions of physical competence and the lack of fulfilment of basic psychological needs (such as having a sense of autonomy or feeling connected to others) associated with motivation were prominent. For example, Calvo and colleagues[45] revealed that constructs associated with self-determination theory such as lower perceptions of relatedness and autonomy, predicted drop-out in the subsequent season. However, contrary to several other studies in this review, Calvo et al. did not find perceptions of competence predicted drop-out. The authors attributed this difference to the high skill level of study participants. Two resource characteristics of the child/adolescent were evident: their actual skill or competence and years of experience. A gender-related difference in reasons for drop-out was evident in Keathley and colleagues' qualitative study[46]; these authors noted that 'Girls were more likely than boys to attribute the decision to leave soccer to negative coaching experiences'.[47] Although age was not used as a direct predictor of drop-out, age-related differences were evident in the findings of several studies. The two large French studies[48] revealed that the rate of drop-out was not even across competition age categories, and three studies[49] revealed age-related differences in reasons for withdrawal. For older adolescents, a lack of skill, low perceptions of competence, and the mediating effect of perceptions on the relationship between skill and drop-out appeared more consistently in the findings. Experience with the sport and a sense of belongingness were more evident for younger adolescents. In the microsystem level of context, interactions with friends, teammates, coaches and aspects of the soccer context (e.g. lack of opportunity to play, low effort-to-reward ratio and lack of enjoyment) were prominent.

The foremost mesosystem factor was competing demands. The high time commitment for soccer interacted with the players' commitments to academic pursuits and to other sports, as well as time to be with their friends. One of the two studies that included parents as respondents[50] revealed several interactions between the family and the sporting organization. Parents of children who dropped out (compared with those that switched clubs) had less favourable attitudes towards the organization and were more influenced by cost and the lack of communication within the organization. Parents also felt their child was affected by intra-team conflicts. Only one exosystem factor was identified; the system of age categories based on the birthdates used by sport organizations. The impact of this factor, termed the relative age effect, was most notable among adolescents rather than children. In the bioecological model, time is conceptualized in several ways.[51] Individuals are situated in a particular historical time, environments can be more or less stable over time, and regular interactions between the individual and the context have more impact. Our findings revealed several time-related factors that could be characterized as interrelationships between the child/adolescent and the soccer environment. Time was clearly an integral part of competing priorities, but time also had an implied presence in the lack of opportunity to play[52] and the adolescents' changing perceptions of the input/outcome ratio across a season.[53] The power and impact of both of these factors are likely influenced by the extent to which players experience these processes on an ongoing basis.

Evidence of proximal and more distal processes

Proximal processes are particular types of interactions (i.e. regular, reciprocal) between the individual and the immediate environment.[54] Although the studies included in this review were generally concerned with the associations between particular personal or environmental antecedents of drop-out, some evidence of the proximal processes were evident. It is notable from the findings presented in Table 1 that adolescents who were discouraged by aspects of soccer training or playing environment were more likely to drop-out. A lack of opportunity to play,[55] not enjoying training or matches,[56] heavy time demands of soccer,[57] and soccer-related peer/teammate difficulties[58] were processes associated with drop-out within the immediate environment. The bioecological model also suggests that the nature and strength of proximal processes vary systematically as function of the characteristics of the developing individual.[59] There was some evidence that age interacted with players' perceptions of competence or actual skill levels to influence drop-out,[60] and that the experience of being coached influenced males and females differently.[61] However, on the whole, how personal characteristics influenced interactions with the immediate environment were not strongly represented in the available literature.

Examination of factors in broader levels of context was largely absent from the studies reviewed. However, the two French studies examining the relative age effect on males and females, clearly show that those born late in the competition age category are overrepresented among those who drop-out of soccer when competition is organized in 2- and 3-year age bands.

Discussion

Bronfenbrenner's bioecological model posits that developmental outcomes are largely driven by regular interactions between the individual and their immediate environment. Further, the impact of these interactions on development is influenced by the characteristics of the individual and the broader social context. This study examined factors associated with drop-out from soccer and classified those factors as personal, contextual or time-related variables and to the extent possible, examined interactions between the individual and their proximal and more distal levels of context. Discrete person factors identified by more than one study were constructs associated with psychological need satisfaction as well as actual or perceived competence. In the immediate environment (microsystem), relationships with friends, teammates or with the coach were important, as were adolescents' perceptions of effort they had to put into soccer in relation to the outcomes/benefits and enjoyment of the soccer environment. These factors have been consistently associated with reasons for withdrawal from sport[62] and serve to remind us that the creation and maintenance of supportive, mastery-orientated environments is crucial for young soccer players' psychosocial well-being.[63]

The two large studies of the relative age effect did not examine aspects of the context or person other than age grouping and age. Delorme and colleagues'[64] findings are consistent with relative age effect studies from other sports[65] that show there are serious disadvantages of having a birthdate later in the competition year. The physical[66] and psychological advantages[67] associated with being older can result in more opportunities for those older players during those developmental years,[68] particularly in terms of game playing time and coach perceptions of the player's potential.[69] Such advantages were documented by Figueireo and colleagues[70] who reported that adolescent soccer players who progressed to an elite level in a two-year period were chronologically and skeletally older, had larger in body size, and scored higher on all tests than those who stayed at the same level or who dropped out in the same time period.

The mesosystem encompasses situations where two or more microsystems come together in some respect, so we classified 'other priorities' as a mesosystem influence on drop-out. It was clear from Keathley and colleagues'[71] work that conflicts between soccer, school work, as well as social and recreational opportunities was a major concern for these relatively high-level players. It was less clear why soccer became the lower priority. One of Keathley and colleagues informants indicated that he/she needed to choose between sports because of the high-time demands and explained that decision by '[soccer] would be the thing that wasn't helping me the most'.[72] It is possible that the player was referring to the input/outcome ratio described in other studies[73]; however further exploration was needed to adequately understand the interrelationships between the microsystems and between the microsystems and time.

Gaps, limitations and research needs

Overall, the sheer volume of studies was limited and 11 of the 14 studies involved fewer than 500 participants. As noted previously, participants were largely male, adolescent and from Europe or the United States. The selection bias in the recruited samples greatly limits the generalizability of the findings. Although four out of the 14 studies included females, they represented 3.1% of the total number of participants. The 2006 FIFA Big Count estimated that 10% of soccer players are women and from 2000 to 2006 there was a 138% increase in registered female amateur players.[74] We know that being male is positively and consistently correlated with children and adolescents' participation in physical activity[75] and the Keathley and others[76] pointed towards gender-based differences in reasons for drop-out from soccer. If, as predicted 'The future of football is feminine'[77] then more studies on girls' involvement and reasons for drop-out are warranted to inform approaches to optimize girls' experiences and retain them in the sport. Similarly, without the two large studies examining the relative age effect, children as a discrete group were virtually absent from this literature. Recent evidence demonstrates marked differences in the correlates of physical activity for children than for adolescents.[78] Sterdt and colleagues synthesis of nine other reviews[79] showed that environmental correlates were more prevalent for children than for adolescents, and there were no consistent psychological correlates of physical activity for children. Sterdt and colleagues findings suggest that further investigation of age-related factors influencing withdrawal is warranted. The other obvious demographic omission relates to world region. Although this study was limited to English language literature, we did not detect any studies from outside of Europe and the United States despite that organized soccer has more than 200 member associations.[80]

Our analysis revealed that the majority of studies prospectively examined personal characteristics of the children and/or adolescents and waited to see if they returned in the subsequent season. Far fewer studies investigated personal and contextual factors simultaneously. For example, Ommundsen and Vaglum[81] found lower peer social integration was directly related to drop-out among 12–13-year-old boys; but they did not examine aspects of the immediate environment (soccer microsystem) that could explain why some boys were less socially integrated than others. Future research could help provide a more comprehensive and integrated picture of why children and adolescents are withdrawing from soccer by including broader aspects of the bioecological framework. As Bronfenbrenner suggests, the principal main effects of bioecological research are generally the interactions.[82] Keathley and colleagues retrospective study[83] suggested that female perceptions of the coaching environment differed from male perceptions, and their subsequent choice to drop-out. Insights such as these will help optimize the coaching environment. In addition to examining the interactions between personal and contextual factors, researchers may wish to consider including multiple perspectives in their research. Proximal processes are not unidirectional, but involve reciprocity.[84] For interpersonal interactions this means that influence comes from both sides. Our analysis revealed no studies where these multiple perspectives were presented. Although Keathley and colleagues'[85] study included both parents and athletes, the parents' perspectives on drop-out were not fully presented; and even though a negative relationship with the coach was reported as a determinant of drop-out,[86] we did not hear from the coaches. The voices of coaches, parents, friends and family, and administrators were notably absent in the available literature.

Practical implications

This synthesis of literature suggests that the motivational climate of the youth soccer experience has a central influence on drop-out from soccer among children and adolescents. Motivational climate refers to the youth's perceptions of the norms and expectations of the environment.[87] For example, the environment can encourage effort and reward personal improvement (mastery environment) or it may promote inter-individual comparison, provide more attention to high-ability players, and/or penalize mistakes (ego-involved environment).[88] Irrespective of the level of competition/player ability in the reviewed papers, researchers recommend that coaches promote a positive motivational climate.[89] Previous research has shown that coaches can foster a positive motivational climate (mastery climate) by providing corrective instruction in a positive way, encouraging players to learn from their mistakes, reinforcing positive behaviours and effort as much as they do results, and through sound technical instruction.[90] Coaches can also encourage players to be supportive of each other and work cooperatively towards team goals.[91] Vazou and colleagues[92] identified 11 areas where adolescents felt their motivation could be affected by their teammates and vice versa. These areas were generally consistent with how adult coaches could create a positive motivational climate, but there were two unique areas mentioned by the adolescents: intra-team conflict (e.g. putdowns and blaming others for poor performance) and relatedness support (e.g. 'look out' for their teammates, feeling part of the whole and having fun with their teammates). Both of these additional areas could be fostered, or addressed, by the coach/coaching staff.

The mastery environments described in the preceding paragraph also foster feelings of enjoyment (or fun) among youth sport participants[93] and 'fun' is the most commonly reported intrinsic motivator for sport participation among children and adolescents.[94] This review revealed that a lack of fun was associated with drop-out from soccer among recreational/club child and adolescent players. A recent study involving child and adolescent soccer players, coaches and parents, that helps to unpack what makes sport fun, mapped 81 practical ideas to enhance feelings of fun.[95] These 81 ideas were also grouped into 11 dimensions. In terms of importance to players, the top five dimensions of making sport fun were: being a good sport (e.g. helping teammates, playing as a team), trying hard (e.g. trying your best, getting in shape), positive coaching (e.g. coach treats players with respect and is a positive role model), learning and improving (e.g. being challenged to improve, ball touches) and games (e.g. getting playing time). Other highly rated ideas were having well-organized practices, getting along with teammates and keeping a positive attitude by participating. The parallels between the body of evidence on positive motivational environments and Visek and colleagues' theoretical framework of fun in sport,[96] emphasize that positive coaching and feeling socially included are key elements of creating enjoyable soccer experiences for children and adolescents.

The findings of this review also supports that the relative age effect influences drop-out from soccer. Although not all children and adolescents with later birthdates are physically, psychologically and socially less mature than earlier born peers in the same competition period, this is the general trend. Suggestions to reduce the impact of having a later birthdate include structural solutions such as building teams based on quarters of birthdates,[97] using the child's birthdate on the day of competition, rather than at the beginning of a season,[98] and education approaches to raise coach awareness of the issue so that they may help their young athletes understand developmental processes.[99] For this latter suggestion, Helsen and suggested that coaches 'should pay more attention to technical and tactical skills when selecting players' rather than primarily focusing on physical characteristics during the developmental years. A commitment to player development such as this may require adjustment in the balance between short-term and longer term outcomes.[100]

Finally, two studies in this review assessed players' intention to drop-out. Coaches and/or soccer clubs may wish to monitor intention to drop-out during the season when there is still the potential to intervene. Quested and colleagues[101] used two questions 'I am thinking of leaving my team' and 'I intend to drop out of soccer at the end of this season' (as well as the positive forms of those questions) to assess intention to drop-out on a five-point scale (1 = strongly disagree, 2 = disagree, 3 = neutral, 4 = agree and 5 = strongly agree). These questions could be paired with an open-ended opportunity (as per the Keathley et al. study[102]) to identify important reasons why players intend to drop-out. To allow children and adolescents to freely share their opinions and concerns, a survey such as this would need to be administered confidentially and anonymously.

Conclusion

Withdrawal, or drop-out, from soccer is likely to be a more complex and multidimensional phenomenon than we are currently able to explain. Bronfenbrenner indicated that the most powerful influences on development are likely to be the interactions between the individual and their context. What is clearly needed are systematic evaluations of reasons for drop-out that consider individual characteristics from a broad demographic populations as they interact with immediate environments. We also need to hear the multiple perspectives and consider more distal institutional, community and policy factors. As with any multidimensional problem, this type of research is difficult and expecting any one study to investigate all personal, contextual and time-related factors as well as the interactions between them is unrealistic. However, within any one study guidance from a bioecological framework may help researchers think more broadly about the interconnections between the individual and the context that are powerful drivers of change.

Disclosure statement

No potential conflict of interest was reported by the authors.

Notes

1. Gould et al., 'Motives for Participating'; Longhurst and Spink, 'Participation Motivation of Australian Children'; Sirard et al., 'Motivational Factors Associated with Sports'; Stern et al., 'Young Children in Recreational Sports'. Wankel and Kreisel, 'Factors Underlying Enjoyment' and Yan and McCullagh, 'Cultural Influence on Youth's Motivation'.
2. Gould et al., 'Motives for Participating'; Sirard et al., 'Motivational Factors Associated with Sports'; Stern et al., 'Young Children in Recreational Sports'; Wankel and Kreisel, 'Factors Underlying Enjoyment' and Whitehead and Biddle, 'Adolescent Girls' Perceptions'.

3. Gould et al., 'Motives for Participating'; Sirard et al., 'Motivational Factors Associated with Sports'; Stern et al., 'Young Children in Recreational Sports' and Wankel and Kreisel, 'Factors Underlying Enjoyment'.
4. Whitehead and Biddle, 'Adolescent Girls' Perceptions'.
5. Allen, 'Social Motivation in Youth Sport'.
6. Gould et al., 'Motives for Participating'; Longhurst and Spink, 'Participation Motivation of Australian Children'; Stern et al., 'Young Children in Recreational Sports'; Wankel and Kreisel, 'Factors Underlying Enjoyment' and Yan and McCullagh. 'Cultural Influence on Youth's Motivation'.
7. Gould et al., 'Motives for Participating'; Longhurst and Spink, 'Participation Motivation of Australian Children'; Sirard et al., 'Motivational Factors Associated with Sports'; Sit, 'Participation Motivation in Sport'; Stern et al., 'Young Children in Recreational Sports' and Yan and McCullagh. 'Cultural Influence on Youth's Motivation'.
8. Perry, 'Factors Contributing to Youth and Adult Dropout'; and Rottensteiner et al., 'Personal Reasons for Withdrawal'.
9. Bronfenbrenner and Morris. 'The Bioecological Model of Human Development'.
10. Fraser-Thomas et al., 'Examining Adolescent Sport Dropout' and Wheeler, 'The Significance of Family Culture'.
11. Patriksson, 'Theoretical and Empirical Analyses'.
12. Sabo and Veliz, 'Go Out and Play'.
13. Delgado and Schwartz, 'SFIA Participation Report'.
14. Cote et al., 'The Benefits of Sampling Sports' and Strachan et al., 'Specializers Versus Samplers'.
15. Bailey, 'Physical Education and Sport'; Fox et al., 'Physical Activity and Sports' and Krustrup et al., 'Executive Summary: The Health and Fitness'.
16. Cleland et al., 'Which domains of childhood'.
17. Kunz, '265 Million Playing Football'.
18. Balish et al., 'Correlates of Youth Sport Attrition'.
19. Balish et al., 'Correlates of Youth Sport Attrition' and Vella et al., 'Socio-ecological Predictors'.
20. Ibid.
21. Bronfenbrenner and Morris, 'The Bioecological Model of Human Development'.
22. Ibid.
23. Ibid.
24. Ibid.
25. Ibid.
26. Ibid.
27. Ibid, 798.
28. Bronfenbrenner, 'Ecological Models of Human Development'.
29. Johns et al., 'Understanding Attrition in Female'.
30. Rosa and Tudge, 'Urie Bronfenbrenner's Theory of Human Development'.
31. Bronfenbrenner and Morris. 'The Bioecological Model of Human Development'.
32. Balish et al., 'Correlates of Youth Sport Attrition' and Vella et al., 'Socio-ecological Predictors'.
33. Molinero et al., 'Dropout Reasons in Young Spanish Athletes' and Rottensteiner et al., 'Personal Reasons for Withdrawal'.
34. Nache et al., 'Predicting Dropout in Male Youth'.
35. Quested et al., 'Intentions to Drop-out' and Van Yperen., 'Inequity and Vulnerability to Dropout'.
36. Van Yperen, 'Inequity and Vulnerability to Dropout'.
37. Delorme et al., 'Relative Age and Dropout in French Male Soccer' Idem, 'Relative Age Effect in Female Sport'.
38. Figueiredo et al., 'Characteristics of Youth Soccer Players'.
39. Delorme et al., 'Relative Age and Dropout in French Male Soccer' Idem, 'Relative Age Effect in Female Sport'.
40. Keathley et al., 'Gender Similarities and Differences'.
41. Nache et al., 'Predicting Dropout in Male Youth'.
42. Van Yperen, 'Inequity and Vulnerability to Dropout'.

43. Keathley et al., 'Gender Similarities and Differences'.
44. Ferreira and Armstrong, 'Parents' Casual Attributions of Youth Soccer Dropout'.
45. Calvo et al., 'Using Self-determination Theory to Explain Sport Persistence'.
46. Keathley et al., 'Gender Similarities and Differences'.
47. Ibid, 171.
48. Delorme et al., 'Relative Age and Dropout in French Male Soccer' Idem, 'Relative Age Effect in Female Sport'.
49. Figueiredo et al., 'Characteristics of Youth Soccer Players'; Ommundsen and Vaglum, 'Low Perceived Soccer and Social Competence' and Ommundsen and Vaglum, 'Competence, Perceived Importance'.
50. Ferreira and Armstrong, 'Parents' Casual Attributions of Youth Soccer Dropout'.
51. Bronfenbrenner and Morris. 'The Bioecological Model of Human Development'.
52. Figueiredo et al., 'Characteristics of Youth Soccer Players' and Skard and Vaglum, 'Psychosocial and Sport Factors'.
53. Van Yperen, 'Inequity and Vulnerability to Dropout'.
54. Bronfenbrenner and Morris. 'The Bioecological Model of Human Development'.
55. Figueiredo et al., 'Characteristics of Youth Soccer Players'.
56. Figueiredo et al., 'Characteristics of Youth Soccer Players' and Ommundsen and Vaglum, 'Low Perceived Soccer and Social Competence'.
57. Figueiredo et al., 'Characteristics of Youth Soccer Players' and Keathley et al., 'Gender Similarities and Differences'.
58. Ommundsen and Vaglum, 'Competence, Perceived Importance' and Skard and Vaglum, 'Psychosocial and Sport Factors'.
59. Bronfenbrenner and Morris. 'The Bioecological Model of Human Development'.
60. Figueiredo et al., 'Characteristics of Youth Soccer Players' and Ommundsen and Vaglum, 'Low Perceived Soccer and Social Competence'.
61. Keathley et al., 'Gender Similarities and Differences'.
62. Molinero et al., 'Dropout Reasons in Young Spanish Athletes' and Rottensteiner et al., 'Personal Reasons for Withdrawal'.
63. Ommundsen et al., 'Parental and Coach Support'.
64. Delorme et al., 'Relative Age and Dropout in French Male Soccer' Idem, 'Relative Age Effect in Female Sport'.
65. Musch and Grondin, 'Unequal Competition as an Impediment'.
66. Malina, 'Physical Growth and Biological Maturation'.
67. Bisanz et al., 'Effects of Age and Schooling'.
68. Balyi and Way, 'Monitoring Growth in Long-term Athlete Development'.
69. Figueiredo et al., 'Characteristics of Youth Soccer Players'; and Helsen et al., 'The Relative Age Effect'.
70. Figueiredo et al., 'Characteristics of Youth Soccer Players'.
71. Keathley et al., 'Gender Similarities and Differences'.
72. Ibid, 180.
73. Figueiredo et al., 'Characteristics of Youth Soccer Players' and Van Yperen, 'Inequity and Vulnerability to Dropout'.
74. Kunz, '265 Million Playing Football'.
75. Sterdt et al., 'Correlates of Physical Activity'.
76. Keathley et al., 'Gender Similarities and Differences'.
77. Kunz, '265 Million Playing Football', 12.
78. Sterdt et al., 'Correlates of Physical Activity'.
79. Ibid.
80. Kunz, '265 Million Playing Football'.
81. Ommundsen and Vaglum, 'Low Perceived Soccer and Social Competence'.
82. Bronfenbrenner and Morris. 'The Bioecological Model of Human Development'.
83. Keathley et al., 'Gender Similarities and Differences'.
84. Bronfenbrenner and Morris. 'The Bioecological Model of Human Development'.
85. Keathley et al., 'Gender Similarities and Differences'.
86. Ibid; and Skard and Vaglum, 'Psychosocial and Sport Factors'.
87. Smith and Smoll, 'Coach-mediated team building'.
88. Ames, 'Achievement Goals, Motivational Climate'.

89. Calvo et al., 'Using Self-determination Theory to Explain Sport Persistence'; Ommundsen and Vaglum, 'Low Perceived Soccer and Social Competence'; Ommundsen and Vaglum, 'Competence, Perceived Importance' and Quested et al., 'Intentions to Drop-out'.
90. Riewald, 'Strategies to Prevent Dropout'; Smith and Smoll, 'Coach-mediated Team Building' and Smith et al., 'Effects of a Motivational Climate'.
91. Smith et al., 'Development and Validation'; and Vazou et al., 'Peer Motivational Climate in Youth Sport'.
92. Vazou et al., 'Peer Motivational Climate in Youth Sport'.
93. Fry and Gano-Overway, 'Exploring the Contribution of the Caring Climate'.
94. Gould et al., 'Motives for Participating'; Sirard et al., 'Motivational Factors Associated with Sports'; Sit, 'Participation Motivation in Sport'; Stern et al., 'Young Children in Recreational Sports'; Wankel and Kreisel, 'Factors Underlying Enjoyment'; Whitehead and Biddle, 'Adolescent Girls' Perceptions' and Yan and McCullagh. 'Cultural Influence on Youth's Motivation'.
95. Visek et al., 'The Fun Integration Theory'.
96. Ibid.
97. Musch and Grondin, 'Unequal Competition as an Impediment'.
98. Balyi and Way, 'Monitoring Growth in Long-term Athlete Development'.
99. Delorme et al., 'Relative Age and Dropout in French Male Soccer'.
100. Ibid.
101. Quested et al., 'Intentions to Drop-out'.
102. Keathley et al., 'Gender Similarities and Differences'.

References

Allen, J.B. 'Social Motivation in Youth Sport'. *Journal of Sport & Exercise Psychology* 25, no. 4 (2003): 551–67.
Ames, C. 'Achievement Goals, Motivational Climate, and Motivational Processes,' Chap. In *Motivation in Sport and Exercise*, ed. G.C. Roberts, 161–76. Champaign, IL: Human Kinetics Books, 1995.
Bailey, R. 'Physical Education and Sport in Schools: A Review of Benefits and Outcomes'. *Journal of School Health* 76, no. 8 (2006): 397–401.
Balish, S.M., C. McLaren, D. Rainham, and C. Blanchard. 'Correlates of Youth Sport Attrition: A Review and Future Directions'. *Psychology of Sport & Exercise* 15, no. 4 (2014): 429–39. doi:10.1016/j.psychsport.2014.04.003.
Balyi, I., and R. Way. *The Role of Monitoring Growth in Long-term Athlete Development*, in Supplement to Canadian Sport for Life. Vancouver: Canadian Sport Centres, 2011. http://www.sportmanitoba.ca/uploads/MonitoringGrowth%281%29.pdf.
Bisanz, J., F. Morrison, and M. Dunn. 'Effects of Age and Schooling on the Acquisition of Elementary Quantitative Skills'. *Developmental Psychology* 31 (1995): 221–36.
Bronfenbrenner, U. 'Ecological Models of Human Development,' Chap. In *International Encyclopedia of Education*, ed. T. Husen and T.N. Postlethwaite, 1643–47. Oxford: Pergamon Press/Elsevier Science, 1994.
Bronfenbrenner, U., and P.A. Morris. 'The Bioecological Model of Human Development,' Chap. In *Handbook of Child Psychology*, ed. R.M. Lerner and W. Damon, 793–828. Hoboken, NJ: Wiley, 2006.
Calvo, T.G., E. Cervelló, R. Jiménez, D. Iglesias, and J.A.M. Murcia. 'Using Self-determination Theory to Explain Sport Persistence and Dropout in Adolescent Athletes'. *The Spanish Journal of Psychology* 13, no. 2 (2010): 677–84. doi:10.1017/S11387416 00002341.
Cleland, V., T. Dwyer, and A. Venn. 'Which Domains of Childhood Physical Activity Predict Physical Activity in Adulthood? A 20-year Prospective Tracking Study'. *British Journal of Sports Medicine* 46, no. 8 (2012): 595–602.
Cote, J., S. Horton, D. MacDonald, and S. Wilkes. 'The Benefits of Sampling Sports during Childhood'. *The Physical and Health Education Journal* 12 (2009): 6–11.
Delgado, F.J., and N. Schwartz. 'SFIA Participation Report'. *SGB* 46, no. 9 (2013): 16–8.

Delorme, N., J. Boiché, and M. Raspaud. 'Relative Age and Dropout in French Male Soccer'. *Journal of Sports Sciences* 28, no. 7 (2010a): 717–22. doi:10.1080/02640411 003663276.

Delorme, N., J. Boiché, and M. Raspaud. 'Relative Age Effect in Female Sport: A Diachronic Examination of Soccer Players'. *Scandinavian Journal of Medicine & Science in Sports* 20, no. 3 (2010b): 509–15. doi:10.1111/j.1600-0838.2009.00979.x.

Ferreira, M., and K.L. Armstrong. 'An Investigation of The Relationship Between Parents' Casual Attributions of Youth Soccer Dropout, Time in Soccer Organisation, Affect Towards Soccer And Soccer Organisation, and Post-soccer Dropout Behaviour'. *Sport Management Review (Sport Management Association of Australia & New Zealand)* 5, no. 2 (2002): 149-78.

Figueiredo, A.J., C.E. Gonçalves, M.J. Coelho e Silva, and R.M. Malina. 'Characteristics of Youth Soccer Players Who Drop Out, Persist or Move Up'. *Journal of Sports Sciences* 27, no. 9 (2009): 883–91.

Fox, C.K., D. Barr-Anderson, D. Neumark-Sztainer, and M. Wall. 'Physical Activity and Sports Team Participation: Associations With Academic Outcomes in Middle School and High School Students'. *Journal of School Health* 80, no. 1 (2010): 31–7.

Fraser-Thomas, J., J. Côté, and J. Deakin. 'Examining Adolescent Sport Dropout and Prolonged Engagement from a Developmental Perspective'. *Journal of Applied Sport Psychology* 20 (2008): 318–33.

Fry, M.D., and L.A. Gano-Overway. 'Exploring the Contribution of the Caring Climate to the Youth Sport Experience'. *Journal of Applied Sport Psychology* 22, no. 3 (2010): 294–304.

Gould, D., D. Feltz, and M. Weiss. 'Motives for Participating in Competitive Youth Swimming'. *International Journal of Sport Psychology* 16 (1985): 126–40.

Helsen, W.F., J. van Winckel, and A.M. Williams. 'The Relative Age Effect in Youth Soccer across Europe'. *Journal of Sports Sciences* 23, no. 6 (2005): 629–36. doi:10.1080/02640410400021310.

Johns, D.P., K.J. Lindner, and K. Wolko. 'Understanding Attrition in Female Competitive Gymnastics: Applying Social Exchange Theory'. *Sociology of Sport Journal* 7 (1990): 158–71.

Keathley, K., M.J. Himelein, and G. Srigley. 'Youth Soccer Participation and Withdrawal: Gender Similarities and Differences'. *Journal of Sport Behavior* 36, no. 2 (2013): 171–88.

Krustrup, P., J. Dvorak, A. Junge, and J. Bangsbo. 'Executive Summary: The Health and Fitness Benefits of Regular Participation in Small-sided Football Games'. *Scandinavian Journal of Medicine & Science in Sports* 20, no. Suppl. 1 (2010): 132–35. doi:10.1111/j.1600-0838.2010.01106.x.

Kunz, M. '265 Million Playing Football'. *FIFA Magazine*, July 2007, 10–5.

Longhurst, K., and K.S. Spink. 'Participation Motivation of Australian Children Involved in Organized Sport'. *Canadian Journal of Sport Science* 12 (1987): 24–30.

Malina, R.M. 'Physical Growth and Biological Maturation of Young Athletes'. *Exercise and Sport Sciences Review* 22 (1994): 389–434.

Molinero, O., A. Salguero, C. Tuero, E. Alvarez, and S. Márquez. 'Dropout Reasons in Young Spanish Athletes: Relationship to Gender, Type of Sport and Level of Competition'. *Journal of Sport Behavior* 29, no. 3 (2006): 255–69.

Musch, J., and S. Grondin. 'Unequal Competition as an Impediment to Personal Development: A Review of the Relative Age Effect in Sport'. *Developmental Review* 21, no. 2 (2001): 147–67. doi:10.1006/drev.2000.0516.

Nache, C.M., M. Bar-Eli, C. Perrin, and L. Laurencelle. 'Predicting Dropout in Male Youth Soccer Using the Theory of Planned Behavior'. *Scandinavian Journal of Medicine & Science in Sports* 15, no. 3 (2005): 188–97. doi:10.1111/j.1600-0838.2004.00416.x.

Ommundsen, Y., G.C. Roberts, P. Lemyre, and B.W. Miller. 'Parental and Coach Support or Pressure on Psychosocial Outcomes of Pediatric Athletes in Soccer'. *Clinical Journal of Sport Medicine* 16, no. 6 (2006): 522–26.

Ommundsen, Y., and P. Vaglum. 'The Influence of Attributional Style on the Soccer-related Self-esteem and Persistence in Soccer of Young Boys'. *Scandinavian Journal of Medicine & Science in Sports* 1, no. 1 (1991): 45–50.

Ommundsen, Y., and P. Vaglum. 'The Influence of Low Perceived Soccer and Social Competence on Later Dropout from Soccer: A Prospective Study of Young Boys'. *Scandinavian Journal of Medicine & Science in Sports* 1, no. 3 (1991): 180–88. doi:10.1111/j.1600-0838.1991.tb00293.x.

Ommundsen, Y., and P. Vaglum. 'Competence, Perceived Importance of Competence and Drop-out from Soccer: A Study of Young Players'. *Scandinavian Journal of Medicine & Science in Sports* 7, no. 6 (1997): 373–83.

Patriksson, G. 'Theoretical and Empirical Analyses of Dropout from Youth Sports in Sweden'. *Scandinavian Journal of Sport Sciences* 10, no. 1 (1988): 29–37.

Perry, M. 'Factors Contributing to Youth and Adult Dropout from Organised Sport and Physical Activity'. *Journal of Science and Medicine in Sport* 16, Suppl. 1 (2013): e81. doi:10.1016/j.jsams.2013.10.194.

Quested, E., N. Ntoumanis, C. Viladrich, E. Haug, Y. Ommundsen, A. Van Hoye, J. Mercé, H.K. Hall, N. Zourbanos, and J.L. Duda. 'Intentions to Drop-out of Youth Soccer: A Test of the Basic Needs Theory among European Youth from Five Countries'. *International Journal of Sport & Exercise Psychology* 11, no. 4 (2013): 395–407.

Riewald, S.T. 'Strategies to Prevent Dropout from Youth Athletics'. *New Studies in Athletics* 18, no. 3 (2003): 21–6.

Rosa, E.M., and J. Tudge. 'Urie Bronfenbrenner's Theory of Human Development: Its Evolution from Ecology to Bioecology'. *Journal of Family Theory & Review* 5, no. 4 (2013): 243–58. doi:10.1111/jftr.12022.

Rottensteiner, C., L. Laakso, T. Pihlaja, and N. Konttinen. 'Personal Reasons for Withdrawal from Team Sports and the Influence of Significant Others among Youth Athletes'. *International Journal of Sports Science & Coaching* 8, no. 1 (2013): 19–32.

Sabo, D., and P. Veliz. *Go Out and Play: Youth Sports in America*. East Meadow, NY: Women's Sports Foundation, 2008.

Sirard, J.R., K.A. Pfeiffer, and R. Pate. 'Motivational Factors Associated with Sports Program Participation in Middle School Students'. *Journal of Adolescent Health* 38 (2006): 696–703.

Sit, H.P.C. *Participation Motivation in Sport : A Comparative Study of Able-bodied and Disabled School-aged Children in Hong Kong*. The University of Hong Kong, Pokfulam, 1998.

Skard, O., and P. Vaglum. 'The Influence of Psychosocial and Sport Factors on Dropout from Boys' Soccer: A Prospective Study'. *Scandinavian Journal of Sports Science* 11, no. 2 (1989): 65–72.

Smith, R.E., S.P. Cumming, and F.L. Smoll. 'Development and Validation of the Motivational Climate Scale for Youth Sports'. *Journal of Applied Sport Psychology* 20, no. 1 (2008): 116–36.

Smith, R.E., and F.L. Smoll. 'Coach-mediated Team Building in Youth Sports'. *Journal of Applied Sport Psychology* 9, no. 1 (1997): 114–32.

Smith, R.E., F.L. Smoll, and S.P. Cumming. 'Effects of a Motivational Climate Intervention for Coaches on Changes in Young Athletes' Achievement Goal Orientations'. *Journal of Clinical Sport Psychology* 1, no. 1 (2007): 23–46.

Sterdt, E., S. Liersch, and U. Walter. 'Correlates of Physical Activity of Children and Adolescents: A Systematic Review Of Reviews'. *Health Education Journal* 73, no. 1 (2014): 72–89. doi:10.1177/0017896912469578.

Stern, H.P., R.H. Bradley, M.T. Prince, and S.E. Stroh. 'Young Children in Recreational Sports: Participation Motivation'. *Clinical Pediatrics* 29, no. 2 (1990): 89–94.

Strachan, L., J. Cote, and J. Deakin. '"Specializers" Versus "Samplers" in Youth Sport: Comparing Experiences and Outcomes'. *The Sport Psychologist* 23 (2009): 77–92.

Ullrich-French, S., and A.L. Smith. 'Social and Motivational Predictors of Continued Youth Sport Participation'. *Psychology of Sport and Exercise* 10, no. 1 (2009): 87–95. doi:10.1016/j.psychsport.2008.06.007.

Van Yperen, N.W. 'Inequity and Vulnerability to Dropout Symptoms: An Exploratory Causal Analysis among Highly Skilled Youth Soccer Players'. *The Sport Psychologist* 11, no. 3 (1997): 318–25.

Vazou, S., N. Ntoumanis, and J.L. Duda. 'Peer Motivational Climate in Youth Sport: A Qualitative Inquiry'. *Psychology of Sport and Exercise* 6, no. 5 (2005): 497–516. doi:10.1016/j.psychsport.2004.03.005.

Vella, S.A, D.P. Cliff, and A.D. Okely. 'Socio-ecological Predictors of Participation and Dropout in Organised Sports during Childhood'. *International Journal of Behavioral Nutrition & Physical Activity* 11, no. 1 (2014): 1–20. doi:10.1186/1479-5868-11-62.

Visek, A.J., S.M. Achrati, H. Manning, K. McDonnell, B.S. Harris, and L. Dipietro. 'The Fun Integration Theory: Towards Sustaining Children and Adolescents Sport Participation'. *Journal of Physical Activity & Health* 12, no. 3 (2015): 424–33. doi:10.1123/jpah.2013-0180.

Wankel, L.M., and P.S.J. Kreisel. 'Factors Underlying Enjoyment of Youth Sports: Sport and Age Group Comparisons'. *Journal of Sport Psychology* 7 (1985): 51–64.

Wheeler, S. 'The Significance of Family Culture for Sports Participation'. *International Review for the Sociology of Sport* 47, no. 2 (2011): 235–52.

Whitehead, S., and S. Biddle. 'Adolescent Girls' Perceptions of Physical Activity: A Focus Group Study'. *European Physical Education Review* 14, no. 2 (2008): 243–62. doi:10.1177/1356336x08090708.

Yan, J.H., and P. McCullagh. 'Cultural Influence on Youth's Motivation of Participation in Physical Activity'. *Journal of Sport Behavior* 27, no. 4 (2004): 378–90.

Transcultural football. Trajectories of belonging among immigrant youth

Max Mauro

Southampton Solent University, UK

Football can play different roles in the lives of immigrant youth. It can be a site for leisure, sport performance and socialization. Even more critically, it can be a place where to negotiate sense of belonging to a local community and to gain access to national sporting cultures. Football can also represent forms of exclusion and discrimination. This article aims to elucidate the meanings that participation in football hold for black immigrant males in a country of recent immigration such as the Republic of Ireland. The article discusses the findings of a long-term ethnographic study with a youth team based in a working-class area of Dublin, the Irish capital. The youth football club plays a special role as a term of identification for the local community. Teenage players of different African backgrounds are presented with the challenge of acquiring different levels of inclusion. They can attempt to appropriate cultural codes that define local working-class men on and off the pitch or they can practice forms of 'resistance' that emphasize their own racialized positioning in Irish society. Overall, these dynamics affirm the importance of grassroots football as a venue for young people's transcultural encounters.

Introduction

In his autobiography, former Manchester United, Aston Villa and Republic of Ireland international Paul McGrath recalls his teenage years spent in a Dublin orphanage in the early 1970s.[1] Born in London to an Irish mother and a Nigerian father, he would become one of the first black athletes to represent the country at international level. According to his memories, football was the place where he felt liberated from his position of 'otherness'.

> I could play soccer. I could stand my ground against anyone in that yard and not feel remotely vulnerable. Within a few days, the change was unbelievable. I was no longer 'Nigger', I was Paul. It was the old cliché about football being the international language. Suddenly I was accepted.[2]

At the time when McGrath was growing up in Dublin, Irish society was not as ethnically diverse as it started to become from the mid-1990s onwards.[3] Nevertheless, his lived experience of football as an alleged 'international language' that appears to minify the racialized social positioning of black youth help us to locate in a historical context the analysis of youth sporting practices in contemporary Ireland. Despite a growing body of literature that critically highlights the role of sport in reproducing social inequalities and racial prejudices,[4] policy-makers and social workers still seem to share the belief in sport's inclusive power. In the last decade, a number of national and international programmes have been promoted across Europe that presuppose the potential of sport, especially football, in fostering 'intercultural dialogue among young people'.[5] Other initiatives aim at promoting 'Integration through sport'[6] for youth of immigrant background, 'Social inclusion through sport'[7] and even 'Football as a shared sense of belonging'.[8] Programmes such as these contribute to the construction of a discourse on sport, and football in particular, seen as a neutral site where differences are lifted, where young people can be made feel 'equal' regardless of their social, ethnic and racial backgrounds. This is a particularly fertile issue in European countries such as the Republic of Ireland and others whose demographic and social landscapes, over the last decades, have been redefined by immigration and questions of 'inclusion' and sense of belonging of youth of immigrant background are debated. Concepts of race and ethnicity within sport are not secondary components in this debate. This is demonstrated by an increasing literature on grassroots football produced in the UK and in mainland Europe. Following the trailblazing study of an amateur 'black club' in Northern England in the early 1990s conducted by Williams,[9] more recently Bradbury has looked at the inclusion of young males in black, Asians and minority ethnic clubs in Leicester and how these clubs still work as sites of 'resistance' for forms of discrimination and racism in the wider society.[10] Attention has been paid to manifestations of racism in grassroots football in England,[11] and to the impact of equality policies in the experience of ethnic minorities in the English grassroots game.[12] A growing literature has emerged in recent years from Germany, often highlighting the role of grassroots football in favouring the 'integration' of immigrants.[13] Yet this literary base is predominantly focussed on adults with little attention paid to youths and children in these contexts.

According to Back, Crabbe and Solomos 'the true significance of sport' lies in 'its ability to bring into focus the lines drawn around belonging, collective identity and exclusion'.[14] This does not happen only at national team level, where national belonging can at the same time be emphasized or challenged by the homogeneous or diverse composition of the team.[15] Belonging is a meaningful factor also at youth and grassroots football, when joining a team or a club can enhance feelings of inclusion to a local community and possibly to the nation.[16] In general terms, as noted by Crawley, 'belonging is usually taken to involve subjective and discursive dimensions of commitment, loyalty and common purpose'.[17] bell hooks emphasizes how belonging is also, and maybe more importantly, a way to define one sense's of place, of feeling 'at home'.[18] In this sense, 'inclusion' is intended not only as the opportunity to fully participate in the life of the local community but also as a way to build feelings of attachment to it.[19] The purpose of this article is to explore the extent to which participation in a grassroots football team can contribute to social inclusion and foster a sense of belonging to the local community. It also aims to emphasize the embodied nature of negotiations around belonging, especially amongst adolescents. In particular, two questions will be addressed: first, what role do racial and ethnic differences play in the football practice of young people in Ireland? Second, to what extent does football serve as a venue for teenagers of immigrant background to negotiate subjective and collective identities, including sense of cultural belonging? The concept of 'transculturation' will provide a theoretical tool to help in making sense of young people's identity formations in a multiethnic city such as the Irish capital. In their comparative study of adolescents growing up in different

European and North-American cities, Hoerder et al. adopted transculturation as a perspective that 'permits ... to re-read homogenized histories that construct belongings as fixed, that essentialize cultural, ethnic, national, gendered, religious, racial, and/or generational dimensions'.[20] Transcultural can also account for the recognition of some shared cultural codes that bridge and challenge different social, ethnic and national backgrounds. This is a central pattern of the discussion, as football is generally portrayed as a 'global game',[21] or the 'most popular global sport'.[22]

My argument will draw mainly upon a seventeen-month-long ethnographic fieldwork with a youth team based in the most ethnically mixed area of Dublin. The Republic of Ireland serves well as a setting at which situate such a scholarly inquiry, since it is one of the youngest countries among the 28 that form the European Union and it is one of the fastest changing countries in Western Europe. Moreover, Ireland is characterized by a rich sporting culture, which has historically been interwoven at different levels with discourses on cultural and national identification. Interestingly, while the intersection between sport and cultural/national identities has been widely addressed by researchers in the north and the south of the island, sporting practices of population of immigrant background remain, so far, largely under-researched.[23] At the same time, literature on children and young people of immigrant background living in Ireland completely overlook sport as a fertile site for socialization and 'multicultural' dialogue,[24] while studies of youth sport practices in Ireland do not pay particular attention to youth of immigrant background.[25] This arguably indicates a research gap that needs to be addressed. I will first introduce the context of my study and my access to this particular 'community', the youth football club. An analysis of the meanings attached to the game and its practice by young players of immigrant background will follow. To start with, however, it is important to outline the methodological challenges one has to face in approaching the study of adolescence in the context of team sports.

Young people voices

The adolescent lives a time 'in-between' – s/he is no longer a child, and not yet and adult – which can be difficult to grasp for the researcher and the adult observer trained in researching childhood or adulthood. In the study of identity formation and cultural difference such a liminal *and* central position of adolescence is particularly intriguing. Adolescence is often the time when such issues become more urgent and relevant for the young person, prompting decisions to pursue peer group membership or to join activities that are not under direct control of parents or teachers. This is the case, for example, of the football team. As confirmed by my study and other research, participation in sport is a terrain within which teenagers can express a degree of autonomy and independence in decision-making.[26] All this impinges on the power dynamics that traditionally characterize research endeavours with young people. In more general terms, according to Raby, 'with adolescence, power relations may become more complicated because teenagers are in a social position that shifts frequently between areas of dependence and independence'.[27]

To overcome these obstacles and to avoid the traps of assumptions of 'neutral' observation I attempted to create a 'dialogue'[28] with my young participants, eliciting conversations on different topics and being as much as possible open and flexible to their inquiries and fleeting interest in me and my role. It was an attempt to practice research *with* rather than *on* youth.[29] Following Norman Denzin's call for 'an ethnographer who functions and writes like a civic or public journalist',[30] for this study I combined traditional tools of ethnographic research such as participant observation and interviewing with journalistic inquiry and the use of a video camera. Arguably, it was the use of the video camera that made a dialogue with my young participants possible. I initially interpreted the use of the video camera as a complementary means of inquiry and as a 'passport'[31] that could give me a role in a community previously unknown to me. In the end, young players find it a 'less-threatening' medium than the notebook, something that most of them related to school or even, in the words of their coach, to a 'police-style' report. The visual cultures of 'digital natives' can be surprisingly rich: as I noted in my study, they are at the same time avid consumers and often producers of images. I further felt that a flexible combination of observation, participation and interviews alongside the critical production of moving and still images allowed me to develop what Bourdieu defines as 'corporeal knowledge', one which 'provides a practical comprehension of the world quite different from the act of conscious decoding that is normally designated by the idea of comprehension'.[32]

My access had been initially negotiated with the adults in charge of the club and the team, namely the chairman and the coach, to whom I introduced myself as a postgraduate student and former journalist interested in following a team with the help of a small video camera. I proposed to film parts of games and trainings, including coach speeches and interactions with players, and I made clear that the footage was not going to be made public but I would share it with them if they wished so. They agreed to this, and permission from families followed, but my level of access was a matter of continuous negotiations. Over the months I was occasionally assigned 'insider's roles, such as linesman or guardian, and invited to play during training sessions. Nevertheless, my position was more often attached to the video camera. Even when I was not using it or carrying it I was still perceived and accepted, especially by the boys, as 'the man with the camera'.[33] In exchange, as a way of 'giving back',[34] I offered to make a DVD with footage of the games and to edit a clip that was eventually uploaded on the club's website.

A local club

The Dublin 15 postal district is one of the most ethnically mixed areas of the Republic of Ireland. In a matter of 10 years, between 1996 and 2006, it almost doubled its population that is today just over 100.000 residents. Immigrants count for about 23%, while the national percentage is 12%. Poland, Lithuania and UK are the most numerous immigrant communities, while Nigeria and DR Congo are the largest among the African nations.[35] At the time of my fieldwork, between January 2009 and June 2010, 10 'Schoolboys' football clubs operated in the area. Every club ran between five to fifteen teams from the age of eight to the age of sixteen. The teams competed either in The Dublin and District Schoolboys League or the North Dublin Schoolboys League. These are possibly the largest association football youth leagues among the 32 that form the Schoolboys Football Association of Ireland (FAI). The SFAI was established in 1943 and declares to represent 'close to 100,000 players from more than 1000 clubs all around the country'.[36]

Greenside Schoolboys Football Club is one of the oldest clubs in Dublin 15.[37] It has a thirty-year history and has grown to one of the most active and successful local clubs. This club is located in a mostly Irish working-class neighbourhood, with indicators of social disadvantage such as proportions of 'youth at risk' and 'people who have never been in paid employment' slightly higher than the national average.[38] To different levels, according to its members, the club provides a strong point of reference for the local community. In one of the many conversations I had with the chairman, Jack, he offered me an insight into the role that the football club plays in the neighbourhood:

> A club has a social value. It is a well-known fact that teenagers who are involved with sport at an early age are less likely to have problems in their adult life. They have people they can count on, coaches, fellow teammates. They are less likely to get in trouble. It's not only about the football, it's about identity, the community.

As noted, during my time spent with club members of different generations the word 'community' emerged as a meaningful one. It was therefore interesting to observe which role the 'newcomers', the boys of immigrant background, would play in it, in the sporting community in particular. My fieldwork was conducted with the Under 13 team as this was a team characterized by a particularly prominent ethnic and racial diversity. At the time I started my fieldwork, this team included five boys of African backgrounds (originally born in DR Congo, Nigeria and Ivory Coast) while the rest of the squad was made of white Irish boys. For a brief period during the following season their number rose to eight (with new players born in Sudan and DR Congo) and then declined again. Also some Irish boys left the team and new ones joined it. Usually, those who felt they were not given enough game time would lose interest in their sport practice and leave the team. However, some would come back after a while. Such fluidity in sport participation appears to be a common trend among male adolescents in Ireland.[39]

The immigrant boys were all born abroad and had been taken to Ireland at different stages of their childhood, between four and ten years of age. Almost all of them were living in the country under refugee status. Their double 'otherness', being black Africans and refugees, made them potential subjects of racialized discourses that in Ireland have often negatively conflated 'African' and 'asylum-seeker' in debates surrounding immigration.[40] Furthermore, in terms of inclusion they were possibly positioned at the fringes of Irish society, as research evidenced that black Africans are most likely to be victims of public racism.[41] All the boys in the team, Irish and those of immigrant background, came from families with at least three or more children, and limited income. Some of the parents were unemployed and living on social support, while quite a few were single parents (at some point I counted that seven among fifteen of the players were either living with a single parent or with a parent and the parent's partner). The immigrant boys had all started playing competitive football after moving to Europe and for most of them Greenside was the first club they had played for. Jimmy, the coach of the Under 13, was locally known to be particularly keen in recruiting new and inexperienced but talented players, regardless of their origin. From the first days of my fieldwork I noticed that there was little resemblance in the team with the practice of 'stacking'. According to Giulianotti,

> In team sports black males are still segregated informally (or stacked) along racist lines. Stacking is the placement of white athletes in central positions associated with intelligence, decision making, leadership, calmness and dependability and the location of non-whites in peripheral positions requiring explosive physical powers (especially speed), unpredictability and infrequent participation.[42]

Giulianotti's analysis resonates here with the profile of the 'impulsive black sportman' articulated by Rosbrok-Thomson in his ethnographic account of a football team's activity in an inner London borough, and with King's discussion of black players lived experience of discrimination in the English game and obviously with the analysis of the history of the black sporting body undertaken by Ben Carrington.[43] The idea of the 'impulsive black sportman' is deeply rooted in the racist colonial past of Europe, and especially of Britain, and despite some signs of improvements across different sports still accompanies many black male youth in their sporting practice. To some degree, my fieldwork with a mixed group of male teenagers in Dublin told a different story. The captain of the U13s was Sam, a midfielder of Nigerian background who had migrated to Ireland at the age of eight. Another black boy played in midfield, two in attack, and a defender was among the substitutes. Apparently, their roles in the team were as diverse as those of the white Irish boys.

Over the two seasons I spent with them, I observed the ways immigrant boys negotiated their place in the team. In doing so, they potentially acquired different levels of inclusion in the local community. This comes as no surprise, as other studies conducted in different countries, have emphasized that sport and physical recreation can effectively play such a role in the lives of young immigrants, especially 'newcomers'.[44] However, sport can also, and maybe more critically, become a site for social exclusion, intended as 'the mechanisms that act to detach groups of people from the social mainstream'.[45] As noted by Doherty and Taylor in their study of the role of sport and physical recreation in the settlement of immigrant youth in Canada, exclusion can occur for different reasons, including language deficiency, lack of familiarity with the rules of the game and ways to practice it, or prejudice from peers. During my first months with the Irish team I observed that, as a point of principle, football practice was based on pure footballing merits, but there were other dynamics at hand that became visible and comprehensible to me over the months.

The serious game (of belonging)

One of the aspects that characterized the teenagers' game at Greenside was its 'seriousness'. For almost everyone the game appeared to be a serious matter. The players gathered to hear the coach's instructions and then entered the pitch with one goal in mind: to win the game (or do the best to win it). This did not mean that they were in any way reproached if they lost a game or did not perform well, on the contrary. Jimmy, the coach and Jack, the chairman occasional assistant coach, were always encouraging them, above all when something went wrong. Among the words most widely used by them was 'unlucky', which would relieve the frustration of the player when a challenge did not work out well. A frequent expression of encouragement was 'well done'. But, for everybody, the game appeared to be a serious matter. 'We want to win', said Sam to me, 'if you win everybody is happy'. In another occasion he let me understand the importance that training has for being (or being considered) a 'good player'. I had asked him how he felt about Darren, an Irish boy who had left the team because he felt the coach had not given him enough game time. 'He was good when he wanted to be. If he trained he was good', Sam said.

On the one hand it was a matter of winning, because winning gives sense to the competition. Already in the first half of the twentieth century Huizinga had observed that even when played by young people emerging out of childhood, the game has arguably almost completely lost its original element of 'play'.[46] Gary Alan Fine came to a similar conclusion in his long-term observation of pre-adolescents playing baseball in the USA.[47] Drawing upon his long-term ethnographic observation of children's sport, Noel Dyck reads the emphasis on 'work' and 'competitiveness' from a more dialectical perspective.[48] He contends that among the factors that make sport attractive to young athletes is the sense of accomplishment that they experience during games and competitions. In this sense, as Sam's words seem to confirm, a certain degree of work commitment is perceived as necessary to fully enjoy the sport experience. On the other hand, in the case of the Irish team 'seriousness' acquired also a different meaning. It underpinned a certain idea of masculinity, of how a young (working-class) local man should be, on and off the pitch. Sam and Kevin, the centre forward of Congolose background, seemed to deeply embrace this attitude of 'seriousness'. They would often be praised by the coach and the chairman for their 'brave' and 'fighting' attitude.

Once, travelling back from a game in the chairman's car, Jack said to me that Kevin and Sam had been the best players that day – they had run and fought without rest. A few minutes later he made what sounded a contradictory comment about 'the black players (in the team) suffering the cold'. In fact, that day James and Eric, respectively, a midfielder and a winger of Nigerian and French-Congolese background, wanted to play with a snood but the coach had asked them to take it off. James was allowed to wear his gloves but not the snood. Neither Sam nor Kevin wore a snood on this occasion, not even gloves, as this was a tacit rule within the game according to the coach. Were the two boys not perceived as 'black'? Along with the rest of the team, Sam and Kevin did not want to be considered 'sissies' by wearing gloves or even a snood. 'Don't be sissies' was a frequent remark that could be heard within the team. Being 'sissies' was essentially associated with a non-fighting, unmanly spirit – to wear gloves and a snood could count as an indicator of such an attitude. In the end, as argued by former Manchester United manager Alex Ferguson, 'real men don't wear snoods'.[49] Why did James and Eric dare to challenge an 'obvious' rule of the game? James had migrated to Ireland at the age of 10 and had soon started playing for Greenside along with Sam. For both of them this was the first club they had played competitive football with as in Nigeria, they recalled, they mainly played 'with friends'. Therefore, he was well aware of the coach's attitude towards snoods, gloves and generally accepted demeanour on and off the pitch. It was arguably a matter of understanding certain cultural codes which defined the local working-class masculine identity, and above all be willing to conform to them.

The meaning of the game

Despite the fact that the club was also proudly home to a girls' team, much of the discourse surrounding the game was blatantly male-oriented. To some extent, this is unsurprising, since football in Ireland emerged in the second half of the nineteenth century under the influence of the game played in Britain, where it was historically rooted in a strong, masculine, urban, (white) working-class culture.[50] It initially developed in urban areas, namely those of Belfast and, later, Dublin. Today, the majority of Dublin youth football clubs are located in the northern side of the city, characterized by a larger working-class/lower class population. For some of the black boys in the Greenside team, to be 'strong', self-controlled and serious was a way to conform to an identity that was primarily that of the game played in the local, Irish, vein. In doing so, they would attempt to appropriate some white coded, urban working-class traits. As emphasized by Archetti in his study of masculinities and sport in Argentina, football can well serve as a catalyst for different embodied identities.[51] My observation resonates here particularly with what Back, Crabbe and Solomos noted in their analysis of the English game. They write:

> What seems to be prevalent in the English game is a reliance on the notion that 'others', whether black, foreign or Asian, should assimilate with the normative, white coded, working class masculinity traits of English Football – unpretentious, self-deprecating, 'honest', committed, hard working, aggressive.[52]

As noted above, in order to be valued as a player, a young man and a rightful member of the local community, the young boys attempted to appropriate some or all the above-mentioned traits. But among the black boys this was something that not everyone felt the urgency to do. For example, Eric did not refrain to speak his mind. He would even make loud jokes about his contested 'blackness'. Because of his slightly lighter skin, and the fact that he had only recently migrated from France, the country where he had been living for a few years with his family after being born in DR Congo, some of his black teammates called him 'Paki', a derogatory term that he did not like. As noted by Hylton, 'the concept 'black' is contested, and there have been many battles over the ownership of suitable identifiers for social groups and names that suitably describe groups of individuals in society'.[53] Eric's frequent use of the term 'black' may appear as a way of, in Stuart Hall's words, 'learning to come into identification'.[54] Once, during the second half of a game Greenside were winning easily, he was removed from the pitch to let another player get some game time. Leaving the pitch Eric made gestures with his hands like a rapper and in a funny tone, looking at the coaches, he shouted: 'Is it because I am black? Are you taking me out because I am black?' There was a moment of embarrassment, then Jimmy and Jack smiled, a timid smile. Later Jack would recall this moment as an example of Eric's unpredictability, to being a 'character'.

In this and other occasions, Eric showed that he was not interested in adhering to the unwritten rules of the game. Even after several months with the team, he would celebrate goals with a long run around the pitch – definitely an eccentric behaviour according to local mores. He would often wear colourful attire and two earrings, while almost all his teammates, white Irish and black immigrants alike, wore the club's tracksuits and rarely earrings. Despite his talent, over the months he was pushed to the margins of the group, and he finally left the team. Having been with the team before his arrival I could follow Eric's trajectory from the start. During the first weeks with Greenside, he looked nervous and studious of the group's dynamics, eager to accustom himself to the general mood. Eric seemed not only to be carefully working his way into the group, a new member in an established football team, but also learning rules of behaviour that were new to him. But as he started scoring goals, seven in his first three games, and getting respect from his teammates and the coach, there was a noticeable change of attitude. He became more confident and vocal, and started joyfully expressing his spontaneity in ways that would 'disturb' the group and the adults in charge of supervising it.

But Eric was not the only one to experience this sort of inner tension. James was also reluctant to 'conform', although he did not have the courage Eric demonstrated in resisting the codes of the 'serious game'. Most of the times, while with the team, he stayed silent. He liked to play with the ball, but was worried about being shouted at if he kept it for too long. The coach insisted that the ball be passed to Kevin, who had to shoot as soon as possible. 'Two touches and shoot', was the coach's instruction to the centre-forward, a classic 'long ball' tactic. James was later to leave Greenside and join a local team run by African coaches operating in the same area and practicing, in the words of their manager, 'football with an African flair'. Sam, on the other hand, was quite the opposite; he was working his way to becoming as much as possible part of the local community, adhering to whatever rules he was presented with. Even though one of his brothers was playing for the immigrants' team, and he also happened to train with them from time to time, he remained faithful to Greenside and to Jimmy, the coach who first invited him to join a team in Ireland. When I visited his house to meet with his mother, I noticed that one of the very few ornaments in the living room was his 'Certificate of Proficiency in the Irish Language'. The mother said he was very proud of that, he preferred to speak Irish rather than Yoruba, his mother-tongue. This was another way to 'perform' belonging, since, as noted by Bell, 'belonging is an achievement at several levels of abstraction'.[55]

But to what extent did his racially marked position allow him to 'belong'? And what do Eric and James's trajectories of exclusion or self-exclusion tell us about the role of sport in identity processes of teenagers living in a multiethnic society? Ben Carrington believes that 'sports contests are more than just significant events … they act as a key signifier for wider questions about identity within racially demarcated societies'.[56] Eric insisted claim of being 'black' and his transformation from the disciplined, compliant young man into a vocal and spontaneous teenager can be interpreted as a way of overtly announcing his 'difference' and in so doing to acknowledge his, and his black peers, racialized position within Irish society. Other ethnographic events reveal a dichotomy that apparently cannot be bridged – you are either 'in' or you are 'out'.

With regard to sense of inclusion and belonging, it can be argued that black immigrants and refugees are positioned at the fringes of Irish society, but there are contrasting narratives that should not be overlooked. For example, what did it mean for a team like Greenside to be captained by a black immigrant boy? As noted, the youth club played a special role in giving a sense of identity to the local community. This was particularly evident when they played and beat teams from more affluent parts of the city. In those occasions, another layer of identity/belonging came to the fore – a particular form of 'neighbourhood nationalism'[57] which appeared to unite lower class Irish nationals and black immigrants. In a way this highlighted a 'common' position of otherness, as according to Loyal, 'lower class Irish nationals are outsiders themselves in relation to higher ranking economic elites whose more secure socio-economic position, class codes and behavioural norms and restraints are expressions of their higher levels of economic and cultural capital'.[58] Games against such teams were especially tense as a strong multi-ethnic team from a working-class area would play against mostly white Irish teams from middle class areas. Two conflicting versions of contemporary Ireland faced each other on the pitch. Greenside embraced the diversity of post-Celtic Tiger Ireland to an extent that clubs from affluent areas of the town did not. This would make the young captain and his black teammates obviously proud. At the same time, Greenside would acquire an image of an area where immigrants could count, at least on the football pitch. The analysis of the next and final 'vignette' will enhance the appreciation and the understanding of embodied dimensions of belonging. While doing this, it will also highlight transcultural dynamics that can take place, and to some extent be facilitated by leisure practices and grassroots sports.

Embodied belongings

The Irish boys in the team sported similar fresh crewcuts which contributed to constructing their own 'working-class' masculine identities.[59] As I personally learned from my first visits to the public park where Greenside trained and played their games, appearance and demeanour helped defining the boundaries of 'inclusion'. Patrick, a winger of Congolose background who had joined Greenside in my second season with them, found initially difficult to adjust to this unspoken hairstyle code. One day he arrived at the pitch sporting his thick curly hair visibly longer on top and shaved on the sides. It was a smaller version of the 'Afro' hairstyle. This did not pass unnoticed and Patrick was immediately called 'Bob Marley' by a club member. That was the joke of the day and almost everybody, both Irish boys and those of African backgrounds, took part in it. The story would not be meaningful for my discussion had it not been for a conversation that involved Patrick and three of his Irish teammates, Keith, Robbie and Shane, a player who had just joined the team and did not know all his teammates yet. Shane asked Patrick if he was really from Jamaica (the country of origin of Bob Marley) like everybody was claiming. The conversation touched upon questions of national and cultural belonging involving football as an 'international' language.

Shane:	How come you are not from Jamaica?
Patrick:	I am from Jamaica.
Shane:	Naa I am from Jamaica … change all things. Where are you from?
Keith:	Congo.
Patrick:	Same country as Eric, same country as Kevin.
Keith:	Kevin is from Nigeria.
Shane (turning to Kevin):	Kevin, where are you from?
Patrick:	My country, Congo!
Keith:	Jamaica.
Shane:	Congo.
Patrick:	Do you know LuaLua?
Shane:	Who?
Patrick:	The fella who used to play for Newcastle.
Keith:	LuaLua, who played for Newcastle.
Patrick:	Yeah, him. He is from Congo as well. We are Congolese man … we are the best.
Shane:	Congolese.
Patrick:	Yeah.
Patrick:	You Irish, Ireland. Congo, Congolese.
Robbie (in a funny tone):	I don't know where is Congo. Fuck that, we are in the Congo team.

This conversation reveals much about the 'transcultural' dialogue that the game of football may engender among teenagers. According to Hoerder et al. it is especially young people living in metropolitan areas with diverse populations that give rise to the 'transcultural'. They believe that 'encounters among youth from different cultural, ethnic, and social contexts produce diasporic public spheres which are neither predominantly emancipatory nor fully controlled, but emerging and therefore contested'.[60] The football team appears to be a site that effectively enables such 'encounters' among young people. The boy from Congo had actually spent half of his life in Ireland and on another occasion he had told me he would gladly play for the Irish national team, if given citizenship, as he said 'I love this country'. In this case he used a footballer as an example of someone from the same origin the Irish boy might know, the former Newcastle United FC player LuaLua. Football functioned here as a common language that everybody could understand. But Patrick was in some way also 'teaching' the Irish boys about the importance of his roots. It was rare to hear such an open declaration of national or racial belonging from a boy of immigrant background, with the exception of Eric. In fact, Keith did erroneously assume that his long-term teammate Kevin was from Nigeria and not from DR Congo.

The question of hairstyle, which originated the discussion, is a vivid example of the embodied nature of negotiations of belonging. The most important things are sometimes unfolding outside of language. Social researchers who want to undertake research with young people should be attentive of the different ways belonging is performed rather than articulated through words. On the other hand, the above-mentioned conversation about the African origin of some of the team's players shows the generative power of younger generations who live, paraphrasing Homi Bhabha, 'in-between cultures'.[61] In this and other occasions, both white Irish and black African teenagers were capable of playing with local modes of behaviour and to some extent challenge their own social and even racial positioning like unpredictable 'agents of diversity'.[62] For example, Eric was the favourite player of the white Irish little kids who attended the team's home games. What to the coach and some of his teammates appeared as 'antics' were what made him special among the little kids who were usually the only spectators at the team's home games. Furthermore, Ross, a white Irish player who was also an amateur rapper, would burn CD copies of his own music inspired by Eminem and Afro-American hip hop artists. When at the club he would not dress any different from the rest of his Irish teammates, but he made nonetheless his passion for hip hop known to anyone.

The extent to which adults accepted these dynamics or influenced young people's agency was, as generally is amongst adolescents, a contextual matter. More importantly, the extent to which their structural positioning in Irish society as black immigrant youth allowed them freedom to 'experiment with cultures' was limited but its potential should not be overlooked. To affirm their 'difference', young people might be asked to enact spontaneous forms of 'resistance' to the status quo, as James and Eric did. Such forms of resistance were not totally ineffective as they challenged the boundaries of 'acceptance' and inclusion in the team and in the local community. On the other hand, the rich dynamics taking place within the team provided the adults in charge of the game – club officials, coaches, adult mentors and game officials – the opportunity to reflect upon and learn about the special role grassroots football can play as a site for negotiations of belonging in a multi-ethnic society. This should be seriously taken into account by football authorities, especially those supervising youth leagues, who could support local clubs and youth coaches in acquiring much needed educational skills to counter the risk of exclusion and discrimination.[63]

Conclusion

The sporting field is a site that serves different needs: that of leisure, of sport performance, but also a site for socialization and a place within which to negotiate sense of belonging. However, this doesn't happen in straight lines. In the case of Greenside, despite the efforts of the young coach and the manager to include everyone regardless of their backgrounds, there were 'conventions' or unwritten rules of behaviour that had little to do with football per se. These informal modes of behaviour were not specifically at work within the football team. Rather, they were part of a set of conventions of demeanour that were followed by local male youth in this neighbourhood. These 'conventions' aimed at the reproduction of a certain idea of Irish working-class masculinity, of being 'strong' and not standing out of the group. They affirmed the embodied nature of negotiations around belonging. As such, they would arguably impinge on the black immigrant boys' subjective sense of inclusion, but the boys could also challenge the 'norm'. At the same time, through their efforts to make the team successful, Irish and immigrant players and officials of Greenside challenged their common lower positioning within the socio-economic landscape of Irish society. This was particularly evident when they beat teams from more affluent areas of the city. In those occasions an ethnically mixed youth football team from a working-class area emphasized the contested nature of belonging. The special role played by grassroots football clubs in enabling negotiations of belonging of immigrant youth is one that needs appreciated to the full. At the same time, it illuminates a line of inquiry that could be taken further in other contexts and countries.

Acknowledgements

I am grateful to Les Back, to the editors of this special issue and to the two anonymous reviewers for their helpful comments.

Disclosure statement

No potential conflict of interest was reported by the author.

Notes

1. The book was co-written with journalist Vincent Hogan.
2. McGrath, *Back From the Brink*, 72.
3. 1996 is the year when the net migration balance of the Republic of Ireland became positive with the influx of foreign population and Irish returning emigrants.
4. Burdsey, 'They Think it's All Over … It Isn't Yet!'; Carrington, *Race, Sport and Politics*. 'Soccer Fields of Cultural [Re]Production'; Giardina, 'Bend it Like Beckam'; Rosbrook-Thomson, *Sport, Difference and Belonging*.
5. Amara et al., *Sport and Multiculturalism*.
6. This is the title of a long-term programme of the German Olympic Sports Federation.
7. This is the slogan of the Irish NGO Sport Against Racism Ireland, www.sari.ie (accessed December 22, 2013).
8. 'Football: a shared sense of belonging?' is the title of a collaborative research project carried out between 2009 and 2012 by the NGO Football Unites, Racism Divides with young asylum seekers and refugees in Sheffield, www.furd.org (accessed January 8, 2014).
9. Williams, 'Rangers is a Black Club'.
10. Bradbury, 'Racism, Resistance and New Youth Inclusions'.
11. Long et al., 'Part of the Game?'.

12. Lusted, 'Playing Games with "Race"'.
13. See for example Demboski, 'Ballfreiheit'; Pilz, 'Rote Karte Statt Integration?'; Soefner and Zifonun, 'Migranten Im Deutschen Vereinfussball'.
14. Back et al., *The Changing Face of Football*, 287.
15. Carter, *In Foreign Fields;* Holmes and Storey, 'Transferring National Allegiances'; Poli, 'The Denationalization of Sport'.
16. Walseth, 'Sport and Belonging'; Rosbrook-Thomson, *Sport, Difference and Belonging.*
17. Quoted in Walseth, 'Sport and Beloning', 449.
18. Hooks, *Belonging. A Culture of Place.*
19. Maxwell et al., 'Social Inclusion in Community Sport'.
20. Hoerder et al., *Negotiating Transcultural Lives*, 14.
21. Giulianotti, *Football: A Sociology of the Global Game.*
22. Goldblatt, *The Ball is Round*, 901.
23. A couple of exceptions: Hassan and McCue, 'The "Silent" Irish'; Mauro, 'A Team Like no "Other"'.
24. Gilligan et al., *In the Frontline of Integration*; Ni Laoire et al., *Childhood and Migration in Europe*; Darmody et al., *The Changing Faces of Ireland.*
25. Connor, *Youth Sport in Ireland*; Delaney and Fahey, *School Children and Sport in Ireland*; Lalor et al., *Young People in Contemporary Ireland*; Woods et al., *The Children's Sport Participation.*
26. Biesta et al., 'Does Sport Make a Difference?'.
27. Raby, 'Across a Great Gulf', 47.
28. Sinha and Back, 'Making Methods Sociable'.
29. Clarke et al., *Understanding Research With Children and Young People.*
30. Denzin, *Interpretive Ethnography*, 282.
31. Rouch and Feld, *Ciné-Ethnography.*
32. Willis and Trondman, 'Manifesto for Ethnography', 394.
33. Loescher, 'Cameras at the Addy'.
34. Clifford, *Routes*; Duneier, *Sidewalk*; Marcus, 'Contemporary Fieldwork'.
35. 2011 National Census.
36. http://www.sfai.ie/ (accessed October 16, 2014).
37. The name of the club as all the names of the participants have been anonymized.
38. In the Greenside area, home to about 8000 people, 22.94% of the population fall into the category of 'youth at risk', while the overall average for Dublin's of 18.3% and the State 20.4% (Ryan, *Socio-Economic Profile of Greenside Parish*).
39. Connor, *Youth Sport in Ireland*, and Faye et al., *School Children and Sport in Ireland.*
40. Lentin and McVeigh, *After Optimism*; Loyal, 'Immigration'.
41. Fannin et al., *Taking Racism Seriously*; Kennedy, *Treated differently?*
42. Giulianotti, *Football: A Sociology of the Global Game*, 74.
43. Rosbrook-Thompson, *Sport, Difference and Belonging*; King, 'Race and Cultural Identity', Carrington, *Race, Sport and Politics.*
44. Doherty and Taylor, 'Sport and Physical Recreation in the Settlement of Immigrant Youth'; Harinen et al. 'Multiculturalism and Young People's Leisure Spaces in Finland'; Stack and Iwasaki, 'The Role of Leisure Pursuits in Adaptation Processes Among Afghan Refugees'; Verma and Larson, 'Examining Adolescent Leisure Time Across Cultures'.
45. Doherty and Taylor, 'Sport and Physical Recreation in the Settlement of Immigrant Youth', 44.
46. Huizinga, *Homo Ludens.*
47. Fine, *With the Boys*, 188.
48. Dyck, *Fields of Play.*
49. Ferguson made his comment in December 2010 and soon afterwards the International Football Association Board banned the use of snoods from professional football. BBC News, 5 March 2011, http://news.bbc.co.uk/sport1/hi/football/9415721.stm (accessed April 30, 2013).
50. Cronin, *Sport and Nationalism in Ireland*; Sugden and Bairner, *Sport, Sectarianism and Society in a Divided Ireland.*
51. Archetti, *Masculinities, Football, Polo, and the Tango in Argentina.*

52. Back et al., *The Changing Face of Football*, 285.
53. Hylton, *'Race' and Sport. Critical Race Theory*, 18.
54. Hall, 'Old and New Identities, Old and New Ethnicities', 205.
55. Bell, *Performativity and Belonging*, 3.
56. Carrington, 'Sport, Masculinity and Black Cultural Resistance', 299.
57. Back, *New Ethnicities and Urban Culture*.
58. Loyal, 'Postmodern Othering or Established-Outsiders Relations?', 142.
59. The hair was shaven to blade one or blade two, usually with a small fringe of longer hair arranged over their foreheads.
60. Hoerder et al., *Negotiating Transcultural Lives*, 15.
61. Bhabha, 'Culture's In-Between'.
62. Mac Dougall, *The Corporeal Image*.
63. This echoes one of the recommendations of the EU Report on Sport and Multiculturalism, Amara et al., *Sport and Multiculturalism*, 85. In 2007, the FAI, with the support of UEFA, launched its first 'Intercultural Plan'. According to Hassan and McCue, 'this plan, which promised so much, has come unstuck due to a weakness in its implementation'; 'Football, Racism and the Irish', 62.

References

Amara, M., D. Aquilina, and I. Henry. *Sport and Multiculturalism*, Bruxelles: European Commission DG Education and Culture, 2004.

Archetti, E. *Masculinities, Football, Polo, and the Tango in Argentina*, Oxford: Berg, 1999.

Back, L. *New Ethnicities and Urban Culture: Racisms and Multiculture in Young Lives*, London: UCL Press, 1996.

Back, L. 'Live Sociology: Social Research and Its Futures'. In *Live Methods*, ed. L. Back and N. Puwar, 18–39. Oxford: Wiley-Blackwell/The Sociological Review, 2012.

Back, L., T. Crabbe, and J. Salomon. *The Changing Face of Football: Racism, Identity and Multiculture in the English Game*. Oxford: Berg, 2001.

Bairner, A., ed. *Sport and the Irish*. Dublin: University College Dublin Press, 2005.

Bell, V. *Performativity and Belonging*, London: Sage, 1999.

Bhabha, H. 'Culture's In-between'. In *Questions of Cultural Identity*, ed. S. Hall and P. du Gay, 53–60. London: Sage, 1996.

Biesta, G., M. Stams, E. Dirks, E.A. Rutten, W. Veugelers, and C. Schuengel. 'Does sport make a difference? An Exploration of the Impact of Sport on the Social Integration of Young People'. In *Values and Norms in Sport*, ed. J. Steenbergen, P. de Knop, and A.H.F. Elling, 95–114. Oxford: Meyer & Meyer Sport, 2001.

Bradbury, S. 'Racism, Resistance and New Youth Inclusions'. In *Race, Ethnicity and Football: Persisting Debates and Emergent Issues*, ed. D. Bursdey, 67–83. London: Routledge, 2011.

Bursdey, D. 'They Think It's All Over... It isn't Yet!' In *Race, Ethnicity and Football: Persisting Debates and Emergent Issues*, ed. D. Bursdey, 3–20. London: Routledge, 2011.

Carrington, B. *Race Sport and Politics. The Sporting Black Diaspora*. London: Sage, 2010.

Carrington, B. 'Sport, Masculinity and Black Cultural Resistance'. In *The Sport Studies Reader*, ed. A. Tomlinson, 298–303. London: Routledge, 2008.

Clark, A., R. Flewitt, M. Hammersley, and M. Robb. *Understanding Research with Children and Young People*. London: Sage, 2014.

Connor, S. *Youth Sport in Ireland*, Dublin: The Liffey Press, 2003.

Cronin, M. *Sport and Nationalism in Ireland: Gaelic Games, Soccer and Irish Identity Since 1884*, Dublin: Four Courts Press, 1999.

Darmody, M., N. Tyrrel, and S. Song. *The Changing Faces of Ireland. Exploring the Lives of Immigrant and Ethnic Minority Children*. Rotterdam: Sense Publishers, 2011.

Denzin, N. *Interpretive Ethnography*. Thousands Oaks, CA: Sage, 1997.

Doherty, A., and T. Taylor. 'Sport and Physical Recreation in the Settlement of Immigrant Youth'. *Leisure/Loisir* 31, no. 1 (2007): 27–55.

Duneier, M. *Sidewalk*, New York: Farrar, Straus and Giroux, 1999.

Dyck, N. *Fields of Play. An Ethnography of Children's Sport*. Toronto, ON: University of Toronto Press, 2013.

Fahey, T., L. Delaney, and B. Gannon. *School Children and Sport in Ireland*, Dublin: The Economic and Social Research Institute, 2005.

Fanning, B., B. Killoran, S. Ní Bhroin, and G. McEvoy. *Taking Racism Seriously*. Dublin: Trinity Immigration Initiative & Immigrant Council of Ireland, 2011.

Fine, G.A. *With the Boys. Little League Baseball and Preadolescent Culture*. Chicago, IL: The University of Chicago Press, 1987.

Giardina, M. '"Bending in Like Beckham" in the Global Popular: Stylish Hybridity, Performativity, and the Politics of Representation'. *Journal of Sport & Social Issues* 27 (2003): 65–82.

Gilligan, R., J. McGrath, M. Ní Raghallaigh, J. J. Scholtz, P. Curry, D. Murphy, M. Rogers, A. Gilligan Quinn. *In the Front Line of Integration: Young People Managing Migration to Ireland*, Dublin: Trinity Immigration Initiative & Integrating Ireland, 2010.

Giulianotti, R. *Football. A Sociology of the Global Game*. Cambridge, MA: Polity Press, 1999.

Goldblatt, D. *The Ball is Round. A Global History of Football*. London: Penguin, 2007.

Hall, S. 'Old and New Identities, Old and New Ethnicities'. In *Theories of Race and Racism*, ed. L.J. Back and J. Solomos, 144–53. London: Routledge, 2009.

Harinen, P.M., M.V. Honkasalo, J.K. Ronkainen, and L.E. Suurpää. 'Multiculturalism and Young People's Leisure Spaces in Finland: Perspectives of Multicultural Youth'. *Leisure Studies* 31, no. 2 (2012): 177–91.

Hassan, D., and K. McCue. 'Football, Racism and the Irish'. In *Race, Ethnicity and Football: Persisting Debates and Emergent Issues*, ed. D. Bursdey, 50–66. London: Routledge, 2011.

Hazel, M., C. Foley, T. Taylor, and C. Burton. 'Social Inclusion in Community Sport: A Case Study of Muslim Women in Australia'. *Journal of Sport Management* 27 (2013): 467–81.

Hoerder, D., Y. Hebert, and I. Schmitt. *Negotiating Transcultural Lives: Belongings and Social Capital among Youth in Comparative Perspective*, Toronto, ON: University of Toronto Press, 2006.

Holmes, M., and D. Storey. 'Transferring National Allegiance: Cultural Affinity or Flag of Convenience?' *Sport in Society* 14, no. 2 (2011): 253–71.

Hooks, Bell. *Belonging. A Culture of Place*, New York: Routledge, 2009.

Huizinga, J. *Homo Ludens: A Study of the Play-element in Culture*. London: Routledge, 1980 [1938].

Hylton, K. *'Race' and Sport. Critical Race Theory*. London: Routledge, 2009.

Kennedy, P. *Treated Differently? Evidence of Racism and Discrimination from a Local Perspective*, Limerick: Doras Luimni, 2013.

King, C. 'Race and Cultural Identity: Playing the Race Game Within Football'. *Leisure/Loisir* 23 (2004): 19–30.

Lalor, K, A. de Roiste and M. Devlin. *Young People in Contemporary Ireland*. Dublin: Gill & Macmillan, 2007.

Lentin, R., and R. McVeigh. *After Optimism? Ireland, Racism and Globalisation*, Dublin: Metro Eireann, 2006.

Loescher, M. 'Cameras at the Addy: Speaking in Pictures with City Kids'. In *Visualizing Anthropology*, ed. A. Grimshaw and A. Ravetz. Bristol: Intellect, 2005.

Long, J., K. Hylton, J. Dart, and M. Welch. *Part of the Game? An Examination of Racism in Grass Roots Football*, London: Kick It Out, 2002.

Loyal, S. 'Postmodern Othering or Established-outsiders Relations Understanding the Reception and Treatment of Immigrants in Ireland'. *Cambio* 1, no. 2 (2011): 135–46.

Loyal, S. 'Immigration'. In *Contemporary Ireland: A Sociological Map*, ed. S. O'Sullivan. Dublin: UCD Press, 2007.

Lusted, J. 'Playing Games with "Race": Understanding Resistance to "Race" Equality Initiatives in English Local Football Governance'. *Soccer & Society* 10, no. 6 (2009): 722–39.

MacDougall, D. *The Corporeal Image. Film, Ethnography and the Senses*. Princeton, NJ: Princeton University Press, 2006.

Marcus, G. 'Contemporary Fieldwork Aesthetics in Art and Anthropology: Experiments in Collaboration and Intervention'. *Visual Anthropology* 23 (2010): 263–77.

Mauro, M. 'A Team Like No "Other". The Racialized Position of Insaka in the Dublin Schoolboys Leagues'. *Soccer & Society* 14, no 3 (2013): 344–64.

McGrath, P. *Back from the Brink*, London: Arrow Books, 2007.

Ni Laoire, C., F. Carpena-Mendez, N. Tyrrel, and A. White. *Childhood and Migration in Europe*. London: Ashgate, 2011.

Pilz, G. 'Rote Karten Statt Integration? Eine Untersuchung Über Fußall Und Ethnische Konflikte, Sport als Mittel der Integration', Duisburg, Sport als Mittel der Integration, Duisburg. http://www.sportwiss.unihannover.de/fileadmin/sport/pdf/onlinepublikationen/pil_eth.pdf (Accessed May 16, 2012).

Poli, R. 'The Denationalization of Sport: De-ethnicization of the Nation and Identity Deterritorialization'. *Sport in Society* 10, no. 4 (2007): 646–61.

Raby, R. 'Across a Great Gulf? Conducting Research with Adolescents'. In *Representing Youth*, ed. A.L. Best. New York: New York University Press, 2007.

Rosbrook-Thomson, J. *Sport, Difference and Belonging: Conceptions of Human Variation in British Sport*, London: Routledge, 2012.

Rouch, J., and S. Feld. *Ciné-ethnography*, Minneapolis: University of Minnesota Press, 2003.

Ryan, K. *Socio-economic Profile of Greenside Parish*, Dublin: Blanchardstown Area Partnership, 2010.

Sinha, S., and L. Back. 'Making Methods Sociable: Dialogue, Ethics and Authorship in Qualitative Research'. *Qualitative Research* (2013): 1–15.

Soeffner, H.G., and D. Zifonou. 'Migranten im Deutschen Vereinfüssball' [Migrants in German Association Football] *Füssball und Integration [Football and Integration]*. Berlin: Heinrich Böll Stiftung, 2006.

Stack, J., and Y. Iwasaki. 'The Role of Leisure Pursuits in Adaptation Processes among Afghan Refugees Who Have Immigrated to Winnipeg, Canada'. *Leisure Studies* 28 (2009): 239–59.

Sugden, J., and A. Bairner. *Sport, Sectarianism and Society in a Divided Ireland*. Leicester: Leicester University Press, 1993.

Swanson, L. 'Soccer Fields of Cultural [Re]Production: Creating "Good Boys" in Suburban America'. *Sociology of Sport Journal* 26 (2009): 404–24.

Verma, S., and R. Larson. 'Examining Adolescent Leisure Time across Cultures'. *New Directions for Child and Adolescent Development* 99 (2003): 1–8.

Walseth, K. 'Sport and Belonging'. *International Review for the Sociology of Sport* 41 (2006): 447–64.

Williams, J. 'Rangers is a Black Club "race", identity and local football in England'. In *Game Without Frontiers: Football, Identity and Modernity*, ed. R. Giulianotti and J. Williams, 153–83. Aldershot: Arena Publications, 2002.

Willis, P., and M. Trondman. 'Manifesto for Ethnography'. *Cultural Studies Critical Methodologies* 2 (2002): 394–402.

Woods, C., N. Moyla, A. Quinlan, D. Tannehill, and J. Walsh. *The Children's Sport Participation and Physical Activity Study*, Dublin: Irish Sports Council, 2010.

A generational divide within the class-based production of girls in American youth soccer

Lisa Swanson

Department of Sociology & Anthropology, Goucher College, Baltimore, MD, USA

By building upon earlier research on social class and soccer, the following study specifically provides insight into American, adolescent girls' experiences with youth soccer (Swanson, 'Complicating the "Soccer Mom"'; Swanson, 'Soccer Fields'; Andrews, 'Contextualizing Suburban Soccer'; and Zwick and Andrews, 'The Suburban Soccer Field'). Driven by Pierre Bourdieu's theoretical concepts regarding social class reproduction, I engaged in ethnographic-style conversations regarding recreational youth soccer with girls ages 11–14 and their Baby-Boom-Generation mothers in order to further understand how the American, middle-class habitus may be contributing to a particular gender-based path in youth sport (Bourdieu, *Distinction*). Additionally, Grossberg's and Giroux's literature on youth and politics of culture informed my understanding of the discrepancies between parents' views and their children's views on youth soccer experiences (Grossberg, 'Cultural Studies'; Giroux, *Stealing Innocence*). In this paper, I recognize American involvement in youth soccer as a class-based form of childrearing as I describe parents' expectations of girls in youth soccer. The participants' thoughts on race, social class, gender, and today's youth as related to their soccer experiences are provided.

Introduction

Youth soccer has been successfully incorporated into the American suburban landscape. The process of white, middle-class Americans ultimately embracing soccer in the latter part of the twentieth century is complex, but can be largely understood as a result of efforts made decades ago by the North American Soccer League (NASL), the impact of Title IX, and the alignment of soccer with the middle-class habitus.[1] NASL, a former professional league from the late 1960s to the mid 1980s, attempted to produce interest in professional soccer through youth involvement. According to Andrews, Pitter, Zwick and Ambrose, NASL's 'comprehensive network of grass-roots youth soccer programmes … contributed to the growing interest in soccer as a participant sport within the crucial suburban market'.[2] During this same time period, the educational amendment Title IX was passed. This legislation furthered ideological support for girls' involvement in sport in general and the production of programmes that allowed for both boys and girls to play. Additionally, the middle-class habitus specifically drives appropriate bodily practices that are aligned with the physical and mental expectations for players involved in youth soccer. Soccer is

---

Department of Sociology, Anthropology, & Criminal Justice, Towson University, Towson, MD, USA.

viewed by middle-class parents as contributing to the production of the desired corporeal aesthetic and culture of competition and teamwork among their children.[3] By the end of the twentieth century, soccer had established itself as the second most popular team sport in the Unites States for children under 12.[4]

According to Lareau 'social class does indeed create distinctive parenting styles'.[5] Middle-class parents' placement of children in organized, youth sport activities is part of a larger effort in childrearing practices that Lareau refers to as 'concerted cultivation'.[6] Placement in organized youth sport supports the 'concerted cultivation' efforts which Lareau describes as 'numerous age-specific organized activities that ... parents view ... as transmitting important life skills to children'.[7] Research can illuminate the efforts middle-class parents make as youth sport is utilized in the process of raising children. Recently produced sociological studies informed by Bourdieu's theories of social class reproduction involving the key concepts of habitus and capital, contribute to the understanding of the impact of social class on youth sport experiences.[8] These research studies shed light on middle-class sport choices, level of involvement, and what parents hope to gain by having their children participate.

I began the following research on girls in youth soccer with the intention of following up on an ethnographic study I conducted on the 'soccer mom' phenomenon.[9] For that study I utilized theoretical work by Pierre Bourdieu in order to understand mothers' placement of their sons into youth soccer programmes as a social-class-based practice.[10] In my prior research on mothers of soccer-playing sons, I overheard conversations mothers had with their daughters whose focus seemed to be on body, fitness and health.[11] As a result, I wondered what kind of specific, gender-based experience American, middle-class girls go through in youth soccer. Furthermore, Zwick noted that gender, while not a focus in his analysis of the intersection of class and race within youth soccer culture, should be a part of future research.[12] By shifting my focus to *girls* in youth soccer for my current study, I planned to extend my qualitative research further by analyzing the mothers' reasons for involving their daughters as class-driven as well.

According to Bourdieu's seminal work *Distinction: A Social Critique of the Judgement of Taste*, members of a specific social class will perceive of and interact within a sport differently from members of another class.[13] This occurs because each social class has its own habitus, and it is this habitus that influences tastes, preferences and lifestyle choices within sport. In regard to analyzing class distribution of sports, Bourdieu stated, 'one would have to take account of the representation which, in terms of their specific schemes of perception and appreciation, the different classes have of the costs ... and benefits'.[14] As described by Bourdieu, the costs and benefits come in economic, cultural and physical forms of capital.

The results of the following study add to the understanding of the possible 'costs' and 'benefits' of participation in soccer, by examining the middle class perception and treatment of soccer among a specific group of 'agents'. According to Bourdieu,

> because agents apprehend objects through the schemes of perception and appreciation of their habitus, it would be naïve to suppose that all practitioners of the same sport (or any other practice) confer the same meaning on their practice or even, strictly speaking, that they are practising the same practice.[15]

Bourdieu emphasized in the above statement that a class member's habitus is clearly going to affect his/her understanding of a particular sport. The 'agents' of interest in this research project were American, middle and upper middle class mothers and their daughters. This study provides insight into American middle and upper middle class habitus by interpreting the agents' understanding of soccer, or more specifically, their own involvement with the sport. Additionally, I recognized these mothers and daughters as two subgroups of agents that share a social-class habitus, but at the same time do not always 'confer the same meaning'.[16] I, therefore, researched the different perspectives between the mothers and daughters on several social issues relevant to the youth soccer experience.

Accessing a social network

My intention was to study a social network of mothers and their daughters involved with youth soccer. I specifically sought out a group of participants who were connected through their youth soccer experiences as a result of having daughters close in age and involved in the same local, recreation council. Fortunately, an acquaintance of mine located in the mid-Atlantic region of the United States knew a few mothers with daughters who played soccer. She had these mothers contact me regarding potential involvement in my research. Once I had access to one mother I followed the 'snowball sampling' technique to gain more participants.[17] I asked the initial participant and each subsequent mother and daughter to suggest another person or two that I should include in the research. Following this method meant that each new participant met me through someone she already knew. My intention was not only to gain access to a particular network through this technique, but also to increase participants' comfort level with me as a result of meeting me through someone each already knew. When to stop pursuing additional participants for the study became clear as I followed my technique of snowball sampling and came to the end of contacts in this particular youth soccer network. I eventually reached the point when mothers were suggesting other mothers who had either already been included or had previously refused involvement in the research. I discontinued the snowball sampling technique and any further inclusion of participants, since my goal was to include members of a group who knew each other and had shared similar experiences in youth soccer in regard to the people involved, location, and organizational structure to which they were exposed. While this limited my understanding of an outsider's viewpoint, it did allow me to hone my focus on their emic perspective and any diversity within the group.

My snowball sampling technique resulted in my working with 21 participants. The mothers who agreed to be involved in the research all had daughters in recreational-level youth soccer. Both the mothers and daughters signed informed consent forms approved by my university's institutional review board. The girls' ages ranged from 11 to 14. The majority of them were 12 turning 13 during the time of this study. The mean age for the mothers was 47 and it was 13 for the daughters. All the girls were Caucasian except for one Asian participant. The mothers identified their families as middle class and upper middle class. All of the girls, except for one, attended public school. Having their daughters in public school meant that the middle school the majority of these girls attended was publicly funded and did not require parents to pay additional expenses beyond taxes supporting the local education system. The particular middle school the girls attended is highly regarded throughout the county and state for its high academic standards and student achievement.

Methods

A number of other studies have indicated the utility of ethnography to understand parental manipulation of children's school and sport experiences.[18] While I would not refer to my study on girls in youth soccer as a comprehensive ethnography since I did not fully immerse myself in their lives, I do consider my research to be ethnographic in style. The ethnographic quality of my method was in the manner in which I gained my information from these mothers and daughters. A fieldworker engaged in ethnography must enter what Van Maanen called the participants' 'home ground'.[19] I worked on building a rapport with the mothers through phone calls and email messages. They allowed me into their homes to conduct extensive and fairly informal interviews over the course of a year. These conversations would most often take place sitting around the kitchen table with the mother and daughter for an hour or two each time. I took great care in 'framing' the interview in a manner that allowed me to develop a good connection with both the mother and daughter.[20] I conducted what I refer to as initial interviews and follow-up interviews. Initial interviews were intended to cover what I considered the basics (i.e. what drew them to be involved in youth soccer and what they got out of it).

My initial interviews were done with both mother and daughter together. Setting up interviews with two participants at a time could potentially illicit more extensive responses from interviewees. When ethnographers arrange an interview in this manner, it 'may make the interview situation less strange for interviewees and thus encourage them to be more forthcoming'.[21] I continued with initial interviews and worked on making sure participants were comfortable with me and my research inquiries. I thought by increasing their comfort level, things might be easier during follow-up discussions about some tougher issues. I needed to gain the mothers' trust during the initial interviews so that when I came back for the follow-up discussions they would allow me to talk with their daughters alone. I designed the follow-up interviews to take place in two stages. I first talked with the daughter alone and then second, I had the mother join the conversation. Setting up the follow-up interview in this manner allowed for me to firstly, give the daughter a chance to have a voice. This was necessary since during initial interviews an interesting dynamic resulted with mothers often talking over daughters or mothers looking to daughters to confirm what they had said. And secondly, setting up the follow-up interview in stages also allowed me to gain separate responses from the mothers and daughters that I could then compare.

I firmly believe in the reflexive process promoted by Bourdieu and Wacquant, Wynne, Alexander and Stake among others, and due to the nature of ethnography, I had to respond to the needs of the research situation as it unfolded.[22] Wynne in discussing the reflexive process notes that

> the researcher(s) will inevitably be faced with decisions regarding the path to be followed next, … Rather than seeing this as a problematic feature of the community study as method, it should be understood as a strength – in that it allows for, and encourages, a continual reflection on the research activity itself.[23]

My research became essentially a compilation of ethnographic *detours* as I worked my way through the process. I needed to respond to the fact that mothers talked over the daughters which is why I shifted the design of the follow-up interviews. Also, I was responding mid-research to what I was learning in regard to different perspectives provided by each sub-group of participants. Hammersley and Atkinson also emphasize the same understanding by noting that research requires 'the exercise of judgement in context'.[24] The ethnographic detours should not be viewed as a negative aspect of method, but instead as a contribution to research since the detours can allow the researcher the opportunity to make the study more extensive and critical. My refined, follow-up interview design still allowed me to achieve the interactive conversations among the mother, daughter and myself as well as gain key insight from each participant.

Results

Early on in my conversations with the participants, I noticed several mothers refused to refer to their daughter as an athlete despite heavy involvement in sports and then an opposing view from the daughter that she was indeed an athlete. This early theme about being an athlete versus not an athlete, did not continue throughout the study, but what I did notice continuing was a pattern of disconnection between mother and daughter. I questioned this generational difference between the Baby-Boom-Generation mothers and their Generation Y daughters. I refer to these generational labels as a means of indicating the time period they were born and their resulting age cohort. Most of the mothers were born in the late 1950s and the daughters were born in the mid 1990s. In a study on teenage daughters of 'suburbia', Kenny explains that her white, upper middle class research participants were 'in the process of learning to silence, defer, and misrecognize. Such is the landscape and culture of privilege'.[25] Interestingly, I seemed to hit upon a moment in time when the daughters in my study could be understood as experiencing that particular process of learning, as the reports on youth soccer from mothers and daughters during the extensive, open-ended interviews revealed differences in the two generations. At times the discussions produced parenting moments when mothers expressed a view that encouraged the 'misrecognition' of particular issues.

Quieting, and therefore, misunderstanding Generation Y

Initial interviews, while proving somewhat difficult, turned quite revealing. As noted by Hammersley and Atkinson:

> group discussions may provide considerable insight into participant culture: in other words, what is lost in terms of information may be compensated for by the illumination that the accounts provide into the perspectives and discourse repertoires of those being interviewed.[26]

The disconnection with and sometimes quieting of the daughters that was illuminated in the group interviews was worth examining.

According to Tedlock, 'ethnography involves an ongoing attempt to place specific encounters, events, and understandings into a fuller, more meaningful context'.[27] I made this ongoing attempt during the research process as I incorporated use of cultural studies literature to understand the participants' division. The generational divide evident among my research participants can be analyzed using Lawrence Grossberg's work which highlights that children in the United States today are under attack. According to Grossberg, there is an insidious war against kids plaguing nearly every aspect of their lives; their words and bodies are increasingly stifled, monitored, disciplined and assaulted.[28] This war is a byproduct of the adult population's misguided understanding and resulting fear of Generation Y. I was certainly not observing in my interviews something nearly as extreme as what Grossberg describes, but his focus on division between generations and his use of Giroux's work on youth and politics of culture seems relevant. As Giroux notes, children are being 'othered' to such an extreme that the rest of the population does not identify with them.[29] This places Generation Y (and society on a whole) in great jeopardy as children are seen as 'the risk to democratic public life'.[30] Giroux refers to this as a 'crisis of youth' which needs to be addressed. I was particularly struck by Grossberg's description of a child who explained 'in class, after Columbine, that she understood how someone who was teased mercilessly could snap'.[31] That empathetic child was suspended from school as a result of her comment. This kind of reaction is disturbing. Our society and particularly our educational system should not fear (and additionally punish) this child as a result of hearing her comment. Alternatively, educators should be encouraging the next generation to be sensitive enough to understand the perspective of other kids who may be experiencing far less than the ideal in their school setting causing them to become angry and violent.

The group of mothers and daughters I was studying experienced youth soccer via their social-class habitus as well as within a broader cultural context. I understood these two subgroups of middle-class agents with ultimately differing views of youth soccer as a way to explicate the divide that Giroux describes as existing at a more grand-scale, societal level.[32] By generating discussions about their perspectives on youth soccer and highlighting significant themes surrounding particular social issues such as race and class, my study was an opportunity to hear from at least the middle class portion of a generation that appears to be misunderstood. During the interviews the girls were sensitive and thoughtful in their responses. I had a chance to give these girls a voice and compare their thoughts to those of their older generation mothers.

Following a gendered path

I talked with the girls and their mothers about the differences I had noticed between what girls experience in sport versus what boys experience. In earlier research, I understood boys' upper middle class parents as using their economic and cultural capital to keep their sons specializing in youth soccer in order to pass on upper middle class habitus and to encourage them to stay out of trouble during their high school years.[33] As my research participants from this former study discussed their sons' participation in soccer, I learned that boys were expected and pressured at around the age of 13 to pick one sport (which was often soccer) and then play it year round.[34] These results coincide with Cote, Horton, MacDonald and Wilkes' assessment of the 'specializing years' to be ages 13–15.[35] Specializing in one sport has become more common among today's youth.[36] On the other hand, when researching mothers with *daughters* in soccer, I learned that these middle-class girls take a particular gendered path within sport; they are generally encouraged to participate in a variety of activities instead of specializing.

The girls I spoke with were regularly involved in, not only soccer, but often basketball, lacrosse, swimming, dance and/or softball as well. The mothers and their daughters were both inclined to continue with a variety of activities and sports even into their planned high school experience. This approach to participation in sport is referred to as 'sampling' by Cote, Horton, MacDonald and Wilkes.[37] Cote et al., noted that while early specialization in youth sport is associated with attrition, it is the sampling approach to youth sport that has been linked to the continuation of physical activity into adulthood.[38] By encouraging these girls in this direction, some negative consequences may be avoided such as burn out and injury, while potentially promoting life-long physical activity.[39]

Interesting responses occurred when I asked why they weren't following the same path in sport as boys their age. Mothers indicated a lack of college scholarship opportunities for girls as a reason why girls would not specialize as the boys typically do. Daughters indicated a lack of professional athletic opportunities for girls as the reason why they would not bother with specialization. Sadly, there was no questioning of these perceived differences of inequality. They just discussed them in a matter of fact way; and as a result, specialization in soccer remained preserved for boys.

As I shared with the participants my previous research results about boys, the mothers indicated they understood that parents may use sport to keep boys out of trouble, but they noted that the reason they had their girls involved with soccer was for them to experience teamwork and exercise. The daughters said they were involved to be with friends, make new friends, and exercise. This information supports Strachan, Cote and Deakin's understanding of the psychosocial benefits gained through sampling youth sport activities.[40] These benefits include 'increased intrapersonal skills, the development of prosocial behaviours and personal identity, the ability to connect with diverse peer groups, and the accruement of social capital'.[41] Two quotes that fairly represent participants' responses overall were the following: one mother noted 'Learning to play the sport and becoming a team player I think is critical' while a daughter noted 'my favourite thing is I get to meet new people' [age 11].

The girls indicated participation in youth soccer could have a positive impact on a variety of things, but at the same time recognized problems inherent within youth soccer or the youth sport experience in general.

Mean and violent kids

I intentionally steered some of our broader conversations about sport and school in general towards issues that Generation Y faces such as bullying and school shootings. We briefly talked about some of the news coverage of kids in these situations. As the participants and I discussed the media's portrayal of kids as violent and mean, most participants noted that the negative portrayals were inaccurate since they didn't represent all kids. But in those same discussions, the girls were quite willing to provide stories of mean kids, abuse, and a variety of problems they encountered on the soccer field. They recognized that sport could actually contribute to the production of a mean or violent child. Girls commented that better players were not as nice to players that aren't as good. For example, one said the following 'if they're really good they could think they're better than someone else and start to push people around' [age 13]. On the other hand, the girls believe participation in youth soccer could benefit kids like those portrayed on television or in the news as angry and depressed. They thought the activity would allow these kinds of kids to get some aggression out as well as provide social support through having a caring adult (i.e. coach) in their life and teammates.

Discussing race and class

In discussing racial and social class relations, the mothers spoke of the soccer field as a place where race and class aren't paid any attention. The daughters on the other hand, made comments that indicated they were quite sensitive to the racial and class differences between themselves and other potential players. For example, one daughter said 'We sort of take for granted that we can play sports and you know it's just thought of that everyday that we can play the sport. We get the uniforms and we get taken for the games, but then a lot of people don't have that ability. Like it's you know like travel, travel is pretty expensive. And a lot of people who are good enough to play travel are even better than the people playing travel [but they] just can't do it' [age 13]. Whereas the following type of comment was common among the mothers 'When they're out on the field, they are all the same cause they are playing the game'. The daughters recognized limitations social class places on experiences within sport, whereas the older generation treated youth soccer as a panacea.

According to Kenny in her analysis of girls in a white, middle and upper middle class, suburban community, 'race neutrality is prized over specific racial identities, by sidestepping race the community actually positions itself and its offspring firmly within a culture of racial privilege'.[42] The mothers in my study claimed the girls didn't notice race out on the soccer field. Clearly they said this with the assumption that this was a good thing. They seemed to be promoting the somewhat dangerous and controversial 'colorblind' perspective.[43] As noted by Hughes in his analysis of corporate culture and race within the management of the National Basketball Association, 'colorblindness' is problematic. This perspective leads to 'failing to reflect on – let alone challenge – the larger social and historical causes of racism from which dominant White interests continue to benefit tacitly'.[44] On the other hand, the daughters' comments indicated they had not ingrained the racial neutrality that Kenny recognized in the suburban community.[45] The girls indicated they recognized the possibility of different experiences a player might encounter due to their race. Many of the girls discussed how they felt it would be difficult for a player who wasn't Caucasian to come out for one of their soccer teams. As one girl said 'they don't feel welcome' [age 13]. Most of the girls offered ideas on how to make a minority player feel included. For example, one of the girls said the following:

> I think that the parents and the coaches should be mature enough to be able to handle that [racial relations] and be able to say, not that they get special treatment, but make sure like they fit in pretty well with everyone else and try to find them a good passing buddy or try to find another person who plays the same position and maybe they could help them out if they need help or that person with different color skin could help someone else out. [age 12]

In regard to social class, again the thought by most mothers was that the youth soccer experience was an equalizer. They discussed how class would not be noticed by the girls. For example, mothers commented that all the girls wear the required soccer uniform which they believed would prevent the girls from recognizing class difference through clothes and labels. Despite these uniforms, the girls claimed that they were still aware of class differences since they could recognize the kind of footwear other girls wore on the soccer field as an indicator of wealth. In addition, the girls definitely noticed a difference among the various levels of youth soccer and how the level might indicate a difference in a player's social class. One girl commented, 'I think that wealthier people do travel-soccer more than non-travel soccer. Maybe because of reputation and they wanna make their kids have reputation' [age 13]. Here, this child clearly recognizes the desired social capital gained through involvement in this particular level of youth soccer.

What kids want adults to know

In order to allow the girls in my study to speak, I had to, as I mentioned above, design a particular style of interviewing. And during these discussions I guided the girls to the various topics of gender, violence, race and class with the intention of really hearing what they had to say. But I wanted to make sure they had an opportunity to say what was important to them. So I posed the simple question 'What should adults know, that they don't know?' The girls responded by saying adults take youth soccer way too seriously. The girls wanted parents and coaches to stop pressuring them while they were on the soccer field.

Conclusion

This study reinforces an understanding of class-specific production of children's lifestyle preferences, bodies, and social connections as it serves as an additional example of a group of American, middle-class parents steering their children in the direction of soccer. More significantly, my results highlight girls' experiences in youth soccer and begin to explicate a generational divide in the understanding of youth soccer and larger social forces connected to the youth sport experience.

My research was an opportunity to engage these girls, get them talking, and start to uncover who the children of Generation Y are. I believe it is through these means that we can understand additional groups of children, and therefore as a result, likely not fear youth as different, violent, expendable, or any number of things Grossberg recognized within the current war against kids.[46] I found it interesting that the girls from this study, who are already aware of a variety of social issues and their impact on sport, and who are out there to have fun, are subjected to the pressure produced by the adults in their lives. The girls described how horrible it felt. They were both emotionally and physically drained by this generational divide, which was a disconnection between themselves and adults about what was important. I conclude with the understanding that we are actually misunderstanding kids and their experiences, thereby producing the disconnection with this younger generation as well as the resulting fear of them.

Future research should further explore the push for girls to approach sport through sampling as opposed to specializing and the resultant impact on the ability to gain social, cultural or economic capital. Different social class and racial groupings of parents and children need to be heard through similar studies. Additionally, there should be continued research into the different generational perspectives on youth soccer experiences.

Disclosure statement

No potential conflict of interest was reported by the author.

Notes

1. Andrews, 'Contextualizing Suburban Soccer'; Swanson, 'Soccer Fields'.
2. Andrews et al., 'Soccer's Racial Frontier', 264.
3. Andrews, 'Contextualizing Suburban Soccer'; Swanson, 'Soccer Fields'.
4. Andrews et al., 'Soccer's Racial Frontier'.
5. Lareau, 'Invisible Inequality', 748.
6. Ibid.; Lareau, *Unequal Childhoods*.
7. Lareau, 'Invisible Inequality', 748.
8. DeLuca, 'Swim Club'; DeLuca, 'Submersed in Social Segregation'; Swanson, 'Complicating the "Soccer Mom"'; Swanson, 'Soccer Fields'; Light and Kirk, 'Australian Cultural Capital'; Andrews, 'Contextualizing Suburban Soccer' and Zwick and Andrews, 'The Suburban Soccer Field'.
9. Swanson, 'Complicating the "Soccer Mom"'; Swanson, 'Soccer Fields'.
10. Bourdieu, 'Sport'; Bourdieu, *Distinction*; Bourdieu, 'The Forms of Capital'; Bourdieu, *Language*; and Bourdieu, *The Field of Cultural Production*.
11. Swanson, 'Complicating the "Soccer Mom"'; Swanson, 'Soccer Fields'.
12. Zwick, 'Sport at the Intersection'.
13. Bourdieu, *Distinction*.
14. Ibid., 20.
15. Ibid., 209–11.
16. Ibid., 211.
17. Singleton, Straits, and Straits, *Approaches to Social Research*, 164.
18. Light and Kirk, 'Australian Cultural Capital'; Chin, 'Sixth Grade Madness'; Tardy, 'But I Am A Good Mom'; Andrews, 'Contextualizing Suburban Soccer' and Shilling, 'Schooling'.
19. Van Maanen, *Tales of the Field*.
20. Fontana and Frey, 'The Interview', 712.
21. Hammersley and Atkinson, *Ethnography*, 144.
22. Bourdieu and Wacquant, 'An Invitation'; Wynne, *Leisure*; Alexander, 'Performance Ethnography' and Stake, 'Qualitative Case Studies'.
23. Wynne, *Leisure*, 1–2.
24. Hammersley and Atkinson, *Ethnography*, 23.
25. Kenny, *Daughters of Suburbia*, 47.
26. Hammersley and Atkinson, *Ethnography*, 147.
27. Tedlock, 'Ethnography', 455.
28. Grossberg, 'Cultural Studies'.
29. Giroux, *Stealing Innocence*; Giroux, 'Public Pedagogy'; Giroux, 'The Abandoned Generation'.
30. Giroux, 'Public Pedagogy', 11; Stephens, 'Children'.
31. Grossberg, 'Cultural Studies', 99.
32. Giroux, 'The Abandoned Generation'.
33. Swanson, 'Complicating the "Soccer Mom"'; Swanson, 'Soccer Fields'.
34. Swanson, 'Soccer Fields'.
35. Cote et al., 'The Benefits of Sampling'.
36. Strachan, Cote, and Deakin, 'Specializers'.
37. Cote et al., 'The Benefits of Sampling'.
38. Ibid.
39. Ibid.
40. Strachan, Cote, and Deakin, 'Specializers'.
41. Ibid., 78.
42. Kenny, *Daughters of Suburbia*, 17.
43. Hughes, 'Managing Black Guys'.
44. Ibid., 178.
45. Kenny, *Daughters of Suburbia*.
46. Grossberg, 'Cultural Studies'.

References

Alexander, B.K. 'Performance Ethnography: The Reenacting and Inciting of Culture'. In *The Sage Handbook of Qualitative Research*, ed. N.K. Denzin and Y.S. Lincoln, 411–42. Thousand Oaks, CA: Sage, 2005.

Andrews, D.L. 'Contextualizing Suburban Soccer: Consumer Culture, Lifestyle Differentiation and Suburban America'. *Culture, Sport, Society* 2, no. 3 (1999): 31–53.

Andrews, D.L., R. Pitter, D. Zwick, and D. Ambrose. 'Soccer's Racial Frontier: Sport and the Segregated Suburbanization of Contemporary America'. In *Entering the Field: New Perspectives on World Football*, ed. G. Armstrong and R. Giulianotti, 261–81. Oxford: Berg, 1997.

Bourdieu, P. *Distinction: A Social Critique of the Judgement of Taste*. Trans. R. Nice. Cambridge, MA: Harvard University Press, 1984.

Bourdieu, P. *The Field of Cultural Production: Essays on Art and Literature*. UK: Polity Press, 1993.

Bourdieu, P. 'The Forms of Capital'. In *Handbook of Theory and Research for the Sociology of Education*, ed. J.G. Richardson, 241–57. New York, NY: Greenwood Press, 1986.

Bourdieu, P. *Language and Symbolic Power*. Cambridge, MA: Harvard University Press, 1991.

Bourdieu, P. 'Sport and Social Class'. *Social Science Information* 17, no. 6 (1978): 819–40.

Bourdieu, P., and L. Wacquant. *An Invitation to Reflexive Sociology*. Chicago: University of Chicago Press, 1992.

Chin, T. '"Sixth Grade Madness": Parental Emotion Work in the Private High School Application Process'. *Journal of Contemporary Ethnography* 29, no. 2 (2000): 124–63.

Cote, J., S. Horton, D. MacDonald, and S. Wilkes. 'The Benefits of Sampling Sports During Childhood'. *Physical and Health Education Journal* 74, no. 4 (2009): 6–11.

DeLuca, J.R. 'Submersed in Social Segregation: The (re)production of Social Capital through Swim Club Membership'. *Journal of Sport & Social Issues* 37, no. 4 (2013): 340–63.

DeLuca, J.R. 'Swim Club Membership and the Reproduction of Happy, Healthy Children'. *Qualitative Research in Sport, Exercise and Health* 5, no. 1 (2013): 58–79.

Fontana, A., and J.H. Frey. 'The Interview: From Neutral Stance to Political Involvement'. In *The Handbook of Qualitative Research*, ed. N.K. Denzin and Y.S. Lincoln, 695–728. Thousand Oaks, CA: Sage, 2005.

Giroux, H.A. *The Abandoned Generation: Democracy beyond the Culture of Fear*. New York: Palgrave Macmillan, 2003.

Giroux, H.A. 'Public Pedagogy and the Responsibility of Intellectuals: Youth, Littleton, and the Loss of Innocence'. *JAC: A Journal of Composition Theory* 20, no. 1 (2000): 9–42.

Giroux, H.A. *Stealing Innocence: Corporate Culture's War on Children*. New York, NY: Palgrave, 2000.

Grossberg, L. 'Cultural Studies, the War against Kids, and the Re-becoming of U.S. Modernity'. In *Contesting Empire Globalizing Dissent: Cultural Studies after 9/11*, ed. N.K. Denzin and M.D. Giardina, 95–120. Boulder, CO: Paradigm, 2007.

Hammersley, M., and P. Atkinson. *Ethnography: Principles in Practice*. London: Routledge, 1995.

Hughes, G. 'Managing Black Guys: Representation, Corporate Culture, and the NBA'. *Sociology of Sport Journal* 21, no. 2 (2004): 163–84.

Kenny, L.D. *Daughters of Suburbia: Growing up White, Middle Class, and Female*. London: Rutgers University Press, 2000.

Lareau, A. 'Invisible Inequality: Social Class and Childrearing in Black Families and White Families'. *American Sociological Review* 67, no. 5 (2002): 747–76.

Lareau, A. *Unequal Childhoods: Class, Race, and Family Life*. Berkeley: University of California Press, 2003.

Light, R., and D. Kirk. 'Australian Cultural Capital – Rugby's Social Meaning: Physical Assets, Social Advantage and Independent Schools'. *Culture, Sport and Society* 4, no. 3 (2001): 81–98.

Shilling, C. 'Schooling and the Production of Physical Capital'. *Discourse* 13, no. 1 (1992): 1–19.

Singleton, R.A., B.C. Straits, and M.M. Straits. *Approaches to Social Research*. New York: Oxford University Press, 1993.

Stake, R.E. 'Qualitative Case Studies'. In *The Sage Handbook of Qualitative Research*, ed. N.K. Denzin and Y.S. Lincoln, 443–66. Thousand Oaks, CA: Sage, 2005.

Stephens, S. 'Children and the Politics of Culture in "Late Capitalism"'. In *Children and the Politics of Culture*, ed. S. Stephens, 3–50. Princeton, NJ: Princeton University Press, 1995.

Strachan, L., J. Cote, and J. Deakin. 'Specializers versus Samplers in Youth Sport: Comparing Experiences and Outcomes'. *The Sport Psychologist* 23, no. 1 (2009): 77–92.

Swanson, L. 'Complicating the "Soccer Mom"'. *Research Quarterly for Exercise and Sport.* 80, no. 2 (2009): 345–54.

Swanson, L. 'Soccer Fields of Cultural [re]-production: Creating "Good Boys" in Suburban America'. *Sociology of Sport Journal* 26, no. 3 (2009): 404–24.

Tardy, R.W. '"But I Am a Good Mom": The Social Construction of Motherhood through Health-Care Conversations'. *Journal of Contemporary Ethnography* 29, no. 4 (2000): 433–73.

Tedlock, B. 'Ethnography and Ethnographic Representation'. In *The Handbook of Qualitative research*, ed. N.K. Denzin and Y.S. Lincoln, 455–86. Thousand Oaks, CA: Sage, 2000.

Van Maanen, J. *Tales of the Field: On Writing Ethnography.* Chicago: University of Chicago Press, 1988.

Wynne, D. *Leisure, Lifestyle, and the New Middle Class: A Case Study.* London: Routledge, 1998.

Zwick, D. 'Sport at the Intersection of Class, Race, and Space: An Ethnographic Case Analysis of Youth Soccer in Memphis, TN'. Masters thesis, 1997.

Zwick, D., and D.L. Andrews. 'The Suburban Soccer Field: Sport and America's Culture of Privilege'. In *Football Cultures and Identities*, ed. G. Armstrong and R. Giulianotti, 211–22. London: Macmillan Press, 1999.

Exploring the everyday realities of grass-roots football coaching: towards a relational perspective

Paul Potrac, Lee Nelson and Jimmy O'Gorman

Department of Sport and Physical Activity, Edge Hill University, Ormskirk, UK

While scholars have increasingly engaged with the (micro)political and emotional experiences of coaches in professional and semi-professional football, little attention has been given to grass-roots coaches' understandings of these issues. The aim of this paper is to outline one possible research agenda that could contribute to the development of a rich and increasingly nuanced understanding of the everyday realities of being a grass-roots football coach. In particular, we consider (volunteer) coaches' participation in grass-roots football to be an inherently relational endeavour. Following the presentation of a creative fiction that is based upon our shared experiences of being grass-roots football coaches, we then illustrate how relational thinking might be productively applied to exploring the social, (micro)political and emotional features of grass-roots football coaching.

Introduction

In recent years, scholars of coaching science have increasingly sought to understand some of the gritty, interactive and problematic realities of coaching.[1] Such inquiry has highlighted how coaching involves not only 'intensive personal interactions'[2], with a range of individuals, but also how coaches operate in settings where 'goals are inherently challenging, variables within the process are many and dynamic, and intended outcomes can never be a foregone conclusion'.[3] With regard to the latter, it has been increasingly suggested that coaching contexts can be characterised by poor coordination and ideological diversity[4] and can be 'riven with actual or potential conflict'.[5]

Alongside these efforts to investigate the frequently (micro)political nature of coaching, there has also been a call for scholars of coaching science to shine an investigative light onto the emotions that coaches experience.[6] In comparison with other fields of inquiry that have established concerted lines of research into the place of emotions in social, organisational and pedagogical relationships, the coaching literature has tended to be largely free of emotionality.[7] This state of affairs is somewhat problematic, as it is arguably impossible for coaches to separate 'affectivity from judgement' and 'feeling from perception'[8] (cf. Nias 1996, 296; Potrac et al. 2013; Nelson et al. 2013). Indeed, by continuing to ignore the emotional features of coaching, we run the risk of further reinforcing some of the strangely inhuman accounts of coaching that have historically predominated in the literature base.[9]

Importantly, the evolving lines of (micro)political and emotional inquiries in coaching have increasingly highlighted how coaches are not free from the constraints and opportunities generated through their relationships with others.[10] While such developments are to be welcomed, much of the available coaching literature examining these topics in the context of football has been situated in professional and semi-professional football settings. In comparison with the work undertaken in these environments, little attention has been given to the experiences of volunteer coaches involved in grass-roots football. This situation is somewhat surprising for two reasons. The first relates to the high number of volunteer coaches who are relied upon to provide high-quality sporting experiences to both children and adults,[11] while the second is concerned with neoliberal and rationalistic trends in sporting organisations[12] that expect volunteers to adopt increasingly professional practices, manage larger workloads and subject themselves to detailed scrutiny and evaluation.[13] Indeed, it is rather unfortunate that we continue to know relatively little about how grass-roots football coaches understand these realities in practice and, relatedly, the ways in which their experiences might impact their decisions to continue their respective participation as coaches.

Given the paucity of literature on this topic, the aim of this paper is to outline one possible research perspective that could contribute to the development of richer and more nuanced understandings of the everyday realities of grass-roots football coaching than currently exists. In particular, we consider the possible merits of viewing volunteer coaches' participation in grass-roots football to be an inherently relational endeavour. In order to achieve this aim, the paper is divided into four sections. Following this introduction, a brief overview of the key tenets of relational sociology is provided. The focus then shifts to explore how we might better consider the inherently relational demands of grass-roots football coaching. Here, a narrative fiction addressing the experience of Chris, a grass-roots football coach, is initially presented to support our case. This is then followed by a relational interpretation of the events, experiences and emotions presented within the story. Finally, we conclude the paper by considering the utility of conceptualising grass-roots football coaching as a relational activity.

Relational sociology: a brief overview

Relational sociologists are primarily concerned with understanding social life in terms of individuals' relationships with, as well as interconnections to one another.[14] Specifically, this intellectual project argues that all social phenomena are processes that are 'constituted by flows of action and interaction, which operate immanently to the life of individuals rather than on a separate order of reality'.[15] As a way of knowing, then, relational sociology is based upon the fundamental premise that social actors are 'always-already enmeshed in relations of interdependency with others and cannot be understood, even theoretically, apart from their relational contexts'.[16] Similarly, Crossley[17] suggested that an individual's thoughts, feelings and actions are not only continuously 'oriented to other actions within the networks in which' he (or she) is embedded. Their reactions and responses to these events are 'influenced by their impact' on them and 'the opportunities and constraints afforded' to them within this particular network of social actors.[18]

At the heart of the relational enterprise is the desire to overcome the dualisms of individual–society and agency–structure that have traditionally dominated the sociological landscape.[19] Researchers employing a relational approach seek to do this 'by conceptualising both individuals and the larger formations in which they participate (like collectives, institutions, social systems) as belonging to the same order of reality, a relational order'.[20] In this regard, social structures, systems and discourses are viewed as the products of relations that exist between interdependent social actors, while individual agency is always located in and through social relations.[21] Thus, individual and society are considered to be clearly identifiable but ultimately inextricably interconnected features of social life, rather than being two separate entities that exist on entirely different planes of reality.[22] Power and identity are also understood in this fashion. In this respect, power is not viewed as a property that some individuals can have more or less off. Instead, it is operationalized as the effect of a network of relationships and interconnections between people.[23] Similarly, identity is also considered to be the effect of the fluid and dynamic processes of identification and differentiation, as opposed to being a 'defining characteristic that each individual carries around with him or her'.[24]

While relational ideas and thoughts can be traced back to a variety of acclaimed and foundational scholars (e.g. Hegel, Marx, Simmel, Elias, Bourdieu, Latour and Foucault), relational sociology, as a clearly demarcated line of academic scholarship, is considered by many[25] to have been greatly influenced by Emirbayer's[26] seminal work entitled 'Manifesto for a relational sociology'. However, rather than being characterised as a uniform and homogenous school of social thought, relational sociology is comprised of various positions and perspectives that differ in terms of how they address fundamental questions regarding what relations are, as well as how they might be understood and investigated.[27] In this paper, we principally drew upon Crossley's[28] thesis on relational sociology, as it closely aligns with the lead authors' largely interactionist inspired roots and beliefs about the nature of social life. We do not, of course, advocate that his work is somehow the 'best', or indeed only, way of understanding the relational nature of grass-roots football coaching. Instead, we believe that it represents one productive means for elevating and refining our scholarly understanding of this little understood and rarely examined aspect of our social world.

Specifically, we were inspired by Crossley's discussion of the importance of social network analysis for symbolic interactionist theorising, and how the tenets of his argument might help to advance our theoretical reading of this creative fiction. Central to Crossley's argument[29] is that doing so might help extend the significance of networks in symbolic interactionist theorising by moving it from the periphery to the centre of this school of sociological thought and explanation. Indeed, his discussions about networks offer symbolic interactionist-inspired researchers new ways of theorising about 'social structure', as well as of thinking about the micro–macro divide. For Crossley,[30] the coming together of these two schools of thought is possible, as there is a natural affinity between the focus and claims of symbolic interactionism and the concepts of social network theory. While he acknowledges that the idea of networks is implicit in the writing of classic symbolic interactionist theorists (e.g. Cooley, Mead, Blumer and Goffman), he suggested that a more pronounced and explicit focus on networks provides symbolic interactionist thinking with an inroad into contemporary debates about complexity, especially those which seek to demonstrate 'that global patterns of order and organization can be explained by reference to finely tuned localized interaction'.[31] Crossley further explained that 'networks are what link the millions of actors in a complex structure' and, in this respect, they also provide 'the link, conceptually, between small groups and large populations', thus bridging the micro and macro divide.[32] Thinking about networks, then, encourages symbolic interactionists to extend beyond relational dyads by giving greater importance to the multitude of interactions that occur within a particular network of people or groups of networks.

The use of creative fiction

In making our case for the development of a relational understanding of grass-roots football coaching, we utilised fictional writing.[33] Unlike traditional empirical forms of inquiry, creative fiction is not based on systematically gathered data or the provision of a so-called 'true' representation of others' experiences.[34] Indeed, rather than being concerned with accurately representing specific people, events and places, fictional writing uses literary, fiction and narrative devices to highlight 'certain aspects of lived experience'.[35] These accounts are, however, developed with the aim of doing more than just telling an interesting story. Instead, they are often produced with the express purpose of stimulating and informing further analysis, discussion and inquiry.[36] For example, Beames and Pike[37] argued that this form of inquiry could valuably assist social scientists' efforts to 'heighten our perception of the [relational] experiences of others in a way that may help us to reflect on our practice and experiences'. This is also a position strongly advocated by Barone,[38] who, in defending the place of creative fiction within the social sciences, argued that it should only be deployed 'in the service of a legitimate research purpose'. In terms of the mission of this paper, our aim was to use fictional writing as a stimulus for evolving the development of a more critical knowledge of grass-roots football coaching than has been achieved to date.[39] In particular, we wish to encourage researchers, practitioners and coach educators to think relationally and, more specifically, to consider grass-roots football coaching from a relational perspective.

The story presented below is based on the amalgamation of the many years that we have, respectively, spent as grass-roots football coaches and as coach learners in this context.[40] As such, like the work of Beames and Pike,[41] the story we present could be considered to be a 'sociology of witness'.[42] When constructing the narrative, we drew upon various events that we participated in and/or observed while working as grass-roots football coaches.[43] Similar to Jones,[44] we sought to create fictional incidents that resembled, as closely as possible, the relational nature of the dilemmas and issues that we encountered in the field. Indeed, it is our understandings of perceived important events, individuals and emotions that provided the cornerstones of this story.[45] Ultimately, we hope that by constructing Chris' story in this way, we may be able to guide the reader into some of 'the previously unexplored depths' of grass-roots football coaching and thus enhance our critical understanding of the social 'life found there'.[46] Our appeal to the reader is, then, based upon a recognition that the issues considered herein not only happen in grass-roots football coaching, but that they have also happened to people like us.[47]

Chris' story

(2nd September) The new best way

Feeling excited! We (the coaches) were introduced to, Barry, an FA Coach Mentor this evening. He will be spending two months working in the club with us to improve our coaching. He introduced the new FA vision for grassroots coaching and the sporting experience that is offered to young players. Geoff, the club secretary, asked if I wanted to put my name down to be one of the coaches that the mentor spent some on 1-on-1 time with. I couldn't say no really, not least because of the support that Geoff has given me over the years that I've been at the club. And how could anyone realistically say no to such help in grassroots football. We've just never had anything like this before. As I watched the mentor deliver a practical demonstration session, I couldn't help but be impressed. His session was fast paced, exciting, and he really seemed to know his stuff. The players certainly seemed to enjoy the session too. Beaming smiles were evident across their faces as they left the practice field. I'd love to be able to put on sessions like his for my team. My time with Barry starts next week. I can't say that I'm not a bit nervous about him coming to watch me coach, but I think I can learn and develop a great deal from this opportunity.

(10th September) Being watched

Well, that was intense! I've never really had anyone of Barry's standing and expertise watch me coach before. It felt like I had a swarm of butterflies in my stomach for the whole time. He seemed like a warm and pleasant person though, which helped a lot. The conversation afterwards was really challenging too. He got me to think about 'what' I was trying to achieve and 'why' I coached like I did. One of the outcomes from the meeting was to try and reduce the number of line drills that I use in my sessions and to get into more free flowing game type situations. Barry gave me a couple of annotated session plans to take home and work with. The more I looked at his session plans and the reasoning behind them the more disappointed I became with my own knowledge. I'm going to try and deliver one of these games like activities in my session next week. I've never done anything like that before. Half of me is determined to try it, but the other half is worried about being able to do it well. What happens if it all goes wrong? What will Barry think of me? What will the parents and players think of me? It's all so public; no private rehearsals. My throat felt increasingly dry as I sipped on my coffee.

(17th September) This isn't easy

Ouch! That didn't go as well as I hoped it would. The line drills went well, but I didn't realise just how hard the game type part of the session would be for me. It felt completely alien. I think it was clear to all watching that I wasn't in control of that part of the session. I tried to exude an appearance of calmness, of being in control, but everything seemed to go by in a bit of a blur. The players seemed to be all over the place and it didn't look as organised as I like to think my sessions normally do. I could see some of the parents weren't buying in to what was happening by the confused and disgruntled looks on their faces. As I packed up the balls and cones, I overheard James' dad ask him what we did in the game type activity. James said that it was about learning how to make decisions as player, but his dad said it looked like a complete mess to him! I wanted to wince, as his comments cut to my core. Barry and some of the other parents had overheard what was said. I could feel them watching me, waiting to see what I would say and do. I felt I had to respond. So I approached James' dad and told him that I was committed to the new activities, that I was doing my best to give James and the other boys a good experience and help them learn, and that I'd appreciate his support. I tried to do it with a smile on my face but I didn't really enjoy the encounter. My increasingly tightening chest, flushed face, and sweaty palms were clear indicators of that. Up until then, I always felt that I'd got on with him. I don't really want to start falling out with anyone.

Credit to Barry though. He was really supportive as we reflected on events over a cup of tea in the club house. It's all about practice and perseverance, apparently. His broad and warm smile help eased some of the inner turmoil that I was experiencing. I could feel the tension and anxiety flushing out of my body as our conversation went on. He told me that some of the parents had commented positively in terms of me trying new things in the session. That also helped to heal my deflated ego a little. But as I drove home afterwards the coward in me came to the fore. I wanted to say that I wasn't good enough to coach in the way he was exploring with me; that he should invest his time with some of the better coaches at the club. Of course, that was all camouflage for the truth. Could I really say that I felt uncomfortable and didn't relish the challenge to Barry, Geoff, and some of the supportive parents and players? That I just wanted to stick with the comfortably familiar because that suited me the most? No, not really. I can't help but think participating in this scheme has upset the normal balance of things.

(28th September) Hope and fear

Just back from attending a region FA course that Barry recommended. It was really stimulating. There were lots of practical demonstrations, clear and understandable explanations from the course tutors, and lots of useful resources to take home and consider. It confirmed all the work that I've been doing with Barry. That said, it has also reinforced my own views of my newly found limitations and weaknesses as a coach. I can't help but feel that I've got lots of learning and improving to do; something that I have to do whilst others watch me.

(17th October) Perseverance and more perseverance!

Well, Barry certainly wasn't wrong with the perseverance thing! I'm still including one 25 min game type activity in my sessions and I think I'm improving (very slowly). I still feel uncomfortable with this part of the session and I'm not convinced that I've won over the doubters on the sidelines. Barry is happy that I'm sticking with it though and does everything he can to help me. At the game on Sunday, I overheard him talking to James' dad about why it was beneficial for the children that I continue to include game and problem solving activities in the training sessions. I know I should be doing these things. The reasons are strikingly obvious from the reading and the work that I've done with Barry. But to say my enthusiasm is waning, is an understatement. The nagging doubts about my ability and the anxiety that accompany every training session are draining. I've had enough of the aching 'butterflies' in my stomach, my racing heart, the nervous sweats, and the feeling of gloom that can surround my coaching. I don't want to tell Barry and Geoff. I don't want them to think that I'm unhappy. But it's hard making myself continually look enthusiastic in their company. What would they think of me if they knew about all of this? I used to enjoy coaching at Erewhon football club. What's more I thought I was quite good at it too. Coaching was my escape from work; a leisure activity. Part of me agrees with James' dad, I wish things could just go back to how they were before the mentoring programme. Another part of me feels ashamed and angered by these thoughts, as I want to develop my coaching and put on good sessions for the kids. I want to do the right things and be seen to be a good coach. And that means not putting me first, doesn't it? It's Barry's last session with me next week and I'm worried what I'll do after he is gone. I don't know whether to stick or twist. Whoever said that change is never easy, was definitely right!

Postscript

After several aborted attempts, I finally dialled the number. As the phone rang, I could feel beads of sweat forming on my palms and my heart raced. 'Hello, Barry. It's Chris. Sorry to call you so late, but I wondered if you had a few minutes to talk?' It was time to be honest with him; to share my inner most feelings and worries with him. No more pretending. I didn't know what this would achieve, but I just felt like I should and, importantly, I wanted to.

Discussion

In making sense of how Chris' thoughts, feelings and actions were grounded in his relations with others, we drew upon Crossley's[48] discussion of 'networks'. In his role as coach of the Erewhon under 10s football team, Chris was required to regularly interact with club officials, the players and their respective parents and guardians. His decision to participate in the mentoring programme meant that he was also expected to attend workshops organised by employees of the FA and interact with a mentor deployed by this organisation. When considered in this way, we would contend that Chris was operating within and across two social networks. While these social networks might be analytically distinguishable (i.e. interactions with social actors from the FA and with his football club), the above narrative suggests that, on a personal level, Chris' concurrent involvement in these networks of relationships meant that he inevitably experienced them in concert and/or in conflict.[49] Indeed, Crossley[50] makes a compelling case for how symbolic interactionist thought might benefit from understandings taken from social network analysis.

While symbolic interactionist thought recognises that actors are tethered to other actors, social network analysis posits that 'these ties form patterns or structure that, in turn, constitute social structures' and that these social structures 'generate opportunities and constraints both in general, for all of those involved, and more specifically for those who occupy particular positions in them'.[51] In the context of Chris' story, Crossley's[52] discussion of networks permits us to understand how the practice guidelines of a macro-organisation, in this case the FA, were relayed to the micro-level environments of its grass-roots coaches. His attendance at FA workshops and subsequent discussions with an assigned regional FA mentor permitted Chris to gain a more detailed appreciation of how his national governing body of sport ultimately wanted him to perform his role. In effect, Chris had entered a new network and was being socialised into the social norms and expectations of the FA through his interactions with its employees. Chris took these guidelines back to his existing sporting network, namely his football club, and started to enact them, despite holding some personal reservations. These concerns focused not only on his beliefs about his ability to cope with the demands of coaching in a different way, but also on his doubts about how various stakeholders at the club might view and react to his changing coaching practice.

Here, we might also usefully draw on the work of Kelchtermans and Ballet[53] and Kelchtermans[54] to better understand why Chris endeavoured to implement the FAs guidelines for practice, as it could be contended that his decision to do so was (micro)politically driven. While originally generated through his analysis of teachers working in Flanders, we believe that Kelchtermans' theorising has considerable utility for understanding the experiences and practices of grass-roots coaches like Chris. Central to Kelchtermans' work is what he termed the *personal interpretive framework* (i.e. a set of cognitions that an individual uses to make sense of his or her particular practice setting, as well as his or her own actions within it). According to Kelchtermans' analysis, the personal interpretive framework comprises two interrelated features. These are an individual's *professional self-understanding* (i.e. the understanding that an individual may have of his or her 'self' at a particular moment in time and how ongoing interactions and experiences influence an individual's sense of 'self') and his or her *subjective educational theory* (i.e. the personal system of knowledge and beliefs that an individual uses to guide his or her practice).

Kelchtermans' exploration of the career stories of teachers led him to suggest that an individual's professional self-understanding is made up of five components. These are *self-image* (i.e. an individual's image of himself or herself as a practitioner), *self-esteem* (i.e. an individual's perception of how well, or not, he or she is performing), *job motivation* (i.e. the drives that make a person choose and continue to practice), *task perception* (i.e. the practitioner's deeply held beliefs about what constitutes 'good' practice) and *future perspective* (i.e. how an individual sees himself or herself as a practitioner in the years ahead). Importantly, Kelchtermans considered an individual's self-understanding in each of these areas also to be influenced by an actor's perception of how other people view him or her in a particular role. That is, an individual's professional sense of self is enmeshed with his or her relations and interconnections to others. While for analytical purposes Kelchtermans' distinguishes between a person's *professional self-understanding* and *subjective educational theory*, it is important to acknowledge that he recognises that an individual's reading of a particular encounter or event 'always implies both the self-understanding and the subjective educational theory'.[55]

When considering Chris' narrative in light of Kelchtermans' theorising, we would contend that his engagement in a formal mentoring programme, while informative, exposed him to ideas and individuals that ultimately led Chris to experience what Kelchtermans'[56] refers to as *vulnerability*, especially as it related to his ability to prove his pedagogical effectiveness to others in his social network. His engagement in these learning and development activities introduced him to ways of thinking and practising that directly challenged aspects of his *subjective educational theory* about coaching and, as such, caused him to question not only his understanding of 'good' coaching, but also his sense of 'self' as a practitioner. Indeed, Chris increasingly questioned his beliefs, practices and motivations for coaching. In terms of his *professional self-understanding* then, his interactions with Barry and the (FA) workshop not only led Chris to question his *task perception* and *subjective educational theory*, but it also had a significant influence on his *self-image* and *self-esteem*. These negative consequences only worsened when he increasingly questioned his ability to effectively elicit desired pedagogical outcomes.

While Chris questioned his ability to deliver new approaches to teaching and learning in his coaching, he was reluctant to share his concerns with his mentor for fear of the repercussions that might ensue and the impact these could have for his *future prospects*. Instead, he chose to conceal his thoughts on this topic from his mentor coach and openly defended the FA's preferred approach when engaging in discussions with those players and parents who were disgruntled with his new coaching practices. In this regard, he felt that it was important not to be seen as questioning the FA's directives, as he was concerned that such behaviours might have consequences for him if they were relayed to, or observed by, his mentor (i.e. Barry) and the club administrators (e.g. Geoff), especially given his understanding of the investment that these individuals had made in assisting his development as a coach. Relatedly, Chris was also wary about how some of his players and their parents, who were supportive of his new approach to coaching, might judge his questioning of the advice of an organisation as prestigious and influential as the FA. Importantly, Kelchtermans'[57] work helps to illuminate how Chris' professional self-understanding was influenced not only by individual self-perception, but also by the responses and messages that others in his network of relations (e.g. parents, players, administrators and mentors) mirrored, or he thought might mirror, back to him. It was clear that Chris considered the feedback of those who supported his new coaching practices (e.g. his mentor, the FA, club administrators and various parents and players) to matter more than those who did not (e.g. James's dad). Chris' efforts to obtain and sustain positive regard from various others in the club setting could, then, bevery much understood as a 'politics of identity'.[58]

Relatedly, Chris' story also highlighted how his engagements in his network of relationships within the football club setting were simultaneously emotional and embodied in nature. Indeed, arguably, he experienced a variety of emotions and sensations that grass-roots football coaches might experience in their everyday practice. These included, but are not limited to, guilt, anxiety, fear, excitement and frustration. In drawing on the work of Heidegger,[59] Crossley[60] argued that 'emotion is not something that is turned on and off, such that we are sometimes emotional and other times not'. While many of our routine interactions might seem affectively neutral then, a relational perspective reminds us that neutrality is an emotional hue in itself.[61] Indeed, emotion is, as Crossley[62] noted, 'a permanent dimension of our being-in-the-world and being-towards-others'.

Of particular interest here is how Chris' emotional and embodied experiences and reactions might be understood 'to do with social relations and interdependencies between embodied persons' rather than being 'things that were internal to the individual and his or her biological constitution'.[63] For example, it could be suggested that Chris' anxieties regarding his ability to deliver his coaching sessions in a different way were produced in his various social (and power) relations with Barry, Geoff, the players and their parents. Indeed, his anxiety arguably stemmed from his perception of actual, or the potential for, damaged or disordered social interactions and relationships in the club setting.[64] Equally, his concerns about what these individuals thought about him, his choices and his actions were clearly not without feeling. In this regard, he experienced a variety of physical sensations, which included an increased heart rate, sweaty palms, a gloomy mood and 'butterflies' in his stomach.[65] From our perspective, such relational thinking has considerable potential in helping us to develop accounts of grass-roots football coaching that better illuminate how practice 'is to do with flesh and blood bodies and selves, actively bound up in power relations and interdependencies, whose embodied expressions and feelings are primarily the outcome of those relations'.[66]

A further feature to consider here is how Chris not only frequently concealed his true thoughts from his mentor and others at the football club, but also often chose not to reveal those emotions that accompanied his experiences. Instead, Chris elected to convey the emotions that he perceived that his mentor coach and the various key contextual stakeholders at his club expected of him. Here, Chris' experiences might be interpreted in light of Hochschild's[67] theory of emotions, which contended that people often purposely manage their emotions when engaging in social encounters. Specifically, she highlighted how, at times, individuals attempt to cope with cultural rules and ideologies regarding behavioural and emotional expectations. Central to Hochschild's discussion of emotions is her exploration of *feeling rules* (i.e. rules about the type, intensity, direction and duration of the emotions that people should feel in a given situation) and *display rules* (i.e. when and how overt expressions of emotion in particular situations are to occur). She also distinguished between two types of emotional management, namely *surface acting* (i.e. intentionally deceiving others through bodily displays to mask how we are feeling without deceiving ourselves) and *deep acting* (i.e. when an individual works on his or her feelings through conscious mental work to the extent that he or she truly believes in the emotions that are being experienced).[68]

When considered in light of Hochschild's theorising, we would contend that throughout his interactions with the various stakeholders mentioned in the vignette, Chris had come to believe that he should think, feel and act positively when talking about and enacting the FA's preferred pedagogical delivery style. While Chris privately came to question aspects of this approach, he chose not to outwardly display his true thoughts and feelings of anxiety and frustration. Instead, he engaged in *surface acting* and, therefore, strove to conduct himself in accordance with what he perceived to be those *display rules* against which various members of the social network in which he was embedded were judging his outward appearance. Although Chris deemed this to be an effective strategy to avoid perceived repercussions, it ultimately came at a significant psychological cost to him. In this regard, it could be suggested that Chris did not have the emotional stamina to sustain the required emotional displays.[69] This psychological cost contributed to a loss of *job motivation*.[70]

While we believe that Hochschild's theorising provides an informative reading of Chris' story, we are mindful that her seminal work has been the subject of critical analysis. For example, Theodosius[71] suggested that Hochschild's thesis does not pay adequate attention to the nuanced and fine-grained relational aspects of emotional experiences. She challenged Hochschild's argument that external feeling rules can always explain how people manage their emotions, and makes the case that this position fails to acknowledge those emotions that are engendered during the social interactions and relationships that occur between two or more people. For example, as alluded to earlier, Chris was initially reluctant to share his innermost thoughts and feelings about his coaching with Barry, Geoff and others present in social network (e.g. parents or players), as he feared damaging his ongoing relationships with them and wished to avoid creating a discredited image of himself in their eyes.[72] However, in this regard, his reluctance to show his true emotions to Geoff, for example, was not solely bound up in his understanding of appropriate external feeling rules, but also his genuine liking of, and gratitude to, this individual that had evolved over his time at the football club.

Burkitt[73] also criticised some aspect of Hochchild's theorising. He argued that Hoschild's theory drives an artificial wedge between the private and the public, self and others, and incorrectly assumes that all emotions have feelings rules imposed on them, which are subsequently transformed through a process of deep or surface acting. While Burkitt acknowledges that emotional work can and does occur, he posits that 'many of our emotional moments with others do not conform to feeling rules and are not well managed in the terms they set out, as we can be deeply affected and moved by others and their emotional predicaments'.[74] In this respect, we acknowledge that not all emotional experiences entail emotional work.[75] Rather, on many occasions, coaches will authentically express their emotions when interacting with others. This was illustrated in Chris' decision to eventually share his 'true' thoughts and feelings about his development as a coach with his mentor, Barry. As such, we urge researchers not to limit their analytical lens solely to the work of Hochschild in their efforts to develop a relational understanding of emotion in grass-roots football coaching. Furthermore, future inquiry would also need to recognise emotion as being located at the interface between self and social structure and acknowledge the multitude of overlapping emotions that are inevitably experienced in the social milieu of grass-roots football coaching, as well as focusing on the social role that emotions play during interactions within this context.[76]

Conclusion

While scholars are becoming increasingly cognizant of the social and interactive nature of coaching, our understanding of the complex network of relations in which grass-roots football coaches are located remains largely undeveloped. As such, the aim of this paper was to make a case for adopting a relational stance to examine and understand the everyday demands, experiences and understood realities of grass-roots football coaching. This perspective offers a potentially valuable lens for not only understanding how and why grass-roots coaches seek to navigate their relationships with a variety of contextual stakeholders in the ways that they do, but that it may also help us to examine the emotions and embodied experiences that are bound up in their interactions and engagements with others. Indeed, we hope that the argument presented herein acts as a stimulus for the development of critical and rich (embodied)accounts of grass-roots football coaching that allow us to better consider the issues of identity, emotion, power, interaction, structure and agency within this setting than has been achieved thus far.[77] Furthermore, the adoption of a relational perspective also allows us to examine the connections between the sporting, working and home lives of grass-roots football coaches. To date, little, if any, attention has been afforded to the interconnections between the multiple social networks in which these coaches are embedded. Arguably then, a relational approach might allow researchers to not only better understand how grass-roots football coaches attempt to manage their various identities, but also the wider social demands that are placed on them.

Finally, in seeking to develop insightful and nuanced relational understandings of grass-roots football coaching, we would encourage scholars to embrace a diverse range of qualitative approaches. Conceivably, realist tales, modified realist tales, (auto)ethnography, participatory network mapping, confessional tales, poetry, ethnodrama, film and photography represent some of the diverse ways in which the lived relational experiences of grass-roots coaches might be understood and represented.[78] That said, it is important to note that 'choosing a form of representation simply because it is novel' will not suffice, rather 'researchers need to choose each form of representation in informed, principled, and disciplined ways'.[79] Of central importance, to us at least, is appropriately employing methodological approaches and forms of representation that help to better articulate the relational demands of grass-roots football coaching.

Disclosure statement

No potential conflict of interest was reported by the authors.

Notes

1. Potrac et al., '"Handshakes, BBQs, and Bullets": Self-interest, Shame and Regret in Football Coaching'; Nelson et al., 'Thinking, Feeling, Acting: The Case of a Semi-professional Soccer Coach'; and Thompson et al., '"I Found out the Hard Way": Micro-political Workings in Professional Football'.
2. cf. Nias, 'Thinking about Feeling: The Emotions in Teaching' 26; Jones et al., *The Sociology of Sports Coaching*.
3. Jones and Wallace, 'Another Bad Day at the Training Ground: Coping with Ambiguity in the Coaching Context': 119.
4. Potrac and Jones, 'Power, Conflict, and Cooperation: Toward a Micropolitics of Coaching', 2009a; Potrac and Jones, 'Micropolitical Workings in Semi-professional Football', 2009b; Potrac et al., '"Handshakes, BBQs, and Bullets": Self-interest, Shame and Regret in Football Coaching'; and Purdy et al., 'Trust, Distrust and Coaching Practice'.
5. Ball, *The Micro-politics of the School*, 19.
6. Potrac et al., 'Coaches, Coaching, and Emotion: A Suggested Research Agenda'; Nelson et al., 'Thinking, Feeling, Acting: The Case of a Semi-professional Soccer Coach'.
7. Ibid.
8. Jones, Edwards, and ViottoFilho, 'Activity Theory, Complexity and Sports Coaching: An Epistemology for a Discipline'.
9. Jones et al., *The Sociology of Sports Coaching*.
10. Jones and Wallace, 'Another Bad Day at the Training Ground: Coping with Ambiguity in the Coaching Context'; Jones, Edwards, and ViottoFilho, 'Activity Theory, Complexity and Sports Coaching: An Epistemology for a Discipline'; and Jones et al., *The Sociology of Sports Coaching*.
11. Lusted and O'Gorman, 'The Impact of New Labour's Modernisation Agenda on the English Grass-roots Football Workforce'.
12. Green and Houlihan, 'Governmentality, Modernization, and the "disciplining" of National Sporting Organizations: Athletics in Australia and the United Kingdom'.
13. O'Gorman, 'The Changing Nature of Sports Volunteering: Modernisation, Policy and Practice'; Robinson and Palmer, *Managing Sports Organisations*.
14. Crossley, *Towards Relational Sociology*; Crossley, 'Networks and Complexity: Directions for Interactionist Research?'
15. Powell and Depelteau, *Conceptualizing Relational Sociology: Ontological and Theoretical Issues*, 2.
16. Ibid.
17. Crossley, *Towards Relational Sociology*; Crossley, 'Networks and Complexity: Directions for Interactionist Research?'
18. Crossley, *Towards Relational Sociology*.
19. Crossley, *Towards Relational Sociology*; Donati, *Relational Sociology: A New Paradigm for the Social Sciences*.
20. Powell and Depelteau, *Conceptualizing Relational Sociology: Ontological and Theoretical Issues*, 3.
21. Crossley, *Towards Relational Sociology*; Donati, *Relational Sociology: A New Pradigm for the Social Sciences*; and Powell and Depelteau, *Conceptualizing Relational Sociology: Ontological and Theoretical issues*.
22. Ibid.

23. Powell and Depelteau, *Conceptualizing Relational Sociology: Ontological and Theoretical Issues*.
24. Ibid., 2.
25. Crossley, *Towards Relational Sociology*; Donati, *Relational Sociology: A New Pradigm for the Social Sciences*; and Powell and Depelteau, *Conceptualizing Relational Sociology: Ontological and Theoretical issues*.
26. Emirbayer, 'Manifesto for a Relational Sociology'.
27. N. Crossley, 'Networks and Complexity: Directions for Interactionist Research?'; Powell and Depelteau, *Conceptualizing Relational Sociology: Ontological and Theoretical issues*.
28. Crossley, *Towards Relational Sociology*; Crossley, 'Networks and Complexity: Directions for Interactionist Research?'.
29. Ibid.
30. Crossley, *Towards Relational Sociology*.
31. Ibid., 342.
32. Ibid.
33. Beames and Pike, 'Goffman Goes Rock Climbing: Using Creative Fiction to Explore the Presentation of Self in Outdoor Education'; Jones, 'Dilemmas, Maintaining "Face," and Paranoia An Average Coaching Life'; and Sparkes, *Telling Tales in Sport and Physical Activity: A Qualitative Journey*.
34. Jones, 'Dilemmas, Maintaining "Face," and Paranoia An Average Coaching Life'.
35. R. Rinehart, 'Fictional Methods of Ethnography: Believability, Specks of Glass, and Chekhov'.
36. Jones, 'Dilemmas, Maintaining "Face," and Paranoia An Average Coaching Life'; Sparkes, *Telling Tales in Sport and Physical Activity: A Qualitative Journey*; Tierney, 'The Cedar Closet 1'.
37. Beames and Pike, 'Goffman Goes Rock Climbing: Using Creative Fiction to Explore the Presentation of Self in Outdoor Education', 5.
38. Barone, 'Among the Chosen: A Collaborative Educational (Auto)biography'.
39. Jones et al., *The Sociology of Sports Coaching*.
40. Beames and Pike, 'Goffman Goes Rock Climbing: Using Creative Fiction to Explore the Presentation of Self in Outdoor Education'; Jones, 'Dilemmas, Maintaining "Face," and Paranoia An Average Coaching Life'.
41. Beames and Pike, 'Goffman Goes Rock Climbing: Using Creative Fiction to Explore the Presentation of Self in Outdoor Education'.
42. Frank, *The Wounded Storyteller: Body, Illness, and Ethics*, 23.
43. Sparkes, *Telling Tales in Sport and Physical Activity: A Qualitative Journey*.
44. Jones, 'Dilemmas, Maintaining "Face," and Paranoia An Average Coaching Life'.
45. Ibid.
46. Ibid., 109.
47. Frank, *The Wounded Storyteller: Body, Illness, and Ethics*, 23; Beames and Pike, 'Goffman Goes Rock Climbing: Using Creative Fiction to Explore the Presentation of Self in Outdoor Education'.
48. Crossley, *Towards Relational Sociology*; Crossley, 'Networks and Complexity: Directions for Interactionist Research?'.
49. Ibid.
50. Crossley, 'Networks and Complexity: Directions for Interactionist Research?'.
51. Ibid., 347.
52. Ibid.
53. Kelchtermans and Ballet, 'The Micropolitics of Teacher Induction. A Narrative-biographical Study on Teacher Socialisation'; Kelchtermans and Ballet, 'Micropolitical Literacy: Reconstructing a Neglected Dimension in Teacher Development.
54. Kelchtermans, 'Who I am in How I Teach is the Message: Self-understanding, Vulnerability and Reflection'.
55. Kelchtermans, 'Career Stories as Gateway to Understanding Teacher Development', 43.
56. Kelchtermans, 'Career Stories as Gateway to Understanding Teacher Development'; Kelchtermans, 'Who I am in How I Teach is the Message: Self-understanding,

Vulnerability and Reflection'; and Kelchtermans, 'Vulnerability in Teaching: The Moral and Political Roots of a Structural Condition'.

57. Ibid.
58. Kelchtermans, and Ballet, 'Micropolitical Literacy: Reconstructing a Neglected Dimension in Teacher Development', 766.
59. Heidegger, *Being and Time*.
60. Crossley, *Towards Relational Sociology*, 33.
61. Ibid.
62. Ibid., 33.
63. Burkitt, *Bodies of Thought: Embodiment, Identity and Modernity*, 127.
64. Burkitt, 'Emotional Reflexivity: Feeling, Emotion and Imagination in Reflexive Dialogues'.
65. Burkitt, *Bodies of Thought: Embodiment, Identity and Modernity*; Burkitt, *Emotions and social relations*.
66. Burkitt, *Bodies of Thought: Embodiment, Identity and Modernity*', 128.
67. Hochschild, *The Managed Heart*.
68. Potrac and Marshall, 'Arlie Russell Hochschild: The Managed Heart, Feeling Rules and Emotional Labour: Coaching as an Emotional Endeavour'.
69. Hochschild, *The Managed Heart*; Turner and Stets, *The Sociology of Emotions*.
70. Kelchtermans and Ballet, 'Micropolitical Literacy: Reconstructing a Neglected Dimension in Teacher Development'.
71. Theodosius, 'Recovering Emotion from Emotion Management', *Sociology* 40, no. 5 (2006): 893–910.
72. Goffman, *The Presentation of Self in Everyday Life*.
73. Burkitt, *Emotions and Social Relations*.
74. Ibid., 149.
75. Nelson et al., 'Carl Rogers, Learning and Educational Practice: Critical Considerations and Applications in Sports Coaching'; Tracy, '*Qualitative Research Methods: Collecting Evidence, Crafting Analysis, Communicating Impact*'.
76. Hunt, Walby, and Spencer, *Emotions Matter: A Relational Approach to Emotions*.
77. Jones et al., *The Sociology of Sports Coaching*.
78. Groom et al., 'Writing and Representing Research'.
79. Ibid., 94.

References

Ball, S.J. *The Micro-politics of the School*. London: Methuen, 1987.

Barone, T. 'Among the Chosen: A Collaborative Educational (Auto)biography'. *Qualitative Inquiry* 3, no. 2 (1997): 222–36.

Beames, S.K., and E.C.J. Pike. 'Goffman Goes Rock Climbing: Using Creative Fiction to Explore the Presentation of Self in Outdoor Education'. *Australian Journal of Outdoor Education* 12, no. 2 (2008): 3–11.

Burkitt, I. *Bodies of Thought: Embodiment, Identity and Modernity*. London: Sage, 1999.

Burkitt, I. 'Emotional Reflexivity: Feeling, Emotion and Imagination in Reflexive Dialogues'. *Sociology* 46, no. 3 (2012): 458–72.

Burkitt, I. *Emotions and Social Relations*. London: Sage, 2014.

Crossley, N. 'Networks and Complexity: Directions for Interactionist Research?' *Symbolic Interaction* 33, no. 3 (2010): 341–63.

Crossley, N. *Towards Relational Sociology*. London: Routledge, 2011.

Donati, P. *Relational Sociology: A New Paradigm for the Social Sciences*. London: Routledge, 2010.

Emirbayer, M. 'Manifesto for a Relational Sociology'. *American Journal of Sociology* 103, no. 2 (1997): 281–317.

Frank, A. *The Wounded Storyteller: Body, Illness, and Ethics*. Chicago, IL: University of Chicago Press, 1995.

Goffman, E. *The Presentation of the Self in Everyday Life*. New York: Doubleday, 1959.

Green, M., and B. Houlihan. 'Governmentality, Modernization, and the "disciplining" of National Sporting Organizations: Athletics in Australia and the United Kingdom'. *Sociology of Sport Journal* 23, no. 1 (2006): 47–71.

Groom, R., L. Nelson, P. Potrac, and B. Smith. 'Writing and Representing Research'. In *Research Methods in Sports Coaching*, ed. L. Nelson, R. Groom, and P. Potrac, 86–97. London: Routledge, 2014.

Heidegger, M. *Being Time*, trans. J. MacQuarrie and E. Robinson. Oxford: Blackwell, 1962/2004.

Hochschild, A.R. *The Managed Heart*. Berkeley: University of California Press, 1983.

Hunt, A., K. Walby, and D. Spencer. *Emotions Matter: A Relational Approach to Emotions*. Toronto: University of Toronto Press, 2012.

Jones, R. 'Dilemmas, Maintaining "Face", and Paranoia An Average Coaching Life'. *Qualitative Inquiry* 12, no. 5 (2006): 1012–21.

Jones, R. L., C. Edwards, and I.T. ViottoFilho. 'Activity Theory, Complexity and Sports Coaching: An Epistemology for a Discipline'. *Sport, Education and Society*, (ahead-of-print) (2014): 1–17.

Jones, R.L., P. Potrac, C. Cushion, and L. Ronglan, eds. *The Sociology of Sports Coaching*. London: Routledge, 2010.

Jones, R.L., and M. Wallace. '"Another Bad Day at the Training Ground": Coping with Ambiguity in the Coaching Context'. *Sport, Education and Society* 10, no. 1 (2005): 119–34.

Kelchtermans, G. 'Career Stories as Gateway to Understanding Teacher Development'. In *Teachers' Career Trajectories and Work Lives*, ed. M. Bayer, U. Brinkkjær, H. Plauborg, and S.Rolls, 29–47. London: Springer, 2009a.

Kelchtermans, G. 'Who I am in How I Teach is the Message: Self-understanding, Vulnerability and Reflection'. *Teachers and Teaching* 15, no. 2 (2009b): 257–72.

Kelchtermans, G. 'Vulnerability in Teaching: The Moral and Political Roots of a Structural Condition'. In *New Understandings of Teacher's Work*, ed. C. Day and J. Lee, 65–82. London: Springer, 2011.

Kelchtermans, G., and K. Ballet. 'Micropolitical Literacy: Reconstructing a Neglected Dimension in Teacher Development'. *International Journal of Educational Research* 37, no. 8 (2002a): 755–67.

Kelchtermans, G., and K. Ballet. 'The Micropolitics of Teacher Induction. A Narrative-biographical Study on Teacher Socialisation'. *Teaching and Teacher Education* 18, no. 1 (2002b): 105–20.

Lusted, J., and J. O'Gorman. 'The Impact of New Labour's Modernisation Agenda on the English Grass-roots Football Workforce'. *Managing Leisure* 15, no. 1–2 (2010): 140–54.

Nelson, L., C.J. Cushion, P. Potrac, and R. Groom. 'Carl Rogers, Learning and Educational Practice: Critical Considerations and Applications in Sports Coaching'. *Sport, Education and Society* 19, no. 5 (2014): 513–31.

Nelson, L., P. Potrac, D. Gilbourne, A. Allanson, L. Gale, and P. Marshall. 'Thinking, Feeling, Acting: The Case of a Semi-professional Soccer Coach'. *Sociology of Sport Journal* 30, no. 4 (2013): 467–86.

Nias, J. 'Thinking about Feeling: The Emotions in Teaching'. *Cambridge Journal of Education* 26, no. 3 (1996): 293–306.

O'Gorman, J. 'The Changing Nature of Sports Volunteering: Modernisation, Policy and Practice'. In *Managing Sport: Social and Cultural Perspectives*, ed. D. Hassan and J. Lusted, 218–438. London: Routledge, 2013.

Potrac, P., and R.L. Jones. 'Power, Conflict, and Cooperation: Toward a Micropolitics of Coaching'. *Quest* 61, no. 2 (2009a): 223–36.

Potrac, P., and R.L. Jones. 'Micropolitical Workings in Semi-professional Football'. *Sociology of Sport Journal* 26, no. 44 (2009b): 557–77.

Potrac, P., and P. Marshall. 'Arlie Russell Hochschild: The Managed Heart, Feeling Rules and Emotional Labour: Coaching as an Emotional Endeavour'. In *The Sociology of Sports Coaching*, ed. R.L. Jones, P. Potrac, C. Cushion, and L.T. Ronglan, 54–116. London: Routledge, 2011.

Potrac, P., R.L. Jones, D. Gilbourne, and L. Nelson. '"Handshakes, BBQs, and Bullets": Self-interest, Shame and Regret in Football Coaching'. *Sports Coaching Review* 1, no. 2 (2012): 79–92.

Potrac, P., R.L. Jones, L. Purdy, J. Nelson, and P. Marshall. 'Coaches, Coaching, and Emotion: A Suggested Research Agenda'. In *Routledge Handbook of Sports Coaching*, ed. P. Potrac, W. Gilbert, and J. Dennison, 235–46. London: Routledge, 2013.

Powell, C., and F. Dépelteau. *Conceptualizing Relational Sociology: Ontological and Theoretical Issues*. London: Palgrave Macmillan, 2013.

Purdy, L. 'Exploring Trust and Distrust in Coaching: A Suggested Research Agenda'. In *Routledge Handbook of Sports Coaching*, ed. P. Potrac, W. Gilbert, and J. Dennison, 309–620. London: Routledge, 2013.

Rinehart, R. 'Fictional Methods in Ethnography: Believability, Specks of Glass, and Chekhov'. *Qualitative Inquiry* 4, no. 2 (1998): 200–24.

Robinson, L., and D. Palmer, eds. *Managing Voluntary Sport Organizations*. London: Routledge, 2010.

Sparkes, A. *Telling Tales in Sport and Physical Activity: A Qualitative Journey*. Champaign, IL: Human Kinetics, 2002.

Theodosius, C. 'Recovering Emotion from Emotion Management'. *Sociology* 40, no. 5 (2006): 893–910.

Tierney, W.G. 'The Cedar Closet 1'. *International Journal of Qualitative Studies in Education* 6, no. 4 (1993): 303–14.

Tracy, S.J. *Qualitative Research Methods: Collecting Evidence, Crafting Analysis, Communicating Impact*. Malden, MA: Wiley, 2012.

Turner, J.H., and J.E. Stets. *The Sociology of Emotions*. Cambridge: Cambridge University Press, 2005.

Index

Note: **Boldface** page numbers refer to figures
and tables, page numbers followed by "n" denote
endnotes

BAME communities *see* Black, Asian, Minority
   Ethnic communities
Batson, Brendon 11
Beckham, David 58
'Bend it Like Beckham' 58, 59
Biskup, C. 52, 62n15
Black, Asian, Minority Ethnic (BAME)
   communities 11
Bourdieu, Pierre: *Distinction: A Social Critique
   of the Judgement of Taste* 107; social class
   reproduction 4, 107
Bronfenbrenner's bioecological theory 65–6, 80

CFAs *see* County Football Associations
Charter Standard Club Programme 8,
   10–12, 15
child-centred approach 14
Coach Bursary programme 11
'concerted cultivation' 107
'corporeal knowledge', Bourdieu's notion of 93
County Football Associations (CFAs) 9
'crisis of youth' 111

Denzin, Norman 92
*Distinction: A Social Critique of the Judgement
   of Taste* (Bourdieu) 107
drop-out of soccer, children and
   adolescents 64–5; Bronfenbrenner's
   bioecological theory 65–6; data extraction and
   synthesis 67; data sources 66; discussion 80;
   inclusion/exclusion criteria 67; limitations
   and research needs 81–2; practical
   implications 82–3; proximal and distal
   processes 79–80; results 67, **68**–**75**, 76, **76**, 78;
   studies investigating **68**–**76**; time-related
   factors associated with **77**–**8**, 78–9
Dublin and District Schoolboys League 93
Dunn, Carrie 3
Dyck, Noel 96

elite female footballers' as role models 3;
   conduct and behaviour 54–5; encouraging
   sporting participation 55–6; and functions
   of 52–4; overview of 51–2; young women's
   football participation 56–60
England: grassroots football in 15–16; mini soccer
   for children 19; teams, development of 10
English Football Association 3; Charter Standard
   Club Programme 8, 10–12, 15; Child Protection
   policy 11; grassroots football, future challenges
   for 15–16; mini soccer 8, 9, 12–15; National
   Game Strategy (2008–2012) 14; overview
   of 8–9; TOP Sport Football Programme 10;
   women's and girls' 9

FA Charter Standard Clubs Award 11
Fairclough, Paul 54, 55
FA Women's Super League (FAWSL) 56, 58, 61
FAWSL *see* FA Women's Super League
FDOs *see* football development officers
Fédération Internationale de Football Association
   (FIFA) 1
female sporting role models 52, 54, 55, 57
Ferguson, Alex 96
FIFA *see* Fédération Internationale de Football
   Association
Fine, Gary Alan 96
Football Association (FA) *see* English Football
   Association
football development officers (FDOs) 9

gendered path within sport 111–12
GirlGuiding UK 52–3, 57, 59–60
girls in American youth soccer 106–7;
   ethnographic research 109–10; gendered path
   within sport 111–12; mean and violent
   kids 112; 'pressure to play' 114; quieting and
   misunderstanding Generation Y 110–11; racial
   and social class relations 113–14; snowball
   sampling technique 108; 'soccer mom'
   phenomenon 107; social class reproduction,
   Bourdieu's analysis 107; social network of
   mothers and daughters 108

Giroux, H.A. 111
Giulianotti, R. 94–5
Greenside Schoolboys Football Club 93–4;
    contested 'blackness' 97; embodied
    belongings 99–100; immigrant
    background 94–5; male-oriented team 96; race
    and ethnicity 95, 97–9; serious game 95–6
Grossberg, Lawrence 110–11

Hall, Stuart 97
Hamm, Mia 59
Hochschild's theory of emotions 127
Howat, G. 58

'impulsive black sportman' 95
Ireland, transcultural context in see Greenside
    Schoolboys Football Club

Junior Club Football 10

Knightley, Keira 58
Kunda, Z. 57

Lareau, A. 107
Levett, Nick 14
Lockwood, P. 57

Mauro, Max 4
McDermott, John 9
McGrath, Paul 90
mini soccer 8, 9, 12–15; audiovisual methods 20;
    critical incidents in 21, 21–2, 29–31;
    incidents with officials 27–9; incidents with
    opposition players 25–7; overview of 18–20;
    players vs. coaches 22–4; players vs. parent
    spectators 24–5
motivational climate, of youth soccer 82
MUGA see multi use games areas
multi use games areas (MUGA) 15
Murray, D. 58

NASL see North American Soccer League
National Game Strategy report 11
National Society for the Prevention of Cruelty to
    Children (NSPCC) 12
NFF see Norwegian Soccer Association
North American Soccer League (NASL) 106
North Dublin Schoolboys League 93
Norwegian Soccer Association (NFF) 35, 45
Norwegian Social Science Data Services 38
Norwegian youth soccer 3; being with friends 41;
    choosing to play sport 41–2, 46; collaborating
    with teammates 41, 44–5; data analysis 39–40;
    data collection 38–9; demonstrating
    mastery of skills 43–4; enjoyment of
    sports 36–7, 40, 44; interview subjects and

sampling procedures 38; learning technical
    skills 43; limitations 46–7; overview
    of 35–6; promoting adolescence physical
    activity project 37–8; self-determination
    theory 46; supportive and attentive coach 42–3
NSPCC see National Society for the Prevention
    of Cruelty to Children

PAPA project see promoting adolescence
    physical activity project
Pfister, G. 52, 62n15
Potrac, P. 5
Powell, Hope 10
PPCT model see process-person-context-time
    model
process-person-context-time (PPCT)
    model 65–6
promoting adolescence physical activity (PAPA)
    project 3, 37–9, 46
proximal processes 65–6, 79–80

relational sociology 5; case study 121–4;
    creative fiction 121; display rules 127;
    emotional inquiries in 118–19; feeling
    rules 127; micropolitical nature of 118; new
    coaching practices 126; overview of 119–21;
    personal interpretive framework 125;
    professional self-understanding 125;
    social network analysis 124; subjective
    educational theory 125; surface and deep
    acting 127
Robinson, Louise 51
Rooney, Wayne 54, 55

Save Our Soccer (SOS) 12
Schoolboys Football Association of Ireland
    (SFAI) 93
Simmons, Kelly 9
'soccer mom' phenomenon 107
SOS see Save Our Soccer
Sport England 9, 13, 15
Stanley, L. 53
subjective educational theory 125
Swanson, L. 4

transcultural football 4; concept of 91–2; Irish
    context see Greenside Schoolboys Football
    Club; race and ethnicity 91; young people
    voices 92–3

Venables, Terry 12

Walvin, James 2
Wilkinson, Howard 8
Winter, Henry 51